THE RIVALS GAME

Inside The British Derby

Douglas Beattie

KNOW THE SCORE BOOKS PUBLICATIONS

CULT HEROES	Author	ISBN
CARLISLE UNITED	Mark Harrison	978-1-905449-09-7
CELTIC	David Potter	978-1-905449-08-8
CHELSEA	Leo Moynihan	1-905449-00-3
MANCHESTER CITY	David Clayton	978-1-905449-05-7
NEWCASTLE	Dylan Younger	1-905449-03-8
NOTTINGHAM FOREST	David McVay	978-1-905449-06-4
RANGERS	Paul Smith	978-1-905449-07-1
SOUTHAMPTON	Jeremy Wilson	1-905449-01-1
WEST BROM	Simon Wright	1-905449-02-X

MATCH OF MY LIFE	Editor	ISBN
DERBY COUNTY	Johnson & Matthews	978-1-905449-68-2
ENGLAND WORLD CUP	Massarella & Moynihan	1-905449-52-6
EUROPEAN CUP FINALS	Ben Lyttleton	1-905449-57-7
FA CUP FINALS 1953-1969	David Saffer	978-1-905449-53-8
FULHAM	Michael Heatley	1-905449-51-8
LEEDS	David Saffer	1-905449-54-2
LIVERPOOL	Leo Moynihan	1-905449-50-X
MANCHESTER UNITED	Ivan Ponting	978-1-905449-59-0
SHEFFIELD UNITED	Nick Johnson	1-905449-62-3
STOKE CITY	Simon Lowe	978-1-905449-55-2
SUNDERLAND	Rob Mason	1-905449-60-7
SPURS	Allen & Massarella	978-1-905449-58-3
WOLVES	Simon Lowe	1-905449-56-9

GENERAL FOOTBALL	Author	ISBN
2006 WORLD CUP DIARY	Harry Harris	1-905449-90-9
2007/08 CHAMPIONS LEAGUE YEARBOOK		978-1-905449-93-4
BURKSEY	Peter Morfoot	1-905449-49-6
The Autobiography of a Football God		
HOLD THE BACK PAGE	Harry Harris	1-905449-91-7
MARTIN JOL: The Inside Story	Harry Harris	978-1-905449-77-4
MY PREMIERSHIP DIARY	Marcus Hahnemann	978-1-905449-33-0
Reading's Season in the Premiership		
OUTCASTS	Steve Menary	978-1-905449-31-6
The Lands FIFA Forgot		

PARISH TO PLANET A History of Football	Eric Midwinter	978-1-905449-30-9
TACKLES LIKE A FERRET (England Cover)	Paul Parker	1-905449-47-X
TACKLES LIKE A FERRET (Manchester United Cover)	Paul Parker	1-905449-46-1
THE RIVALS GAME Inside The British Derby	Douglas Beattie	978-1-905449-79-8
UNITED THROUGH TRIUMPH AND TRAGEDY		
	Bill Foulkes	978-1-905449-78-1

CRICKET	Author	ISBN
MOML: THE ASHES	Pilger & Wightman	1-905449-63-1
GROVEL!	David Tossell	978-1-905449-43-9
The Summer & Legacy of the 1976 West IndiesTour of England		
MY AUTOBIOGRAPHY	Shaun Udal	978-1-905449-42-2
WASTED?	Paul Smith	978-1-905449-45-3
LEAGUE CRICKET YEARBOOK North West edition	Andy Searle	978-1-905449-70-5
LEAGUE CRICKET YEARBOOK Midlands edition	Andy Searle	978-1-905449-72-9

RUGBY LEAGUE	Editor	ISBN
MOML: LEEDS RHINOS	Phil Caplan & David Saffer	978-1-905449-69-9
MOML: WIGAN WARRIORS	David Kuzio	978-1-905449-66-8

FORTHCOMING PUBLICATIONS

GENERAL FOOTBALL	Author	ISBN
THE BOOK OF FOOTBALL OBITUARIES		
	Ivan Ponting	978-1-905449-82-2
THE DOOG: DEREK DOUGAN	Gordos & Harrison	978-1-905449-02-9
The Incredible Story of Football's Most Controversial Character		

THE RIVALS GAME

Inside The British Derby

Douglas Beattie

www.knowthescorebooks.com

First published in the United Kingdom
by Know The Score Books Limited, 2008

Know The Score Books Limited
118 Alcester Road
Studley
Warwickshire
B80 7NT
01527 454482
info@knowthescorebooks.com

www.knowthescorebooks.com

A CIP catalogue record is available for this book from the British Library
ISBN: 978-1-905449-79-8

Jacket design by Graham Hales

Printed and bound in Great Britain by Cromwell Press

Mixed Sources
Product group from well-managed
forests and other controlled sources
www.fsc.org Cert no. TT-COC-2082
© 1996 Forest Stewardship Council
FSC

Jacket image reproduced by kind permission of Action Images

Author's Acknowledgements

IT IS NO UNDERSTATEMENT to say that without the help of dozens of people *The Rivals Game* would never have been written. Almost everyone I approached was kind enough to freely give their time: journalists, politicians, clergymen, lawyers, authors, fanzine writers, historians and the countless supporters on the street who were buttonholed to air their views. Many went far beyond the call of duty to assist and advise.

In particular my sincere thanks and best wishes go to all of those individuals quoted in the text. They were not alone, indeed, some of the most illuminating conversations were held with people who did not wish to be named (for various reasons). All I can say is you know who you are – oh, and the drinks are on me the next time we meet.

A considerable amount of faith was shown by my publishers Know The Score Books and my editor, Simon Lowe, who was constantly helpful and thoroughly supportive. Thanks a million. May you long leap from the sofa!

This book draws some inspiration from those who have gone before me, in particular Simon Kuper in *Football Against The Enemy*. Simon is owed an immense debt of gratitude for his kindness in writing the foreword to this volume. It meant a great deal, Simon. Thank you.

To the rest of you, thanks one and all for your time, support, views, and – in some cases – all that we have shared down the years. In Sheffield: Richard Batho, Keith Farnsworth, Karl Taylor, Jan Wilson, Andrew Gilligan, Andrea Neville and especially Gary Armstrong. In Birmingham: Bill Howell, Roger Blake, Andy Davis. In north London: Barry Baker, Bernard Corcoran, Vic Wright, Bernie Kingsley, Ken and Stevie Benjamin. In Manchester: Andy Mitten and Dave Wallace. In Liverpool: Bernard and Suzanne at the Feathers, Simon Favour, Ben, Veronica and (the one and only) Nick Astor. In Glasgow: Val Lemmon, Stephen Townsend, Joe Ferrari, Barry McKinnon. In Edinburgh: Tam Wright, Rhona Crawford, Jane Reid at St Patrick's. In the North-East: Colin Patterson, Roger Fairlie, Kevin Douglas, John Clayson, Louise Wanless and Gary Oliver.

Never to be forgotten: Jason Hall, Franny Graham, Russell Bell, Clive Scott, Danny Cotter, 'Big Deev' McVittie, John Rae Elliot, Graeme Cooper, Nick and Sarah Harvey, Alan Guy, Gilly Bavington, Lucy Marrs, Georgie Steele, Lennox McBay, Duncan Ritchie, Stephen Rae, Gordon Stewart, David Ewart, Neil Gill, Natasha Serlin, Amelia Hill, Jenni Doggett, Ed Grenby, Ruth 'Rocket' Isherwood, William Cadogan, Simon Coulson, the McP Blues Agenda, Steve Bottomley, Tom Hodgkinson, Paul English, Donald Graham, Mark Anker, the cricket writer Simon Lister (for endless good advice), all my friends at *Kalendar* and in the Radio Newsroom (forever the unsung heroes) and the finest of BBC Journalists, Mick Robson and Anthony Birchley.

Although it is often ignored by the supposed great and good of the game – without you there would be no football. Good luck to all your teams.

Douglas Beattie
February 2008

THIS BOOK IS DEDICATED TO K M BEATTIE (WHO
GAVE ME THE CHANCE) AND LINDSEY (FOR THOSE
AMAZING EYES AND ALWAYS BELIEVING)

Contents

FOREWORD

BY SIMON KUPER

A FEW YEARS AGO I went to watch Spurs play Arsenal with some friends who happened to be Gunners fans. We sat in the away end at White Hart Lane and, when Dennis Bergkamp scored in the goal in front of us, my friends – who all had yuppie London jobs – gesticulated madly at the entire stadium while everyone else threatened to kill us.

Though I knew that Spurs and Arsenal fans were enemies, it baffled me. At 16 I had returned from the Netherlands, where I grew up, to live in a London neighbourhood about halfway between the Spurs and Arsenal grounds. Some of the locals supported Spurs, and others Arsenal, but what struck me is that they seemed to be exactly the same people. There was nothing in their origins – not religion or class or anything else – that determined which club of the two they chose. Rather, it was an apparently random decision. My friends that day happened to have chosen Arsenal, and so they despised the people who happened to have chosen Spurs. They even despised each other in the same vocabulary. I had a friend, a Tottenham fan, who used to wander around absentmindedly chanting "We beat the scum, 3-1" in honour of the famous FA Cup semi-final of 1991. However, in this eye-opening book Douglas Beattie describes Arsenal fans at another derby singing: "You're scum and you know you are."

Beattie's book is a pursuit of that strange beast, the British derby. There is probably no other footballing nation with as many inner-city rivalries, and British ones are spicy enough to have drawn in the whole world. People in Shanghai or Soweto will live Everton versus Liverpool as fully as if they grew up just off Stanley Park. Yet south of the Scottish border it's usually impossible to discern what these derbies are about. Is all this passion really random and pointless? Beattie tries to find out.

In other European countries, it tends to be clear what derbies are about, or at least what they were originally about. When Milan played Inter, for instance, Milan used to draw their supporters from the poorer migrants to the city, while Inter's tended to come from the better-established indigenous middle class. In France, where I live now, the regional derby between Lyon and St-Etienne sets a wealthy bourgeois city against a post-industrial working-class one. At a recent game, Lyon fans unfurled a banner that said: "We invented cinema when your fathers were dying in the mines.

In Glasgow, of course, the derby was about religion. Beattie also makes a typically energetic visit to Edinburgh, where he shows that the Hearts-Hibs derby is drenched in class. As one Hibs fan tells him: "If you look back over the board of Hearts compared to the board of Hibs, Hearts was very much, until the 1980s, successful businessmen, lawyers, but also people who were brought in from major businesses like the banks. For Hibs it has always been small businessmen, bookmakers, guys with building firms, and before that, bakers, more artisan successful tradesmen."

Beattie has traipsed round this island and sought out fans whose voices you seldom hear, except when they are chanting: the hardcore, the local supporters who care most. Nick Hornbys they are not, but they are the people who give these derbies their passion – or, to drop the euphemism, their venom. But Beattie is enterprising and willing to range: outside Lime Street station in Liverpool he runs into Michael Howard, Liverpool fan and former leader of the Conservative party, and asks him what he thinks.

Thanks to all this legwork, he builds a distinctive picture of each derby, with charming detail. Only in Liverpool, for instance, could there have been a Charity Shield match like this: "The teams came out together with Ray Wilson of Everton and Liverpool's Roger Hunt parading the World Cup they had won with England that summer. Then, together, both sides showed off their winnings from the previous season – Everton had the FA Cup and Liverpool the league championship."

Beattie has ended up writing a book not just about football, but about Britain – and in particular, its unlovely provincial cities, the ones nobody would notice unless, if walking through the little streets, you didn't suddenly hit upon a football ground and then, just a mile or two away, another.

INTRODUCTION

A WISE MAN ONCE WROTE: 'hardly anyone seems to query the importance attached to the game. For those who do the kicking and those who watch it so avidly, the whole matter is taken for granted. Football is football...'*

Quite so. Football is now a sport and a spectacle for billions around the globe. I have been fortunate enough to play it with people from all classes, colours and religions. Whenever possible I try to spend Friday afternoons down in Wapping on the banks of the Thames or Monday evenings in Ladbroke Grove often breathless, but always happy in 'the game'.

At the moment our teams are made up of Englishmen and Scots, but also of Algerians, Nigerians and Irishmen. At times we have also fielded various South Americans, Lithuanians and Italians. There though, sadly, similarities with the majority of teams in the Premiership ends.

Things were very different a century and half ago when the sport, a new sport – that of Association football – was about to spread its wings. The embryonic clubs which were successful then are the ones which we think of as great institutions today. Often they would have to fight for success in their own towns and cities, sometimes even swallowing up other local teams, before reaching wider acclaim. These are the stories you will find here: of rivalry and how these were forged and shaped. Always it was the people, mainly the unknown supporters in their tens of thousands, who said 'this is my team', while rejecting all others. Football unites, but if we are honest, it also divides. It always has.

That is why I wanted to write this book. Growing up in Scotland I had always been fascinated by the idea of rivalry. It first grabbed me when I watched the Scottish Cup final of 1980 and the riot which followed. I was wide-eyed and open-mouthed, unable to

* Desmond Morris, *The Soccer Tribe*

comprehend what had caused such violence. I knew something had gone terribly wrong, but a small part of me wondered if this was what Celtic and Rangers fans did after every Old Firm match.

Even before that day, though, I had perhaps been aware of footballing rivalry and its emotional power through watching the annual Auld Enemy fixture between Scotland and England on wild dusty summer days during the late 1970s when London would fall into the hands of a very drunk Tartan Army; though more often than not England remained the masters. There followed some wonderful celebrations, but also afternoons of great pain (on both sides no doubt). The solution was to go out and kick a ball. Hard.

Also, I wanted to look – properly look, digging down into corners – to better understand the way these clubs and the people of their cities related to each other. What did they 'stand for'? What separated them and did anything unite? Could it be class, or family, religion or maybe politics? Perhaps it was just the colour of a certain team's kit? All of this and more I set out to try and discover. It was never easy, but slowly the picture would emerge, often laying waste to expected conclusions.

I had long grown tired of hearing football commentators and pundits say things like: "we've all been looking forward to this match today; one of the great derbies..." I wondered how the protagonists had come to be rivals, why and sometimes whether they still were, and what characterised their rivalry, both today and in years gone by? I wanted to know what it was which made someone, for instance, a Manchester City or a Manchester United supporter.

Then there were questions about the effect these games have on the life of each city and on the people living there; how the teams and the grounds were used as places of expression and communion?

What I can be sure of is that history plays a large part in all these rivalries. The fans, to varying degrees, are quite aware of this. It helps to shape the present-day relationships while confirming the past. More than that, it allows supporters to define themselves and also the way in which they view their rivals.

I was strict in my choice of matches. These had to be between long-standing rivals from the same major British cities where football has always been overwhelmingly important. The glaringly obvious exception to that is Sunderland versus Newcastle. There I wanted to see the effect of a derby between cities where there is only one club, but a historical rival close by. The North-East fitted this bill perfectly and, being undeniably one of the heartlands of English football, it could hardly be ignored.

So apologies to fans of other clubs not featured. I certainly thought about Bristol Rovers and Bristol City, but ruled it out on the grounds that it has not really been a major derby for some considerable time. The same applied to Nottingham Forest against Notts County and to Stoke versus Port Vale. Indeed, many others came close, such as those in Belfast, Dundee, East Anglia, south Wales, Portsmouth and Southampton. In the end, I only went to one match outside the top English and Scottish leagues. The others may well be tackled in the future, should the reader demand.

SHEFFIELD:

In The Beginning There Was Steel

"Sheffield has a unique place in the history of football."

K Farnsworth – *Sheffield Football, A History*

ON THE 15TH OF FEBRUARY 2006 Shaun Rhodes and Stephen Fairbank were killed in a car crash. Both aged just 24, they were on their way home from Sheffield Wednesday's away match against Coventry City. Wednesday immediately declared that a minute's silence would be held before the kick-off of their next home game as a tribute to the tragic and untimely deaths of two loyal supporters. That fixture happened to be against Sheffield United, three days later. This was the Steel City derby – with no quarter given, nor asked for, on or off the pitch.

The clubs, the two managers, senior players and various local sages appealed for calm and respect. Sheffield as a city, was about to test its mettle. How would the United fans take to this public show of grief for two supporters of their great rivals, and how would the 27,000 Wednesdayites in the ground react if the United contingent failed to observe the silence?

This was the backdrop to the second Sheffield derby of the 2005/06 season. Add to the mix the fact that the fortunes of the teams could not have been more contrasting. United, it seemed, were on the verge of automatic promotion to England's top division, the Premiership. Wednesday were scrapping to stay in the Championship, hovering just above the relegation zone. For everyone involved it could well turn out to be the defining point of the season, perhaps even the decade.

Not that the eyes of the world were upon the city that weekend, nor anything like it. No, Sheffield had slipped off the average fan's radar, certainly since the highest profile meeting in recent years, the 1993 FA Cup semi-final at Wembley. Neither of the senior sides had graced the Premiership in five seasons. Partly as a consequence, Sheffield's profile had fallen away in the national media and, as ever, there was local competition from Leeds for airtime and column inches. I got the distinct impression that pride had been more than a little bruised when Trevor Braithwait, the editor of the Wednesday fanzine *Out of the Blue*, told me that I had arrived in "the Bermuda Triangle of Football."

Trevor and his fellow Sheffielders have seen many changes over the past three decades, few of them welcome. Football aside, Sheffield's name was, quite literally, forged in the mass production of steel. The city once led the world in that field, being mentioned as long ago as Chaucer's *Canterbury Tales* as a thriving market town known for producing knives. Despite the collapse of the industry during the 1980s, more steel than ever is now made there, but automation means it provides just a tenth of the jobs. Large numbers work in the retail, business and tourism sectors, while a burgeoning student population helps to keep the local economy buoyant. The local authority is anxious to promote what it calls 'the greenest city in England', a cultured and vibrant place in which to live, visit or do business – one which has seen house prices rise by well over a-hundred per cent in five years.

It may be hidden among the rows of cranes reaching up from seemingly endless building sites, but another Sheffield remains. This is the city of sink estates, depravation, strip clubs, junkies and heavy drinking. A recent documentary film – *Fucking Sheffield* – focused on people living in a place totally at odds with that of the new luxury apartments, offices and wine bars. The local council admitted to me that economic divisions remain between the city centre, the highly affluent area of Hallam and the many outlying wards, which still require as much help as they can get.

Sheffield has also been keen to market itself as a sports city. It has hosted the World Student Games, while the English Institute for Sport and the World Snooker Championships are both based there. Cricket, basketball and ice hockey are also popular. Yet, over-whelmingly football is, and has always been, the only game in town.

The oldest football club in the world was formed there in 1855 – giving Sheffield the title – the home of association football. Sheffield

FC, set up by ex-pupils of the local Collegiate School, is still in existence today. Every Boxing Day the club play their neighbours, Hallam, in the oldest derby in football. Within five years there were more than a dozen clubs in the town. In time, amid great smoking factories of steel, they would be joined by Wednesday and United, clubs which would truly leave their mark on the game. Not that they, or Sheffield FC, had arrived in a vacuum.

Football has been around for centuries. Not football as we know it, but more a deeply violent form of rugby, played for hours on end by a cast of dozens. These 'folk football' or 'mob' games still occur annually up and down the United Kingdom, often tied to ancient festivals. It was the Victorians who changed things, making games respectable, structured and central to education.

The new winter game which was to become Association football was first organised in, and then zealously carried out of, the finest public schools and universities from the middle years of the 19th century. At some schools success on the field was viewed as the greatest possible achievement, a way of disciplining oneself and governing others. These young men would join the professions or go into business, then literally club together to continue playing the game. More than any other group they moved football away from the narrow sphere of private education. By the 1880s, thanks to the establishment of, first, a national cup competition – The FA Cup – and then a national league competition – The Football League – football had exploded into the popular imagination.

The background to this was the British empire and the urbanisation which fed it. By the end of the century a fifth of the population lived in cities of over 200,000 people and another fifth in London. The country was quickly changing, with ever greater numbers experiencing life in the factories. Gradual improvements in both conditions and wages helped the game grow during this period. For the first time a good many people had a little to spend on leisure at the end of the working week.

The social impact of football was not lost on the writer and playwright, JB Priestley, who claimed, in his 1929 novel *The Good Companions*, it "turned you into a member of a new community, all brothers together for an hour and a half... you were there, cheering together, thumping one and another on the shoulders, swapping judgments like lords of the earth, having pushed your way through a turnstile into another and altogether more splendid kind of life."

In 1863 a group of old-boys clubs in the London area met to decide on the best way of playing each other. They came up with a name for their organisation – the Football Association. The FA's new unifying code adopted, with some minor adjustments, the rules drawn up by Sheffield FC. At this point modern football was born.

It's not clear why the first club emerged in Sheffield, but those behind it would have been socially privileged young gentlemen who understood how the game had been played in the schools. Their influence and that of the independent Sheffield FA was crucial. Corner kicks, free-kicks for handball, fixed crossbars, shin-guards and the referee's whistle are all believed to have come from Sheffield; as did the principle of the team first to be drawn being given home advantage in cup matches. By any standards that is a remarkable list. History, however, has never been quite enough, the fresh thrill of glory is also required.

I WAS SURPRISED THAT the only evidence of the derby on the streets the next morning was in the local press. The newsagent was a young Asian man, a Liverpool fan. This is relatively unusual – here the biggest teams in the country do not dominate. You will see very few Liverpool, Manchester United, Chelsea or Arsenal shirts in and around Sheffield. The blue and red of the local teams are much more common. This saturation of support means there is no escape, any supporter whose team loses the derby will be reminded constantly of the fact at home, at work and at play.

I paid for my newspaper and left, having been mordantly warned that "hell will go on fire, if Wednesday or United lose today". I headed out to Hillsborough on the Supertram hoping for a draw. Outside the ground a United fan issued another warning, telling me that she'd seen supporters "kicking hell" out of the family section buses on one occasion.

Fans are mainly split along family lines, with people choosing to support the club their fathers and grandfathers followed. Also, it's not unusual to find supporters of both clubs within the same families, living harmoniously most of the time, as Trevor Braithwait explained. "Traditionally you will love one and hate the other, it's as simple as that. I don't hate Sheffield United. But there are a lot of people who do despise them, and vice versa. You could have five adults from the same family go to the match together and come home together but three will be on one side and two on the other. Just friendly fun, but two hundred yards down the road you might see a chair flying through a window among sworn enemies."

It seemed I was being told contradictory things. Families supporting Wednesday, United, or a mix of both were able to go to the derby peacefully together, but there was also the distinct possibility of outright violence. The fact is there are two highly entrenched camps in the city, blue and white, and red and white, making anything possible on derby day.

Why things developed in this way isn't at all clear. There doesn't seem to be any great political or cultural differences between the fans; not these days at least. That itself may be the key. Sheffield never experienced any large scale immigration and so, compared to other major British cities, it has remained relatively isolated. It's not difficult to imagine how football became a natural outlet for young men's passions, where small historical differences between the clubs were magnified.

There's no escaping the fact that Wednesday are the elder club. They were formed in 1867 – twenty-two years before United. One evening in September of that year, on the site of what is now the Crucible Theatre, members of the Wednesday Cricket Club gathered to discuss what to do during the winter. Football was their solution. The playing colours of blue and white were chosen and within a month the Wednesday football team was up and running.

Wednesday won a number of competitions before United were even in existence and were often said to have what might be described as the 'vision thing'. During the early part of the 20th century Hillsborough was built into one of the leading grounds in the country. It was subsequently revamped in time for both the 1966 World Cup and the 1996 European Championships. Also, from the outset, the club saw itself as the moral guardians of the game, slowly and reluctantly accepting professionalism.

Wednesday have always been traditional in outlook, affluent, well-connected in local politics and to the national FA; altogether a bit stuffy. In contrast United have played the role of the younger, disreputable brother. The feeling has long been that one aspired to Wednesday, but simply inherited United.

This view is echoed by a rather unlikely source, Neil Warnock, the United manager – and renowned Blades fan – at the time of my visit. He believes Sheffield derbies are "the best games in the world", but admits United have been overshadowed by their neighbours for much of their history. "I started supporting United as a youngster because Wednesday were the massive club and everyone supported Wednesday, so I wanted to be the black sheep of the family and support the lesser club. We have always had lesser crowds than Wednesday... you are talking now about twenty or thirty years of dominance that Wednesday have had, so we've got to try and get up to the promised land and stay there and that's the only way of getting the next generation [to back United rather than Wednesday]."*

Warnock was right, Wednesday have often been in the ascendant, but not always, and many youngsters have tended to support whichever team was the more successful during their own formative years.

Outside the main entrance of the South Stand, I met Dan Hammond, a schoolteacher and well-known Wednesdayite. He feels that historically there has been something of a class element to the rivalry. "I don't wish to be stereotyping here, but the lower or left-wing worker may have chosen United in the early days and the more middle-class, perhaps the businessmen, may have chosen Wednesday. The club, Wednesday, was set up by a group of men who owned their own businesses. And the only time they had off was a Wednesday afternoon, so they played then and that was the cricket club as well. They were butchers and bankers and all that, rather than manual workers."

Officially Wednesday describe those who formed the football section as 'primarily local craftsmen'.** So Wednesday hardly began as an establishment club, but cultivated the image over time. Even though their founders weren't from what could be described as 'old money', nor even great 'new' industrial money, the fact they were tradesmen of varying descriptions allowed an independence from factory life.

---

* Neil Warnock, speaking on *Sky News*
** Sheffield Wednesday Official Website

United's earliest fans were probably something of a mixed bunch, comprised of supporters from failing teams, non-Wednesdayites and people close to Bramall Lane on the southern edge of the city centre, well away from Hillsborough. To a limited extent they have always seen themselves as the underdogs, which is not necessarily the same thing as being the smaller club. They feel United truly represent football in Sheffield, claiming their support has always been more localised than that of their rivals.

United, they say, come from the city centre, or close to it – Wednesday from the northern edge of Sheffield and have always relied on supporters coming in from nearby towns to bolster their numbers. Both sides now have fans scattered throughout the city and well beyond. The old zonal dividing lines of the past have blurred greatly.

Wednesdayites scoff at the idea of United having more fans from Sheffield, suggesting that claim is based on nothing more than an inferiority complex. Whatever the truth, it is clear United are well aware of their status as a major institution in the community. In 2001, as part of the redevelopment of Bramall Lane, the club opened an enterprise centre, providing accommodation for small businesses. It is a commercial project, but one with obvious benefits to the city.

Here history winks at us and smiles. United's ground came into being as a sporting arena away from the smog of the steel factories, a place where games could be played and watched by all. But it was Wednesday who originally played at what was to become the home of their rivals, hiring it from the United Cricket Club.

Strangely it was the actions of the Wednesday footballers which brought about the creation of their rivals. The Wednesday committee felt they were losing out by having to rent a ground and were also paying too much for the privilege. The obvious solution was to find their own place and by the start of the 1887 season they were gone. This was a big financial blow. United knew how popular football was becoming and the kind of money it could generate. They were forced to move to fill the gap left by Wednesday. The FA Cup semi-final of 1889 was played at Bramall Lane and the high attendance that day rammed home the point that United really needed their own football team. Within a week Sheffield United had been formed.

The prospect of having to share the city with another team caused deep unhappiness in the Wednesday ranks and many people wondered whether Sheffield was big enough to provide for both clubs. Dark conspiracies were also circulating about United's motives – were they simply trying to frighten Wednesday back to Bramall Lane by claiming to have set-up their own club? The answer was no. Sheffield United soon became part of the sporting landscape, being given the name The Cutlers, to reflect their roots. Amazingly at this time Wednesday were known – in reference to the Steel City's knife-making heritage – as The Blades, the name now so firmly associated with United. Wednesday dropped this shortly after moving to Hillsborough, in Owlerton, where they became 'the Owls'.

These then, were the ideal building blocks in the formation of a serious rivalry, something made clear in a United match pro-gramme of the mid-1930s: "Feelings arose well nigh to human hate and passion, which football is capable of rousing. It is scarcely an exaggeration to say that business bargains and relationships were influenced, private friendships shattered and even families divided owing to claims of jealous football clubs … there was between the partisans of United and Wednesday, jealousy, rancour and unchar-itableness."*

United, having begun their football club, were determined it should work and tried desperately to make themselves more popular than their rivals. Season ticket prices to watch Wednesday in 1890 were 7 shillings and 6 pence. On learning this United, priced theirs at just 5 shillings and, better still, would charge just three pence admission for matches which clashed with Wednesday's home games. The tactics were simple, they would undercut Wednesday in a blatant attempt to win fans over to their side. The constant niggling between the clubs until this point had made it impossible for a derby match to take place. Wednesday had made their feelings on the matter clear; the first Sheffield derby would take place at Olive Grove, their home ground at the time, or not at all. In 1890, during the run up to Christmas, United agreed, with one newspaper describing the atmosphere at the match as "raw and

* Sheffield Wednesday Official Website

slightly laden with fog and smoke. The light was bad and the outlook altogether far from agreeable. Yet everybody was in good spirits".*

The outlook was indeed disagreeable for United supporters among the ten thousand or so who turned up. The first derby was heading for a 1-1 draw when Wednesday, in the drawing gloom of the afternoon, scored a late winner. The senior club had triumphed.

Even so Wednesday were not about to reach out with an olive branch from Olive Grove. In 1892 they refused to play a local cup final against United at Bramall Lane on the grounds that this would not be a neutral venue. Perhaps this was understandable given that, the previous October, United had extracted stinging revenge for their defeat in the first Sheffield derby, cuffing Wednesday 5-0 in the rematch. Relations were not helped when, in the wake of that triumph, their supporters circulated this funeral notice throughout the town:

'In loving Remembrance of
the
SHEFFIELD WEDNESDAY FOOTBALL TEAM
who were safely put to rest on Monday October the 26th
at Bramall Lane
Poor old Wednesday were fairly done,
When United beat them five to none;
Although they lost, they did their best,
So let them quietly take their rest.
(Friends of the above kindly accept this intimation).**

Wednesday officials were so outraged at the defeat that an emergency meeting was called. Three weeks later United were beaten 4-1 at Olive Grove, prompting a new funeral card:

* *Sheffield Football, A History*, K Farnsworth
** *Sheffield Football, A History*, K Farnsworth

'In pitiful remembrance of
Our idols, the
SHEFFIELD UNITED FOOTBALL TEAM
who departed their football life,
Struggling to the end,
At Olive Grove on Monday November 16th 1891.
When United died, they struggled hard
Enough to live a brighter and longer life;
Do as they would they could not ward
Neat kicks by Wednesday, and thus the strife
Ended, thus closed famous United's reign;
Sheffield now mourns their death the more,
Dying as they did -- ne'er to rise again.
And kick for fame at Wednesday's door.
Yes United have lost four to one.' *

THE JAGGED NATURE OF their relationship was further complicated when the clubs first gained entry to the Football League. Wednesday went straight into Division One while United started in the Second Division, an injustice in their eyes. To Wednesday this initial difference in league status simply confirmed their superiority. United would be back on equal terms the following year, however, having won promotion. The rest of the century – and the next – would see a constant battle for supremacy in the city.

In 1898 United, boasting famous names such as England half-back Ernest 'Nudger' Needham and the gargantuan goalkeeper William 'Fatty' Foulke, became the first Sheffield team to rise to be the champions of England. They won the FA Cup the following season and again in 1902, 1915 and 1925. Since then they have taken silverware during promotion campaigns and have been losing FA Cup finalists. United have sunk as low as the bottom division of the Football League, but were in the Premiership at its inception, although they were relegated in its second season, 1994. Their story is, to some extent, that of nearly men.

* *Sheffield Football, A History,* K Farnsworth

It is a tag which can also be attached to Wednesday. Since 1900 they have won the league championship on four occasions, the last in 1930. They have also won Division Two five times and the FA Cup in 1896, 1907 and 1935 – their last major success before beating Manchester United 1-0 in the final to take the League Cup in 1991.

Two years later the Sheffield clubs took over 75,000 fans to Wembley for the semi-final of the FA Cup. The match was sold out two days before tickets had even been due to go on sale after police became worried about the large numbers of people who were already queuing at the grounds. The Football Association had wanted the tie to be played at Elland Road, Leeds. An intense rivalry also exists between the two Yorkshire cities so this was the last place Sheffielders wanted their biggest ever derby to be staged. The other semi-final, between Spurs and Arsenal, was scheduled for Wembley; the Sheffield clubs and their fans demanded, and got, the same venue.

The match is fondly remembered by the vast majority of those who were there, especially the Wednesday contingent, who saw their team win 2-1 after extra time. Off the field the whole event had been a triumph. Fans mixed on the way to London and this was, without doubt, one of the friendliest, if not the friendliest Steel City derby ever staged. A carnival mood prospered amid the unusual setting, a contrast to the atmosphere more often associated with the matches in Sheffield.

As recently as 2000 and again in 2002 fans were arrested and some jailed after serious derby day fighting in the city centre. The fact that the teams are not always competing in the same division can make this situation more flammable; the lack of derbies seems to lead to an enormous discharge of aggression when the sides do clash. Lessons have been learned and extra police are now always on duty before during and after these fixtures.

But the phenomenon is not new. As far back as 1892 players from both sides joined the fighting among a large number of spec-tators, before dozens of police waded in to stop the violence. The players restricted themselves to on-field violence during an uncompromising FA Cup clash at the end of the 19th century. It became so much of a battle that the local paper said: "the play degenerated into a bitter feud in which retribution was the name of the game."*

THERE HAVE BEEN MANY other famous meetings and incidents. Yet when I asked supporters, one derby dominated their thoughts, even though it took place at the close of the 1970s. The biggest crowd ever to gather in the old Third Division – over 49,000 – saw the first match between the sides for eight years. It was Boxing Day 1979.

The city council had been so worried about the potential for violence that the kick-off at Hillsborough was brought forward to 11am, before the pubs opened. The biggest police operation ever seen in Sheffield at that time was mounted, with officers describing it as a military operation. A local TV report explained why: "with a capacity crowd expected it could also mean the kind of crowd trouble which almost inevitably accompanies such occasions."**

In the end it all passed off peacefully, the only violence done was to Sheffield United's reputation in what came to be known as the Boxing Day Massacre. It turned out to be the most important post-war match between the clubs.

That season United had looked a good bet for promotion and were leading the table going into the match, Wednesday were not among the top sides. What followed, in the 100th Sheffield derby in league and cup competition, was exceptional. Wednesday took the lead from long-range shortly before half-time. The expected second-half comeback by United never materialised – Wednesday scoring two goals in as many minutes and one more, a penalty, three minutes before the end. It was an historic and highly significant victory.

Four goals against United without reply sparked an ailing side into action. While United crumpled, winning only another four matches in the league, Wednesday were propelled forward, promoted to Division Two at the end of the season, and eventually back into the top division under Howard Wilkinson. United finished well down the table, and were relegated the following year. The match is now part of Wednesday lore:

* *Sheffield Football, A History,* K Farnsworth
** *Look North,* December 1979

'Hark now hear the Wednesday sing
United ran away
And we will fight for evermore
Because of Boxing Day.'

The Massacre changed the fortunes of United and Wednesday for years to come. It has also had a lasting effect on the psyche of both sets of supporters. Wednesdayites, in 2006, were seriously worried about the prospect of taking on United. It wasn't just that they felt they could lose to a better team, but the possible margin of victory which really troubled them. Trevor Braithwait spelt it out. "United will one day avenge that four-nil massacre of '79 and you just don't know when it's going to come and you don't want to be there to see it. To do it in our backyard would be even worse."

Wednesday fans were clearly uncomfortable at the prospect of facing a resurgent United, desperate for more promotion points. But the meeting at Hillsborough would also increase the pressure on United. Just as in 1979 they were the form team on the cusp of success; a success which would see them move ahead of their rivals into a higher division and confirm their status as the best side in the city. They badly wanted to reach the high plains of the Premiership, from where they would be able to look down on Wednesday.

A sustained period in that league would give United the exposure they craved and remove any underlying feeling of inferiority. Whichever way you looked at it there was a lot to play for in that particular corner of S6 that Saturday afternoon.

Hillsborough is hardly modern, but remains an impressive stadium with single-tiered stands sloping gently down to the pitch. The pre-match derby atmosphere seemed like the real thing, noisy and aggressive. James Shield follows United for the *Sheffield Star* newspaper. He's originally from London and told me he hadn't initially realised the importance of the match. "The first time I covered this game it was quite a surprise just how intense and passionate it was. The funny thing is, and this surprised me even at work, the people in the print room and that kind of thing will quite happily work together during the week, but you can almost see the personas changing a couple of days coming up to this. It gets intense, very antagonistic, very, very partisan and it does get a little bit like a mini war type of thing – and that's on the pitch as well."

From the back of the South Stand I could see what he was getting at. It was still a good half-hour before kick-off and already both sets of fans were trying to out-sing each other and doing their best to encourage or intimidate the players. Today's match would be the biggest attendance in the Championship all season. Wednesday fans tend to turn out in numbers. Despite their lowly league position they regularly get crowds at home of well over 20,000. But these healthy attendances belie the fact that it is easy to spot that the club is now under considerable financial pressure. Everything is sponsored in a bid to squeeze as much cash as possible out of the marketing of match days, even the time added at the end of each half. I shuddered at this, for a club of Wednesday's size it was all distinctly small-fry.

It's not difficult to pin-point exactly when things began to go wrong. In 1997 the directors, with an eye on eventually floating on the Stock Exchange, asked an investment bank – Charterhouse Development Capital – to come on board in return for a significant holding. Wednesday were already in debt and the idea was that new money from Charterhouse would help balance the books and bolster the training facilities, the ground and the squad. The move was designed to make Wednesday more attractive in the long-run but the terms of the deal enraged the fans. More than 35 per-cent of one of the biggest clubs in England had been sold off to venture capitalists for a stunningly low sum – £15.6 million. Getting into bed with the investors would, in time, have its consequences. Supporters groups felt they were the wrong partner at the wrong time, and certainly at the wrong price. In short, the club could have got more for its money, a commodity which was soon to be needed like never before at Sheffield Wednesday.

On the pitch there was an incident which made national headlines, though hardly for the best of reasons. In September 1998 the talented but temperamental Italian, Paulo Di Canio, pushed referee Paul Alcock. He staggered backwards for what seemed like an age, before eventually landing on his backside. It looked funny on *Match Of The Day*, but for the club and the player the aftermath wasn't – Di Canio was banned for eleven matches and left Wednesday within months.

He was soon replaced by more high-profile imports on bumper salaries. The football which followed didn't mirror their first-class reputations. The feeling was these players were happy to sit back and take the money rather than fight for points. In 2000 they were relegated and sank into the First Division. The club had no choice but to keep paying Premiership-sized wages to those same players, all on long contracts, but without the money generated by being in the top league. They spent the next three seasons in Division One before being relegated again. All of this was financially shattering, and something from which they are yet to recover. Wednesday continue to battle debts of around £25 million.

The problems at Hillsborough may have been mocked by fans on the other side of the city, but in truth, financial insecurity was nothing new at Bramall Lane either. Over time the cricket pavilion, a remnant of the club's beginnings and which had seen an Ashes Test match at the ground in 1902, had been joined by three football stands. At the turn of the 1970s, with United newly promoted back to the top flight and boasting the likes of the mercurial midfielder Tony Currie and England keeper Alan Hodgkinson in their side, those in charge felt a revamp was needed in order to compete at the highest level. The ground would be turned into a 'normal' four-sided stadium. It was a gamble which failed to pay off and almost ruined Sheffield United.

The last cricket match was played at Bramall Lane in 1973. Two years later a new South Stand was built. The cost of the renovation was high and went well over budget. United did well in 1975, just failing to qualify for Europe. But the next season they were relegated; there had not been sufficient investment in the team because of the high cost of ground improvements. It would be difficult to pay off the debts of the new stand while out of the top flight. The solution was even greater frugality on the pitch, but less quality there led to more misfortune, United were relegated to Division Four in 1981, having missed a penalty in the last minute of the final game of the season, which would have kept them up. They then pin-balled up and down the divisions, but were back in the old Division One by the beginning of the 1990s and in 1992 became a founder member of the Premier League at a time when serious money was about to flood into the game. They stayed there only until 1994, and have since been regular candidates to come back up, only to miss out and in doing so place the board under increasing fiscal strain. This time, surely, they would make it.

AROUND 7,000 UNITEDITES had come across the city and were packed into the Leppings Lane end. I have to admit I couldn't look at them without thinking of how 96 Liverpool fans had lost their lives there seventeen years earlier. A disastrous combination of what can, at best, be described as highly questionable policing and grossly inadequate safety measures inside the ground left dozens unable to breathe in a terrifying crush. From time to time football has a way of reminding us that for all it is loved, there are more important things. That was true in 1989 and was also the case for the derby I'd come to see.

As the teams gathered around the centre circle just before kick-off no-one could have been in any doubt that the Blades fans were about to be examined every bit as much as their players would be once the ball was rolling. There was a burst of applause as the stadium announcer explained what was happening...

'A one-minute silence for two Wednesday supporters killed in mid-week will begin when the referee sounds his whistle.'

The moments which followed would clearly set the tone for the rest of the afternoon. I was nervous. Since I'd been told that the derby was 'like a religion' and 'the passion of the city' I was in two minds as to how the away end would react. Many United fans had said they hated Wednesday and they didn't expect the silence to hold. Others were prepared to 'take the mick' about the deaths, but would remain quiet during the silence. They had no time for Wednesday, but didn't want to see their fans dying.

The crowd hushed, there was a collective intake of breath as the referee gave a single long blast on his whistle and ...

Nothing, not a sound. Around me Wednesday fans stood, their heads bowed. Hands were fumbled with or clasped behind backs. Then slowly a banner was raised high in the away end – black letters on a white background, it said simply 'SHAUN STEPHEN' – the forenames of the two dead Wednesday boys. This was a real touch of class, a grand gesture, when what had been expected was a scabrous disregard for the feelings of the Wednesday supporters. There was another blast from the whistle and the roar which followed signalled that honour had been satisfied. Sheffield collectively exhaled.

Really the match wasn't much of a contest. There was a pretty relentless flow towards the Wednesday goal. The United fans were enjoying themselves. Hemmed in by blue, but dominant on the pitch, they took the lead from a free-kick and made it 2-0 shortly before half-time:

'Stand up if you're going up... Stand up if your going up...'

This was followed, to general grumblings around me, by: 'You're so shit it's unbelievable.'

United also had the best of the second half and could easily have been four ahead – a score to chill Wednesdayites to the marrow. There were varied reactions from the home support. Many just seemed to accept they were being outplayed, while others were furious. I heard one shout of "kill him" as a Wednesday player went in for a crunching tackle. There was no real malice in this, it was more about the need to atone for some sloppy defending. The Wednesday manager, Paul Sturrock, was also told to "get a fucking goalkeeper." Rather more disturbing, given the context of the match, was the Wednesday chant:

'Die die United, die die, singing die die...'

From both sides there were constant shouts about 'Pigs'. Fans in Sheffield often refer to each other in this way. This is unusual, since in most other rivalries there are distinct terms of abusive for the opposition. Supporters are unsure about the origin of the term and which side used it first, though it's an accepted fact that the expression dates back to around the 1960s. United fans claim to have been the original authors. The suggestion is they began using the name because Wednesday call themselves The Owls. Blades fans are said to have decided that a pig – traditionally seen as the lowest animal – would be more appropriate. One group of Unitedites sung me their song which goes: 'Oh I've never felt more like swinging a pig, from Hyde Park flats to Wadsley Bridge'. Hyde Park flats are considered to be in the United end of the city, Wadsley Bridge is Wednesday territory.

Wednesday supporters are just as convinced they first used the name. These claims seem to centre on the consumption of bacon, strangely enough. It has long been said that Owls fans wouldn't eat bacon on Sunday if United had won the day before. Dan Hammond thinks there's some truth in that. "I've had this argument so many times, my mates will say to me 'oh Wednesday are the original pigs', but my Dad always used to say that when he was young he didn't eat bacon because it was red and white, bacon comes from a pig and United play in red and white. The other thing is, if you mix red and white together, you get pink, which is the colour of a pig. So they are the true pigs."

It looked very much as though the traditional English breakfast was unlikely to be served in many Wednesdayite homes that weekend. Their fans must have begun to wonder whether their team would ever really have a go, but the noise around me increased considerably from the moment Steven MacLean slotted away a penalty to make it 2-1. It continued throughout almost all of the ten minutes which remained as Wednesday battled away and had two goal-bound efforts swept off the United line. Having been so dominant, the Blades had to hang on for the points, but just before full-time, realising they were about to triumph, they sang:

'Warnock, Warnock gives us a wave ...'

Furtively, down on the touchline, flailing and pointing at his players like a drunken puppet, the United manager obliged. This was more than the Wednesday crowd could take. They responded with a rousing chorus:

'Fuck all, you've never won fuck all.'

AS THE REFEREE BROUGHT THe proceedings to a close the unofficial United anthem – *The Greasy Chip Butty Song* – was belted out across Hillsborough, to the tune of *Annie's Song* by John Denver:

'You fill up my senses
Like a gallon of Magnet
Like a packet of Woodbine
Like a good pinch of snuff
Like a night out in Sheffield

Like a greasy chip butty
Like Sheffield United
Come thrill me again….
Na na na na na oooooooooooooo….'

Neil Warnock went onto the pitch to congratulate his men and acknowledge the supporters. His fist was high, his arm curled. He punched the air and walked away grinning. More than anyone else at the club he symbolised United. He is reviled by Owls fans. One described him to me as a 'petty, small-minded man'.

I didn't have long to wait to see him at close quarters. Half an hour after the match, forty of us were downstairs in the small press room. The United manager appeared first. Warnock was statesman-like, full of cheer, speaking quietly and cracking jokes. He mentioned the silent tribute and looked genuinely moved by the conduct of the fans. After a few questions he slipped into a side room.

A deflated Paul Sturrock took his place. He sounded flat, almost pained. As he was talking about his team having "thirteen cup finals left" to save their place in the division, the door behind him opened and out came Warnock, flashing another smile in our direction. Sturrock momentarily turned his head to look, and there in that cameo was the moment which summed up the day, the hurt of defeat on the one hand, maybe even a little jealousy, and, on the other, simple joy at a job done.

As I left, groups of journalists were swarming around players looking for an angle or a good quote. Being unsure of the geography of Hillsborough I managed to turn into a very narrow white-washed corridor, at the end of which I could see daylight. This turned out to be the players' entrance. My path was blocked by a female steward who had her back to me. In front of her, doing their best to get in, were three men. My first thought was that they were old-school Blades lads trying their luck. I had no choice but to wait until these obviously uninvited guests were dealt with. The one doing the talking was wearing a baseball cap. He was tall and slim and had blonde hair sticking out over his shoulders. With the total conviction of someone in authority the steward scolded him: "Look, you can't come in this way. It doesn't matter WHO you are, you can't come in here."

She was given a pleading look and an engaging smile, but still stood firm. The three then tried to laugh as if they didn't care, turned and marched off. I followed, only then realising that the person apparently trying the old 'don't you know who I am' line, was the Hollywood star and well known Blades fan, Sean Bean. Obviously status, riches and success hadn't changed the way he felt about beating Wednesday, something he'd been keen to tell the United team first-hand.

For the Wednesday fans it must have been a sombre journey home. Their prospects of avoiding relegation had hardly been improved and on top of that – on their own ground and at their expense – United had taken another step towards a place among the glamour boys. Wednesdayites didn't like the fact that their rivals were heading for the Premiership, but knew that they had been beaten by a better side.

The actions of the United fans during the silence had also proved that, when circumstances demand it, even old enmities can be put aside, in the short term at least. This was very short in some cases. The day after the match United's Irish international Alan Quinn was arrested on suspicion of assault in connection with a fight in a pub in the city which left a man in hospital. The 26 year-old, who didn't even play in the derby, was asked by police about claims he had attacked the man during a game of pool. One witness spoke of a brawl of up to twenty people. Another said... "it was terrible, very frightening, like something out of a film. I've never seen any-thing so appalling in my life." *

The news that one of his players had apparently been in a fight just hours after the match did not fill Neil Warnock with joy. He immediately banned the squad from drinking in pubs for their own safety, saying he'd "ask Alan to look at himself. He goes out to find a pool table in a Sheffield Wednesday pub the day after we'd beaten our bitter rivals at Hillsborough. Hello Alan – work it out for yourself, son. It doesn't seem to have been the brightest idea he's ever had, that's for sure."** Certainly, it would have been impossible for

* *Sheffield Star, February 2006*
** Neil Warnock, quoted on *eleven-a-side.com*, April 2006

Quinn to plead ignorance, having previously spent seven years in the colours of a certain Sheffield Wednesday.

SHEFFIELD UNITED MADE IT into the Premiership at the end of the 2005/06 season, although a turbulent campaign would end in instant relegation. But for now there was only glee at making it back into the big time for the first time in 12 years. They finished in second place in the Championship and were promoted along with Reading and play-off winners Watford. Wednesday managed to avoid relegation, but not by much. They finished 19th, three places from the drop, but faced a battle the following season to remain in a position which would allow them to again try to challenge their neighbours. The old underdogs had shown Wednesday they had learned some new tricks in that never ending scrap for pre-eminence in the city of steel.

BIRMINGHAM:

An Unquiet Easter

"The atmosphere reminded me of when I played in Turkey, where it can be really hostile … everyone was really ready for it."

Steve Bruce – *Birmingham Mail, April 2006*
(talking about the first derby of the 21st century in 2002).

THE WOMAN ON THE OTHER end of the phone would not be moved. No, I couldn't buy a ticket for Aston Villa against Birmingham City, even though there were still some available. I asked why and was told it was police advice for a local derby, only people already on Villa's official database could have them. In turn, the police said it wasn't a case of them telling the club what to do, but a 'general agreement' to stop rival fans ending up in the home end.

To be fair both Aston Villa and the good officers of the West Midlands force had reason to be jumpy. This would be the eighth meeting between the teams since they were reunited in the Premiership in 2002. With Birmingham's return to the top division old wounds had not so much been reopened, but torn apart.

September the 16th that year was a black day, or rather night, in the history of the fixture. The match was being televised live and had been built-up beforehand, principally because the clubs had spent sixteen years in different divisions. The last time they'd played league football against each other Diego Maradona was about to win the World Cup for Argentina, with a 'hand-of-God' goal along the way, Margaret Thatcher was coming to the end of her second term as Prime Minister and Duran Duran, the new romantics from Birmingham, were still one of the biggest bands in the world. That season Birmingham City were relegated, though not before comfortably winning the last derby at Villa Park.

It was to be an inglorious return for the fixture. When Birmingham's Clinton Morrison gave the home side the lead after half an hour dozens of their fans ran onto the pitch in celebration. The same thing happened after the break when the Villa goalkeeper, Peter Enckelman, mis-kicked a throw-in, letting the ball roll into an empty net. He was taunted by invading fans, one at particularly close range.

Birmingham made it 3-0 in the dying minutes and again the supporters flooded onto the pitch. The Football Association immediately charged Birmingham City over the behaviour of their fans. They were fined £25,000, one supporter was jailed for four months and another fifteen appeared before magistrates charged with violent disorder. The club's chairman, David Gold, was not amused by the scenes, but refused to class them as pitch invasions: "It was a handful of fans in pure jubilation. This was not an invasion where fans were fighting each other or were attacking players ... In all the great matches you are, from time to time, going to get some fans on the pitch."*

So, would the situation be different when they met for the second time that season in another evening kick-off? Not a chance. The following March the Blues beat Villa again, this time 2-0 at Villa Park. Things were just as fractions, with clashes between fans both inside and outside the stadium. There were reports of supporters still fighting at midnight and during the match a handful again managed to get onto the pitch. The ill-feeling spread all too easily to the players, with several squaring up. Two were sent off and there was an alleged spitting incident just for good measure. After the match, death threats were made against Birmingham's Welsh midfielder, Robbie Savage, and the FA held another inquiry.

From then on, kick-off times for the derby would be carefully managed, early on a Sunday being the optimum time for order to be maintained if not a cracking football match to break out. It was felt the late starts had given the fans time to consume too much alcohol, giving rise to the violence. West Midlands Police were determined

* David Gold, *The Independent*, September 2002

to be seen to be doing everything possible to avoid any repetition. The following season they told the media that known hooligans could be put under house arrest before the derby and only released when the game was over.

AN OPENLY ADMITTED HATRED BETWEEN the fans lies at the heart of the trouble. Once Birmingham had re-joined Villa in the Premiership their fans were desperate to show they deserved to be there. Those first matches were acutely tribal and emotional affairs. The lack of league matches between the two in more than a decade and half meant there had been no pressure valve to release this tension, no catharsis. The authorities were simply over-whelmed by the reaction of the supporters.

The second derby of the 2005/06 season was scheduled for Easter Sunday – April 16th – kick-off at the very sober hour of midday. One local vicar, the Rev Andy Jolley, was not, despite his name, at all happy about the timing. His church, and many others in the area, were aggrieved that it was being played during one of the most important services in the Christian calendar. Mr Jolley admitted to me that the match had "a history of difficulties", with violence the previous season spreading into the city centre. Yet, he was mystified as to why the game had to be played at midday on Sunday rather than at that time on Saturday. Goodness knows what the forefathers of the clubs would have made of the situation. Certainly they would have had great difficulty in accepting or understanding how or why they were playing on Easter Sunday, since both Aston Villa and Birmingham City had emerged from local churches.

Early in 1874 a group of around a dozen young Methodists – members of the Villa Cross Wesleyan Chapel – gathered under a street light along Heathfield Road, close to Villa Park. It's a romantic image, but one which no-one doubts is the true origin of Aston Villa. The men, who were really cricketers, are said to have watched a kick-about and decided to get involved in the new game. Just as in Sheffield, they saw football as a means of staying together during the winter.

In the autumn of 1875 cricketers from a church (variously described as Holy Cross and Holy Trinity) based in Bordesley Green near Small Heath formed a football club for the same reason. They were known then as Small Heath Alliance, but would become, in turn, Small Heath, Birmingham FC and, by the middle of the 20th century, Birmingham City FC.

It should be stressed that neither club held onto their religious background in any meaningful sense. They were founded by ordinary members of the church rather than the clergy themselves and, though they were religious men, football was the only real purpose of their activities. They were not trying to build clubs for their churches and these nominal religious ties fell away completely as interest in the game expanded rapidly throughout the region. Just as in the other great industrial centres, football had gripped the Second City of the UK, the Workshop of the World, the City of a Thousand Trades.

The old industries have now faded, but Birmingham, it seems, is continuing to thrive. The day before the match I found the main shopping area of New Street bustling with happy consumers clutching large plastic bags bearing the names of every high street brand imaginable. In the twilight I reached the Bull Ring, a part of central Birmingham with a vexed history. This spot has been the heartbeat of the city since the middle ages. Here, as the name suggests, the rather cruel sport by today's standards of bull 'baiting' or killing took place, and possibly the more exotic art of bull running, a practice seen across southern France and northern Spain to this day, and one which would certainly give Britain's Health and Safety officers a collective heart attack. More importantly it became the site of a long-standing market.

In the 1960s the Bull Ring shopping centre was built. Its modernist, concrete architecture and maze of subways was meant to herald a bright new dawn after the physical destruction of the bombs which rained down during the Second World War. It was soon detested by the pubic and fell into disrepair. From its ruins sprang, in 2003, the new Bull Ring complex complete with the breathtaking, futuristic Selfridges building; decorated with thousands of aluminium panels it looks every inch the alien spacecraft of a child's imagination.

THE NEXT MORNING, FROM A now uninhabited New Street, I took a taxi out onto empty dual carriageways, past blocks of flats and old warehouses into Aston in the north-east of the city. The general perception is that the area is rundown, suffering from all the usual problems associated with poorer urban areas. The most high-profile example being the fatal shooting of the teenagers, Letisha Shakespeare and Charlene Ellis, in the neighbouring Lozells district in early January 2003. It also has a burgeoning and highly visible Muslim community. Here, in backstreets next to shops selling Halal meat, exotic fruit and every conceivable fabric, you will find the modern home of what was, a century ago, the greatest football club in the world – Aston Villa.

When Villa moved there in 1897 they felt it would be the perfect platform for a club without parallel, one which had become nothing less than a winning machine. Villa's early history is dominated by two things, trophies and Scots. George Ramsey captained the team which won the club's first trophy in 1880. He'd seen the players knocking a ball around in Aston Park and begged them for a game. He revolutionised Villa's outlook and was the force behind what would come to be seen as their golden age. Archie Hunter took Villa to their first FA Cup win in 1887; while their director, William McGregor, secured his place in the history books by becoming the founder of the Football League. It was from the influence of these men that Villa took their crest – The Lion Rampant of Scotland – and their Presbyterian motto – Prepared.

By the outbreak of the Great War, six league championships and five FA Cups had been won. Not only were they the most popular club in Birmingham, they were loved throughout England. The Villans were the aristocrats of football, complete with clones such as West Ham United and Burnley, who copied their claret and blue colours in the hope of intimidating the opposition.

The men in charge of Villa at this time certainly felt the club was what we today might describe as a 'brand leader'. Before the war intervened, a stadium with a capacity of 130,000 was under serious consideration. It was a hugely ambitious plan for the time, and one intended to cement their success for generations to come. Yet in 1936 the unthinkable happened, they were relegated. This was an event which, even when seen through the grainy kaleidoscope of history, takes on seismic proportions. It was the equivalent of Real Madrid or Manchester United being demoted today, almost impossible to imagine.

Villa would bounce back, but never really to quite the same heights. Since those days they have, with some significant exceptions, sailed mainly on the undulating seas of mediocrity. Their captains have lifted the FA Cup, the League Cup and even the championship again in 1981. The last of these was a precursor to their greatest moment in the second-half of the 20th century – beating Bayern Munich in the European Cup final. But those achievements have been offset by relegation, not only to Division Two, but as low as the old Third Division. Since the late 1980s Villa, at least, have not been out of the highest division, finishing as runners-up on one occasion, although other seasons have seen yet more frantic struggles to avoid the drop.

If Villa's history has been of rise and fall, for their rivals it has been more about failure to scale the heights. Birmingham City, for most of their existence, have been very much the poor relations. However, they have had their occasional moments of success. One of these was the first ever match against Villa in 1879. Small Heath, as they were known, won by what was described at the time as 'a single goal and a disputed goal to nil'. The fixture was not quite the David against Goliath meeting we may imagine. Small Heath had been founded just a year after Villa themselves and were popular enough, using enclosed football grounds within their first two seasons. Since then Blues have been FA Cup finalists twice and champions of Division Two five times. But the club has won just one major trophy, the League Cup in 1963. It must have been a sweet victory though, beating Villa 3-1 on aggregate in the final. This triumph was not totally without precedent. Birmingham also edged out Villa to take the Football League Championship (South) on goal difference in 1945/46. It may sound a little arcane now, but was no mean feat. Before the return of 'proper' peacetime football, clubs played on a regional basis and this league involved all the pre-war First and Second Division clubs south of Derby, including Arsenal, Spurs and Portsmouth, winners of two post-war titles.

Perhaps their finest season was 1956, when Blues lost to Manchester City in the final of the Cup after finishing the season in sixth place, their best to date. This was the beginning of a fine run for the club over the next decade. In 1960 they became the first British club to reach a European final, losing the Fairs Cup to Barcelona and again to Roma the following year. Then came that first major trophy. The 1970s saw the team spearheaded by the young Trevor Francis, who would go on to become the first player transferred for £1 million.

Though Birmingham did not always succeed on the field of play, their activities in the boardroom were another matter. It's said that, back in the 1880s, they were the first club in the country to turn professional and had also been the first to form a limited company with directors formally appointed to run things. They often struggled with debts during this period too. It seems a bizarre practice today, but on at least two occasions they quite legally took money from opponents to give up home advantage.

You don't have to look too hard to uncover the obvious frustration that has built-up at the club and there have been desperate efforts to turn their fortunes around. Some of the most bizarre of these are linked to the story of the gypsy curse. Legend has it that their ground, St Andrew's, was built on a Romany encampment and the team was cursed to fail by the travellers who were forced to make room for the new ground. It's really not clear whether there is any truth in the story, but it is has haunted Birmingham right into the modern era, sometimes in the most amusing ways – to all but the Blues support.

Just imagine you are the manager of the club. The team is struggling, you're worried. It's not that the players simply aren't up to the job – no, it's the curse again. That was the conclusion of Ron Saunders in the 1980s when he had crucifixes hung from the floodlights and the soles of the players boots painted red. Barry Fry went one better, personally urinating in each corner of the pitch in the belief that it would improve matters.

City's bad luck has not just been restricted to events on the pitch. There was also an unfortunate mishap during the Second World War when the main stand was damaged by fire, not at the hands of the German Luftwaffe, but rather when a fire warden decided to douse a small blaze with a bucket of petrol, believing it to be water.

Most fans will say that they don't really believe in the curse, though that doesn't dilute its power. Supporters tend to invoke it when things are not going well and so it remains, hanging over St Andrew's. Eventually one group decided to take matters into their own hands. If they could not be rid of the curse then they would make damn sure their rivals also had to endure it. There were rumours that Birmingham fans working on the rebuilding of Villa's

Trinity Road Stand at the start of this century managed to steal some concrete from St Andrew's and embed it there. Much to the delight of their rivals, Villa cannot claim to truly have had an outstanding season since.

Putting sorcery to one side, in principle everything required for Birmingham City to be successful seems in place. The club has always been reasonably well supported, based as it is, in one of the largest conurbations in the country. But the truth is Villa's great early triumphs and popularity made it vastly more difficult for others to blossom. Birmingham, too, did not always find it easy to win approval with the local authorities. Perhaps the best example of this came shortly after the outbreak of World War II. The area around St Andrew's was deemed to be a danger zone and the club was banned from playing there. When the Home Secretary reversed the decision in March 1940, allowing them to return, the local chief constable and eight members of the council were furious. It was hardly a gesture of support on their part.

Also, they had long wished to change their name from Birmingham FC to Birmingham City FC. This had first been tried in 1905. Then, a director proposed the new title because, he said, the Blues were the only Football League club playing within the historic boundaries of Birmingham. At the time the Small Heath shareholders rejected the suggestion, but a compromise was found and the team became Birmingham FC. Tony Matthews, in his book, *Birmingham City, The Complete Record*, claims this produced plenty of critics. "Some people did not take wholeheartedly to the change and one reporter referred to 'the Small Heath club now masquerading as Birmingham'."

The issue never quite went away and eventually, amid booming gates at the end of the Second World War, the club achieved its objective, gaining the title we know them by today. While all this sounds straightforward enough, it wasn't by any means. The directors had been reluctant to add the word City to their name without the backing of the council and a campaign lasting almost thirty years was necessary before agreement was reached.

There may have been a number of reasons why this took so long. Without doubt there were those who felt Birmingham FC hadn't won sufficient honours to represent the 'city of Birmingham' and didn't like the idea. There are Blues fans, though, who maintain that the lack of support for their new title among the city fathers was prompted by the hidden hand – or rather muscle – of Villa being flexed behind the scenes, unhappy that the name suggested Birmingham City were the club connected root and branch to people there. Villa's own name didn't have the same local connotations. Whatever the case may have been it didn't change the course of events; the Blues remained the second club of the Second City, something which has been a vital element in the rivalry.

Birmingham supporters claim Villa have an elitist attitude, an inability to let go of their early history, retaining 'ideas above their station'. Villa fans counter that they know they are living on their history, but, unlike Birmingham, they have much of it to be proud of. Not only that, they say the Blues support has a collective chip on its shoulder over the continual failings of their own team.

Birmingham fans do tend to get exasperated at the mention of Villa's past. One season-ticket holder made this clear, saying: "I just hate everything about them. They have got silver spoons in their mouths, their mouths are too big, and to be fair, they need to shut it." It's understandable that Blues fans don't like the fact they've never truly had a period to rival Villa's success, but at the same time they have been able to carve out their own niche as the city's working-class club.

Admittedly class is a difficult concept to pin down these days, but most of those who go to St Andrew's are happy to identify with what they see as their traditional outlook on football and an association with the city's poorer communities. This may be more than mere perception. Fans I spoke to claimed their club was, at heart, working-class, while Villa's supporters used the word 'posher' to describe why they were different to their rivals. The accusation from Birmingham supporters is that they are still solidly based in the south and east of the city, while many season ticket holders at Villa Park are now drawn from areas outside Birmingham, particularly to the north, which have become more affluent. Villa, it is said, are the team of the suburbs and therefore of the middle-classes.

AT THE GATES LEADING INTO the North Stand I met a bearded, cheery, middle-aged man. This was Ivan Barnsley, from the wonderfully-named Birmingham City Historical Society. Ivan has been following the team since 1953. He told me that these claims about class were not new, but had been voiced more frequently in recent seasons. To illustrate this he pointed to a queue of Villa glitterati who were waiting to drive into the ground in BMW's and 4x4 jeeps. "If you look at the car-park now, these are the sort of quality of cars. If you go down the Blues you've still got the bangers, the Volvos, the Hillman Imps and that sort of thing."

Ivan also told me how a recent survey had shown there was still a wide gap between the average salary of Aston Villa and Birmingham City fans. "That gulf is becoming wider, although I'm sure Villa do have a fair number of working-class fans and Birmingham will have a few middle-class fans. The heart of the club is working-class people. Steve Bruce [the then manager] has been making quite an issue out of this recently, the fact that he senses what they [the supporters] are, and that they are looking for effort and guts from the players. If they give that the fans don't seem to mind."

It's true that many Villa fans no longer live in Birmingham, but should that debar them from remaining strongly attached to their club? People living relatively comfortable lives outside the city may very well use the team as a link back to their own youth and cultural background. Birmingham fans see it differently. To them Villa's support has sold out by moving out.

In actual fact there are still plenty of Villa fans in town, but they tend to be dominated by the other side. This is how Caroline Gall, the author of *Zulus* (about Birmingham City's infamous hooligan firm) sees it: "Aston Villa lads know they have to watch their backs if they go into Birmingham city centre at times. They have to think twice about drinking there or they used to. Their pubs are just outside the city centre, whereas Birmingham is the city centre. It is Birmingham and they totally represent that." I was about to get my own personal tutorial on the Zulus, which would affirm this view.

VILLA PARK IS NOT UNUSUAL in that the entrance for the away fans is the area least cared for, in this case grimy and a bit rundown. At the corner of the North Stand and the Witton Lane Stand the Birmingham support was congregating. It was twenty minutes before kick-off. They were clearly agitated, constantly chanting and shouting. Few of them were wearing their team's colours and I'm not sure I saw even a single woman. They certainly looked and sounded very different to the average home supporter.

I approached a large group of men, all white, many in baseball caps, some heavily overweight. Each wore a large round pin-badge which carried the message – Fuck the Villa – complete with the image of a fat middle finger extended upwards from a fist. Tentatively I introduced myself and asked why they supported the Blues rather than their cross-city rivals. These were the responses, delivered in aggressive, staccato style:

"We were born in Birmingham, that's why we support the Blues. They are from the dirty side of town really. We are proper Birmingham."

"Basically, it's like they are the prawn sandwich brigade. I mean, Prince William supports them and all that."

"They are not from Birmingham. Aston is a little suburb of West Bromwich. There's only one Birmingham club and that's Birmingham City."

"We all stick together and they are all shit. Tossers basically, they don't do the name of Birmingham any good whatsoever."

"Villa have always been moan, moan, moan. They have always been up in the top, but always middling, doing nothing. They hate us. But we hate them more than they hate us."

"We are proper lads, they are maggots."

As we were talking, their attention was taken by a knot of black men who'd arrived. There were plenty of others scattered among us, but the fans were making a fuss over this particular group, shaking their hands, keen to be acknowledged by them. My curiosity got the better of me. I wandered over and asked if they would like to speak. No problem.

So what were these derby matches like? There was a pause, the tallest among them, well over six-foot, with large sunken eyes and immense cheek bones, looked down and said he didn't know, they:

"hadn't been out for ten years." Cue laughter. Suddenly, I knew exactly who I was talking to. These were the Zulus or the remnants of them – a gang which had fought, stabbed, maimed and robbed their way to the forefront of organised inter-city football violence.

We were being pressed in on all sides by police, determined to squeeze the away support into the ground as soon as possible. There was no easy way to back off even if I had wanted to. I asked again what the derby matches were like? "Well it would be better if Villa fans weren't so racist. They are a bunch of racists. They started off their firm with the C-Crew. And that was to rival what was the Zulus, and because Birmingham has got a lot of coloured lads and ethnics. There is no divide at Birmingham. At Villa there's a big divide, Villa are a lot of racist pigs.

If you come across to Birmingham City, you can come up in one section and you will see the most blacks, mixed-race, Asians, whatever. It doesn't really matter, because it's all football. Like, we have all grown up together, we all know each other, and whether you are black, whether you are white – it doesn't matter – because wherever you come from you'll have black mates, white mates, Asian mates. And that's what it's really like with Birmingham City."

Fans at St Andrew's are rightly proud of their multi-cultural attitudes. It is true different ethnic groups have existed side by side among Blues fans for decades, mostly without any great problems; the violence being reserved for the opposition. This can be traced back to the late 1970s when the club attracted skinhead gangs with National Front sympathies. That picture changed in the 1980s, when the Zulus began to make headlines. A large number of black men were involved with the group from the very beginning, but really it was both a black and white gang.

More than that, Birmingham's stadium is still a highly polarised and unusual place to watch football, one in which it's possible to encounter people from every political walk of life, many of them extremists of one kind or another. The same crowd is able to house Irish republicans, Anti-Nazi League members, BNP supporters, Trotskyites and so on. Perhaps the one thing these groups have in common is that their activists tend to come from working-class backgrounds.

Yet this is also a city of entrenched and sometimes serious ethnic problems. In the autumn of 2005 these broke into outright violence on the streets of Lozells after a rumour that a black girl had been raped by a gang of Asians swept through the area. Groups of young Asian and black men fought running battles, with the police in the middle. A 23 year-old black man – Isaiah Young-Sam – who had nothing to do with the fighting was stabbed to death. The three Asian men who killed him were each sentenced to a minimum of 25 years in jail. The judge said Isaiah had been killed for no other reason than the colour of his skin.

In the immediate aftermath of the attack, elders in the black community suggested that Asian and black people were living side by side, in mutual exclusion. A race campaigner in the city compared the situation to that of the Apartheid regime in South Africa saying it was a society where "you have got white on top, Asians in the middle and then black at the bottom, particularly in economic terms."*

None of this seems to matter at the Blues. As far as they are concerned it's much more important to be Birmingham City supporters. Some of the lads from the Zulus are connected with the different gangs, but that is just not a problem in any significant way at St Andrew's.

It would also be deeply unfair to characterise Villa's fans as racist. They are not in the main. In fact they tend to be more mainstream than their Blues counterparts and broadly apolitical. However, there is a well established minority linked to their hooligan groups, who do display far-right tendencies. My new friend from the Zulus was insistent on that point. "I'm not being funny, but they have got a little racist contingent. They have got their little racists. Seriously, that's a fact. But you know you do get the Asians and blacks going to Villa Park, but looking at it, it was always like that, well you would see the odd one here and there."

I assumed this had been the reason he chose to support Birmingham? "No I wouldn't even say that, it was that I just grew up never liking Villa. I suppose you just play football when you grow up and you see where it's at and we are from the city, the city centre. But don't get me wrong, you could live in that part of the

* Maxine Hayes, *BBC News and website*, May 2006

city and support the Blues, or live in our part and support Villa, but you would be coming literally across the city to get to your team."

He smiled and wondered if I was coming in with them, tugging my jacket. It was seductive, the appeal of the street fighter, taking on the establishment – in this case both Villa and the cops. I thanked him, made my apologies and squeezed through the advancing police lines.

Really, I had no choice, my ticket was for the Villa end and I'd been incredibly lucky to get it. A friend had called an hour before the match to say he knew someone at the club who could get me in. I jumped at the chance and with five minutes to spare before kick-off I was climbing high into the Trinity Road Stand.

THE VILLA ENDS WERE NOISY and antagonistic, though not without reason. Both teams were stuck at the wrong end of the Premiership, with Birmingham teetering on the brink of relegation and Villa not quite safe. A win for the home side would see the Blues all but sent down, while victory for Birmingham would drag Villa back into the fight for survival. Local journalists had described the match as the most important fixture between the sides in 36 years.

The Villa boss, David O'Leary, had been showing the strain of that kind of pressure, igniting the wrath of his own fans by describing them as fickle. It's one thing for a manager whose team are winning everything in sight to feel he can criticise the paying customer, but quite another if you're venting spleen from the wrong end of the division. O'Leary had also said his players were "desperate to win" the derby and didn't think he would cry if Birmingham were relegated.* Steve Bruce, the Blues manager, who had in the past been hit by objects thrown from the home supporters at Villa's ground, was doing his best to play it cool, joking: "I always enjoy my trips to Villa Park. It's a happy hunting ground for me."**

As I took my seat, the referee's whistle was met with a din of encouragement from 41,000 throats. I'd been warned that the players were "like ants" from the back of the stand, but as it turned

---

* Aston Villa match day programme
** *Birmingham Sunday Mercury*, April 2006

out I was in a good position to see every corner of the stadium, which is still one of the finest in the land.

The Birmingham contingent, about 4,000 of them, were penned into the corner of the Doug Ellis Stand (though everyone still calls it the Witton Lane Stand), and behind the goal of the North Stand. They just stood, and sang, then sang some more, while around me people were on their feet gleefully chanting: 'Shit on the City, shit on the City below, below...'

Then the Villa fans turned on Steve Bruce, who was looking agitated even in the opening minutes:

'Sit down potato head, sit down potato head.'

The football itself was fast and untidy, neither side being able to strike anything approaching a considered passing rhythm. But drama wasn't far away. After just ten minutes Villa went in front. Three sides of the ground celebrated by singing and pointing at the away end:

'The shit are going down, the shit are going down.'

It looked bad, very bad for Birmingham, but they settled and started to knock the ball around. For all that, Villa still created chances to go further ahead, and were soon given cause to regret not taking them. That old warhorse Chris Sutton fired in the equaliser from a scramble in the box ... down to my left dozens of Birmingham fans rushed forward, pouring out of their seats and onto the running track beside the pitch. Advertising boards were knocked or kicked over and the stewards tried desperately to contain them.

Deep inside the Villa half, almost as far as they could be from their own fans, the Birmingham players congratulated Sutton. Strange, I thought, that such an important goal, was celebrated in so quiet a fashion, no grand gestures, no rush to the crowd, nothing elaborate, just hugs, handshakes and smiles.

The Villa fans around me were on their feet and some were standing on seats. They were no longer looking at the pitch, but to the centre of the stand. Despite the best-laid ticketing plans, a few Blues supporters had covertly made it into the home end and had, unlike the players, been unable to contain themselves. It was hard to tell amid the booing and pointing, but it looked as though the transgressors were being hauled away for their own safety.

The Birmingham contingent were jubilant and their famous old battle hymn *Keep Right on Till the End of the Road* resounded around the ground. This was followed by the rather less eloquent 'You're the shit of Birmingham' and 'Shit on the Villa.'

Things changed again just after the break. An acrobatic volley from Gary Cahill in front of the Holte End sent Villa back into the lead, prompting their players to rush into the arms of the crowd. When things calmed down at least one struggling fan was dragged off by police. Birmingham had chances to get back on terms before Villa finally got a third to kill them off. As the match grew near to its close, their play became increasingly fractured. This desperation was reflected by the away supporters, who called for anything that looked vaguely like a free-kick or a penalty. Meanwhile the Villa fans were in raptures, singing:

'The Shits are going down, the shits are going down, and now you're gonna believe us, the shits are going down.'

There is a strange scatological aspect to the rivalry. In 1995 the Birmingham midfielder, Paul Tait, on scoring in the final of the Football League Trophy at Wembley, pulled off his club shirt to reveal a T-shirt which said 'Birmingham City… Shit on the Villa'. It prompted a controversy in the local and national media. Tait claims he has subsequently had dog excrement posted to him, a bottle smashed over his head, a glass shoved in his face and has received numerous death threats. He also claims that after the match the Birmingham owner, David Sullivan, demanded to know where he'd got the T-shirt. Tait told him: "it was just there."* Sullivan, apparently, said he needed to know, not because he would be admonishing its creator, but because they would be able to sell loads in the official club shop.

* Paul Tait, *Birmingham Post*, 15 April 2006

At the final whistle a platoon of orange-jacketed stewards immediately fanned out across the pitch, forming two separate lines stretching from one touchline to the other. This was a well-rehearsed operation and without doubt designed to stop away supporters getting near the Villa fans. Meanwhile the Villa players danced and sang inside their half of the pitch, safe in the knowledge that they would be playing Premiership football once again the following season, while their Birmingham counterparts trudged off, heads bowed.

A FEW MINUTES LATER I emerged into the crowded Trinity Road just in time to see a gang of around two hundred Blues marching straight into the thousands of Villa supporters, who were walking in the opposite direction. A helicopter was beating overhead, and there were police on the ground, though not nearly enough. This was far from the nice shiny Premiership of Sky TV. It looked like trouble, pure and simple.

Or perhaps not, certainly had this group wanted to they could have carried out an attack, randomly on any number of Villa fans. They didn't, not because they were in any way concerned about being outnumbered, but rather, I suspect, because these were just ordinary fans making their way home, not the Villa crew. This was more a show of defiance in the face of defeat. Nevertheless it provoked a reaction. Some Villa supporters were obviously scared and got out of the way, there were shouts from others who watched as police, some of the four hundred officers on duty at the match, shepherded the gang up and over Aston Park. Deeper into the streets of Aston there were groups of police patrolling on foot while sirens screamed in the distance. Violence, it seems, is always on offer at these derbies.

Most students of the matches will tell you that the rivalry really took off during the 1970s and became nasty in the 1980s. However there is evidence that the antipathy between the clubs was well established decades earlier. In 1898/99 they were drawn together in the FA Cup and the football author, Peter Morris, writing in the

---

* *Aston Villa*, Peter Morris

early 1960s, talks about it being "the tie with Villa's old rivals across the city."* Morris also says there was "pandemonium on the terraces" during a derby in 1926 and reports how fighting broke out among local boys when they dared to switch their allegiance to Birmingham during Villa's dark hour of relegation in 1936. *

I noticed that both before and after the match the fans kept their distance, there was really no mingling and no coming nor going together. Supporters on both sides made it clear there is no common unity; they will not support their rivals in Cup finals or against teams from other cities. One Villa fan told me he was "fucking delighted" at the prospect of Birmingham being relegated. It didn't look like he would have long to wait to see that wish fulfilled. Easter 2006 belonged emphatically to Villa and their fans and I was invited to have a few celebratory drinks with some of them in a Villa watering hole, the Barton's Arms. Minutes before I arrived a group of around fifty Blues had turned up looking for more than a drink. An older fan, his hand shaking as he drank, told me the whole thing had been "dodgy as hell".

I was meeting Dave Woodhall, the editor of the fanzine *Heroes and Villans* and author of several books about the club. In an upstairs room where the team from the magazine had gathered, Dave called for silence before slamming his pint on the table. Bent backwards, hands thrown high into the air, he screamed "Fuckingggg.......Yeeeeessssss!"

What had he made of the match? "It's everything isn't it, a game like that. Everybody wanted to win it so badly because of the position they are in, we could relegate them. This is the only derby in the Premier League certainly where two clubs really go for it hell for leather."

He went on to describe the derby as both evil and hateful, but believes there are differences between the supporters. "Villa fans, tend to be, well you know, people have seen us win everything, championships, the European Cup, play in Europe regularly, seen some great players. Birmingham have only really got their hooliganism to be proud of and I was looking at their support today, and

* *Aston Villa*, Peter Morris

honestly, they don't seem to have kids. Nearly everyone I looked at in that crowd of theirs seemed to be a hardcore hooligan or capable of it. Birmingham supporters do seem to be a bit more earthy than Villa fans. I think Birmingham fans revel in the fact that they are aggressive. They haven't grown out of this sort of 'we are from Birmingham' mentality. You will see more old-school Villa hooligans today than you will have for years. You just see them, I mean our hooligans turn out for just one game – with Birmingham. You get the feeling theirs are in there week in week out."

Dave's final comment was the one which really stayed with me, though. It wasn't at all about hating Blues, or being happy that Villa had won, but much more about the state of the game, the view from the terracing, as it were. "The problem with modern-day football supporters is that they are not bothered about history, all they are bothered with is the present. I saw four guys today who'd won the European Cup with Villa walking over the Trinity Road, and no-one so much as recognised them. The big problem with English football now is that people support teams, they don't support clubs. All they are interested in is winning today. Now that's a shame."

BIRMINGHAM CITY WERE RELEGATED two weeks later. Unusually for these times, Steve Bruce kept his job, but across the city, David O'Leary lost his, despite Villa retaining their position in the Premier League, being replaced by Martin O'Neil. After years trying to find the right man, and several sackings along the way, octogenarian chairman Ellis had the legacy he so desired – the Midas-like managerial talents of the Ulsterman, bequeathed to Villa, as a parting gift. All of this further ramped up the pressure on the Blues to keep their nerve and ride out what, in the end, would prove to be a single season in the Championship. Their rivals now had serious amounts of money to spend, a revamped ground and one of the most coveted managers in football. Villa fans, for the first time this century, began to believe a sustained challenge at the top of the game and a return to those far off days of glory could again be possible. Birmingham's followers were left wondering exactly when their luck might change.

NORTH LONDON:
Land, Lies And Lasagne

"If you were only going to win two games in the season, they had to be the two against Arsenal. There was no way you would do anything less than go out and die against the Gunners. Crossing over to Highbury I found the attitude just as strong."

Pat Jennings – *The Great Derby Matches, Arsenal vs Tottenham Hotspur*, Michael Heatley and Ian Welch.

THE COMPUTER AT THE Premier League HQ in central London is programmed to come up with the fixtures for each season. It does so coldly without any consideration for how the circumstances of the time might affect players, management and supporters. By this method Arsenal and Tottenham Hotspur, the traditional north London rivals, were paired to play each other on the 22nd of April, just three matches from the end of the 2005/06 season. For the first time in several years they were joined together near the top of the league at this point in the campaign. Arsenal were heading towards the showpiece final of the Champions League and at the same time fighting to secure a spot in the tournament the following season. Standing in their way in the race for that all-important fourth place were Spurs, rejuvenated under Martin Jol. With three games remaining they were two points clear, meaning victory would all but seal qualification.

So, the derby wasn't quite all or nothing, but it would go a long way towards deciding which of these teams would capture that vital spot as England's representatives among the elite of the continent. There was an added significance in that, for decades, Tottenham had sent teams to play Arsenal in their own corner of north London, now they were coming to bid a less than fond farewell. For over ninety years, until the summer of 2006, Highbury was known the world over as the home of Arsenal. But no longer, the Gunners were moving to a new state-of-the-art arena five hundred meters away. The last ever north London derby at that art-deco monument to the people's game would be a mighty occasion full of rage against the dying of the light.

THE TRAIN DOORS SLID open and I followed the exit signs upstairs into a narrow, dimly lit corridor in the depths of Arsenal underground station. Mural images depicting historic days in the life of the stadium adorned the walls leading to the ticket barriers in the distance. This was the first physical acknowledgement that Highbury, shoehorned in beside residential streets, was coming to the end of a slow death. Outside on Gillespie Road the street vendors had mountains of unofficial Highbury memorabilia ready for sale, countless scarves and badges carried the slogan, apparently with no hint of irony, Highbury N5 – Home of the Gunners. A notice in the window of the stadium shop read – How Will You Say Goodbye? Season ticket holders were even being offered the chance to take their seat home, encouraged, it was hoped, by posters showing how one had been incorporated into a child's go-cart. Eventually there would be a Highbury auction site, where fans could bid for miscellaneous bits and pieces. Well, every penny counts.

The club is, without doubt, among the leading English and European names, generating millions of pounds annually. Football is, as the truism goes, 'big business' and this was the main reason Arsenal were shipping out. The directors had come to the conclusion, some years before, that the famous old ground was simply too small to compete with other clubs at home and abroad, purely in terms of the money taken at the gate.

In 1999 the board, having seriously considered options outside the local borough of Islington, announced their intention to build a new stadium at nearby Ashburton Grove. Construction began in 2004 after concerted and continual opposition from fans, local residents, businesses, trade unions and councillors. Some of these groups had also successfully campaigned against plans to revamp Highbury. They now feared a much bigger stadium and the upheaval that would bring. What they really wanted was the continuation of the status quo, arguing that Arsenal had no pressing need to relocate, and were doing so simply to make money. It's hardly surprising that with a season ticket waiting list of around 20,000 Arsenal saw things differently.

All in all it was a bitter fight, but for better or worse, one which Arsenal ultimately won. The stadium project, heavily sponsored by the Dubai-based Emirates Airlines, would cost nigh on £400 million by the time it was completed and came with several strings attached. Arsenal had to shell out £60 million on a new rubbish disposal plant to replace the dump their new ground was built on, they also had to buy up land for the development of a series of flats, some of which would be set aside for what was termed as 'affordable homes'. There were also promises to modernise local underground and rail links. In all, the club claims to have spent a £100 million on redeveloping "half of Islington" but not everyone is happy.* There have been claims, vigorously denied by Arsenal, that they reneged on the full extent of the initial agreements. Also, residents have angrily complained about travel problems on match days and the volume of rubbish generated by the increased numbers of supporters.

Then there are the houses. The further you walk down Hornsey Street, the road which leads to the tip, the more aware you become of the heavy sourness which hangs in the air. Over a thousand cars, vans and lorries carrying rubbish rumble up and down there every day of the week. There are almost five hundred homes for key workers and poorer people. Many of these are situated next to the waste disposal unit, a matter of yards away, with a view to the other side of the east-coast mainline railway to Scotland. I went there as the development was being completed and was told by one site worker that the flats were "good inside, but are sometimes you know", he wafts his fingers past his nose, "smelly."

Highbury itself had been saved, after a fashion. The finest football stadium in England was also being turned into flats. Here again, some properties were set aside for key community workers, but the prices meant people would need a salary of at least £40,000 a year to

---

* Ken Friar, *BBC Radio 4 World Tonight, 26 October 2006*

afford them. Otherwise, they cost in the region of between £250,000 and £500,000. Not a bad little earner for Arsenal.

The East and West stands were incorporated into the project, since even football clubs can't knock down listed buildings. Indeed, Arsenal were quite aware of how special their old stadium was. As those inside were readying to leave, the club's official website was still promoting tours telling fans they could "… Relive the glorious history of the unique venue and marvel in the splendour of its tradition, which sets Highbury apart from any other stadium in the Premiership…Take a look behind the scenes and experience the intricate architectural design characteristic of the East Stand, contrasted with the modern elegance of the North Bank, which differentiates the stadium from any other in our domestic game."* The schizophrenia didn't stop there. The club's managing director Keith Edelman was effusive about the development saying: "…This is our home. It's our home and we want to see this done beautifully and properly to end the Highbury era."**

T HE IDEA THAT THE CLUB had to move on was accepted by the majority of fans, though a good many still had their doubts, a nagging feeling about whether they should be jettisoning a building which had been such a large part of Arsenal's sense of itself. The official Arsenal Supporters Club can be found just behind the North Bank on St Thomas' Road. There I met Peggy Goulding. Despite her sixty-eight years she runs the supporters shop single-handed and has been a regular at Arsenal for almost four decades. If anyone represents the grassroots Arsenal fan it is her. We talked about leaving the stadium as she took mugs and hats out of boxes. "In lots of ways I'm really sad that we are going because it's like my second home. I'm just very sad because you have got your memories, but I know it's inevitable because the ground is too small, and it's going to be a fantastic stadium, it's going to be really something special, so I think we have just got to do it. I suppose it must be the right thing because we are going to have 60,000. We've only got 38,500 here. It's got to be better.

* *Arsenal Official Website, 19 January 2006*
** *Sunday Telegraph, 30 October 2005*

I think it's the memories more than anything else. This is the place my husband brought me to, game after game. I'm going to go and sit in the new stadium with no memories of him there. So in lots of ways I'm sad, but I know it's inevitable. I'm full of sadness really that it is the last time we are going to meet this particular team at this particular ground. But you have to move on, so you hope it's not going to be a game that you are going to regret, because you are going to get played off the park. We always want to beat [Tottenham]. It is the one game you don't want to lose, it doesn't matter where it is, you just don't like to be beaten by Spurs because it is such an important game."

Many supporters spoke to me about the derby and depth of emotion they expected the few remaining games at Highbury to generate. While this undoubtedly would be the case, it was also true that Arsenal were leaving the ground in exactly the same manner which they'd arrived, shrouded in opposition and controversy. 2006, as I would discover, was simply an echo of things past.

Back on Gillespie Road the street vendors were enjoying themselves, their souvenirs of what was soon to be Arsenal's past were selling quickly among the crowd now constantly spewing out of the underground into the late morning sun. Groups of men were also positioned across the street next to the station. To everyone who passed they would say, mechanically, in a shout of a whisper: 'buy any tickets'. I was approached by one man in his forties, accompanied by a teenager. He grumbled that getting a ticket was proving to be difficult and "they" were asking £300 for one. I took that to mean the touts and asked if he was Arsenal or Spurs – "Chelsea", he said. In fact he was a tout moaning about what supporters were demanding for a change, and wondered if I would be prepared to buy at that price? I was shown no ticket though, no-one was selling.

I'd imagined that sampling the pre-match atmosphere was as good as things would get. Fans from both sides had laughed when I'd asked their advice on finding a ticket. Some agencies, called as a last resort, said I'd have to pay in the region of £400, even more for the Spurs end. Eventually I was rescued by Peggy who kindly took me to a small hut next to her shop. There I was asked if I was a Spurs fan – I said no – then, amazingly, was given a ticket for the North Bank. The price was £31.

What was supposed to be a queue for the turnstiles was bordering on an old-fashioned crush by the time I arrived. Many fans were the worse for the combination of sunshine and booze. A chant went up behind me about how we 'have foreskins' – clearly a reference to Tottenham's Jewish heritage. No-one voiced their disproval.

The thought crossed my mind, as I eventually came through the squeeze and navigated the turnstile, that I was a fraud. My ticket, today of all days, should have gone to a life-long Arsenal supporter, not a mere interested observer. Then again, my conscience told me, it hadn't fallen into the hands of a tout; neither had it been sold for profit and was a genuine spare which would have been left unused.

The North Bank was, as I had expected, vibrant, boisterous and full of colour. My seat faced the corner flag directly opposite the Spurs fans who were crammed low into the far side of the Clock End. They too were in good voice, shouting forcefully in flat tones:

'Yids Yids Yids' … 'Yid Army, Yid Army'

For that season both teams had departed, to varying degrees, from their traditional colours. Arsenal, commemorating the first side to play at Highbury, had swapped their famous scarlet tops with white sleeves for something described by people who know about such matters as 'Redcurrant'. Tottenham had diluted their traditional spotless white tops, strangely choosing to add navy sleeves.

At the kick-off on the stroke of 12:45 there were fevered cries from all sides which suggested a savage desire to win and an equally brutal determination not to lose. The mood reflected comments made by the Arsenal manager, Arsène Wenger, earlier that week when he'd said: "there was never a game where there was so much at stake, for both teams, of course. It is our biggest game of the season. It's not a war, in terms of a war that people get killed, but yes, there is a lot at stake."*

* *The Sportsman, 22 April 2006*

If that was so then it was surprising that he'd left out his young midfield conductor, Spain's Cesc Fabregas, and the mainstay of the side, the sublimely brilliant French attacker, Thierry Henry. This was no aberration on Wenger's part, but rather, a conscious decision to dilute his first-choice XI with the second-leg of the Champions League semi-final just four days away.

Wenger's plan was soon in pieces as Tottenham battered Arsenal in that first-half. Spurs certainly looked capable of leaving Highbury with points for the first time in seven years. The fans around me knew it too. There are times when the frustration of being a supporter, trapped on the terraces, with no real power other than the expression of collective will becomes too much. Close to half-time, with Spurs dictating the pace and shape of the game, some in Arsenal colours could take no more. Just behind me three fans, all in their twenties, were suddenly on their feet, shouting, not at the play but at each other. One had been overly critical of the Arsenal performance and the others had taken exception. Heads turned from the match to the back of the stand. There was some shoving and fists were raised before the stewards moved in to calm things down.

During half-time I noticed that over my right shoulder, in the gap between the West Stand and the North Bank, I could literally see the future. There, baking in the heat haze of the mid-distance, was the Emirates Stadium. The new ground was a vast, dark jewel, out of reach, but only for the moment. There were issues to be settled before the great de-coupling form Highbury.

During the second half Arsenal began edging ever-more into things. Then, in the 66th minute came utter chaos. Arsenal's Gilberto Silva and Emmanuel Eboue crashed into each other, losing the ball in the centre-circle. With the pair still prostrate, the play slowed, almost to a stop, with Spurs in possession. Arsenal expected the ball to be put out of play to allow treatment to their stricken players. But no, the England midfielder, Michael Carrick, out on the touchline and urged on by his manager, swept the ball to Edgar Davids. The referee glanced at the two Arsenal players, and ushered the play forward.

Spurs were breaking at speed. Their Irish striker, Robbie Keane, scampered at an angle across the box in front of the Clock End. Timing his run perfectly he side-footed Davids' inch-perfect ball low into the Arsenal net. Hands raised in triumph he ran on, behind the goal, to the away fans tumbling down the stand in celebration towards him. Such joy was not confined to the main Spurs contingent. As Arsenal players jostled opponents and beseeched the referee, unprecedented scenes were being played out in the directors' box. There a group of people were leaping around, totally at odds with the traditional reserve of that area. It later emerged that Keith Edelman, had threatened to evict the official Spurs party because of the exuberance of their celebrations.

This incident tells you everything about the importance of winning the fixture, especially when there is something tangible to play for, like the cold hard millions of guaranteed Champions League cash. Yet the break with protocol among the Spurs directors is all the more surprising given that one of the defining characteristics of the derby has been the good working relationship which has existed between the boards in recent times. Ancient rivalry, it seems, cannot get in the way of cupid's arrows. Connections between the clubs were strengthened in 2002 by the marriage of the Arsenal vice-chairman David Dein's son, to the daughter of the Spurs vice-chairman, David Buchler. A cause for celebration, but rather different to the time when, in 1987, Tottenham sent champagne to the Arsenal dressing room after they had beaten Spurs in the replayed semi-final of the League Cup at White Hart Lane. This would have been an exquisite gesture under any circumstances in sport, but was especially so in the moments following a major defeat against their rivals.

Also that year, to mark the 100th league derby, the two teams got together for a photo-shoot for the match programme, under the slogan, Friendly Foes. This, it has to be said, could only have been dreamt up by the directors. The fans would never have conceived of it, and really, they were not alone. Both managers – Martin Jol and Arsène Wenger – as men with reputations for being urbane and professional would no doubt subscribe to the Friendly Foe maxim. The heat of this derby exposed such notions as myth.

In the wake of the Spurs goal Wenger, in shirt and tie, and a track-suited Jol, went nose-to-nose in the no-man's land between the two dug-outs. Wenger demanded to know why Jol had not called for his players to put the ball out of play in the build up to the goal. Jol, borrowing an well-worn line from Wenger's own phrasebook, said he "didn't see" the Arsenal players clash. After the match Wenger refused to shake the hand of the Spurs man and openly claimed he was a liar. "Their first goal was a disgrace. They lie when they say they didn't see it. I can't believe they didn't see it. Of course they lie. I find it very disappointing and it's a shame that a thing like that can happen."*

There was another side to this story. "Irrespective of the rights and wrongs I don't think a manager should behave like that. He called me a liar. I have not seen it [the collision] because I was watching Edgar Davids." This was Jol's response and television replays backed him up. ** Menacingly he also warned Wenger not to confront him in future. "He should not act like that. I had to hold back because he doesn't know how strong I am."*** Jol was not voted 'manager most feared by Premiership fans' by a landslide majority for nothing.

Regardless of the circumstances, Spurs deserved to be in front. Their supporters knew it and rubbed it in with chants of 'one nil to the England'. They, unlike Arsenal, were sending several players to the World Cup with the national team that summer. In fact Arsenal did not have a single Englishman in their side, nor even on the bench.

The home side did not lie down in the face of what they believed to be a gross injustice. They were fuelled by it, and the immediate arrival of Henry and Fabregas. Now the balance of the play changed and with just six minutes remaining Henry was clear, surfing over the Highbury pitch at top speed, the ball at his feet. His movement was so slick, the danger so apparent, that he seemed to pull the whole game towards him deep inside the opposition half. Around me there was the dull rippling echo of thousands of seats closing as their erstwhile occupants sprang to their feet. Henry had reached the edge of the penalty box. In an instant he drew the advancing goalkeeper and defender, flicking the ball gloriously to his right, into the far corner of the net. On the North Bank thousands of hands shot into the air, silhouetted against the pitch. The

* *BBC website, 22 April 2006*
** *Independent On Sunday, 23 April 2006*
*** *Independent On Sunday, 23 April 2006*

fans grabbed who and what they could in giddy celebration and some fell laughing against the seats.

The Spurs players were left frozen where they had been at the culmination of Henry's goal, hands on hips, heads slumped into chests. Some sat on the pitch, disbelieving. They had played well and come very close to taking all three, vital points. Henry and his cohorts enjoyed a moment of unguarded celebration in front of us and then another closer to the Spurs fans.

Minutes later the atmosphere changed again. Arsenal tried, but could not get a winner. The draw was of greater benefit to Spurs and on the other side of the ground their fans were driving the point home. For Arsenal this was not the way the last Highbury derby was supposed to have ended. Their fans sang 'You're scum and you know you are' – Tottenham responded with 'Stand up if you hate Arsenal.'

After six straight defeats at Highbury, Spurs had won a point. In reality it was much more – finishing the season above Arsenal and grabbing a place in the Champions League at their expense seemed now firmly within their grasp. But even with Spurs fans still making merry in the background there was no more than a slow trickle away from Highbury. Arsenal supporters went down, as close to the pitch as they could, taking photos and videos with their mobile phones as the nets were being taken down and the goal frame dismantled by the groundstaff. For many it would have been their last moments inside the old ground.

A WHILE LATER I JOINED a couple of hundred people outside the East Stand. We were kept back by metal barriers. Parked close to the main entrance was the Tottenham team bus: black, sleek, mirrored. Some of those who'd stayed behind were tourists, but most were Arsenal fans, determined to let off some steam. One, who arrived shortly after I did, addressed us with a rhetorical question. "Ah, is that the Spurs coach ... where are all the bricks when you need them? Please, please has anyone got a brick? I'll buy a brick off anyone." He took a swig from his can of lager and smiled.

Almost everyone who came out of the building was booed and ridiculed, just in case they were Tottenham officials or supporters. One of the Spurs technical staff, a tall, strong looking woman with red hair repeatedly went to and from the bus, while being called things such as a 'fucking ginger minger'. Not once did she show even the slightest interest.

Eventually the players emerged, including the goal-scorer, Robbie Keane, who marched quickly aboard without making eye-contact. He was followed by Edgar Davids, who'd been sent off in the closing moments and had played a crucial part in the opening goal. The whistles and shouting increased and some kind of liquid was thrown. The little pit-bull stopped, looked over the heads to the back of the crowd, smiled and defiantly pulled at the Tottenham crest on his jacket.

A moment later the last of the Spurs party could be seen talking to someone just inside the main door. Martin Jol seemed startled as he stepped over the threshold and stood for a moment looking at the crowd, taking in their insults and gestures with jutting chin and wild staring eyes – half Brando, half Mussolini. Seconds later he was on the bus. Its doors then closed with a mechanical hiss before it slid out of the shadows, through the Arsenal fans and away down the rubbish-strewn Avenell Road. Spurs had left Highbury for the last time. All in all they had made quite an impression.

THOSE WHO FOLLOW TOTTENHAM Hotspur and Arsenal are not so different. Broadly speaking they come from the same areas of north London, Hertfordshire and Essex, they attend the same schools, drink in the same pubs and generally live happily together, cheek by jowl. However, there are a series of historical pressure points which define their rivalry and can, on match days lead to declarations of loyalty, assertions of legitimacy and from time to time, violence.

The clubs are located at opposite ends of the Seven Sisters Road. It cuts through residential areas dominated by immigrant communities both old and new. Spurs are situated in a district which has received substantial funding from the European Union for economic and social development. Arsenal, around four miles further south, have a similar constituency, but border more affluent, middle-class areas in Islington and Camden.

The clubs first played each other back in 1887 in a friendly on the Tottenham Marshes. The game had to be abandoned due to bad light, with Spurs in the lead. It was not, however, a north London derby. There's no escaping the fact Arsenal are not originally from that part of the city. Back then they went by the grand, but incongruous, name of Royal Arsenal and played their football out of Plumstead, south of the river Thames in south London, on the border with Kent. The Gunners' origins are distinctly working class, being formed by employees at the Arsenal munitions factory in Woolwich. Historians are unable to agree upon the exact date at which Arsenal came into being, principally because they emerged out of various teams at the works, such as Dial Square. Sometime in the autumn of 1886 is the best guess.

Spurs at this time were happily plugging away in and around the same area in which we find them today. Even though the two sides were separated by the sprawl of the city, matches between them were popular. Spurs were prompted to find a new ground after 14,000 turned up to see them take on Arsenal in 1889. Dozens climbed on top of a refreshment stand to get a better view, causing it to collapse. Amazingly, no-one was killed and few were injured.

Arsenal had some initial success, winning trophies in a range of local competitions, but the first time they came to wider public attention was in 1891. Now called Woolwich Arsenal, they decided to turn professional in a game which was still largely amateur outside northern England. Such was the outcry that the club was immediately banned from all London and Kent competitions, making themselves the subversives of football in south-east England. It wouldn't be the last time they were mired in controversy.

By the close of the first decade of the 20th century Arsenal's board were forced into action over what had become a desperate financial plight. They were bankrupt; their gates had been falling since the outbreak of the Boer War in 1899, which forced the local munitions factory to go into overdrive, taking away many of their regular supporters. After half a dozen of their top players were sold off in 1908 the situation became nigh-on hopeless. None of this was helped by an accident of geography. Public transport links to Plumstead and Woolwich were relatively poor and Arsenal's natural constituency was halved by a great sweep of the Thames. Things have improved greatly during the intervening decades, but the picture painted by George Allison, a sports journalist who'd go on to manage the club, shows just how remote Arsenal were. "Other sports writers were more than happy when I offered to undertake all the reporting of Arsenal's home games. The payment I received softened the monotony of the long and tedious journey. One could travel on the South Eastern and Chatham Railway from London Bridge, Cannon Street or Charing Cross. The trains stopped at every station. There were the same halts on the return journey, with the added difficulty that no-one knew where the trains were going."*

Into this picture stepped the man who for decades would be the great bogeyman to Spurs fans; the figure who transformed Arsenal, and whose methods electrified their rivalry with Tottenham. Sir Henry Norris. Norris took control of struggling Arsenal in 1910. He had built a fortune as a property developer in south-west London. MP, mayor and knight of the realm, to those who knew him Norris was also a bully and a man unwilling to listen to advice. More than that, he was a football visionary. When Norris came into contact with Arsenal he was already the chairman of Second Division Fulham and now planned a merger. The League vetoed that idea, and a further proposal, to have Fulham and Arsenal play at Craven Cottage on alternate Saturday's was also rejected

There was a simple motive behind these revolutionary ideas – Norris was desperate to create a team in London which could take on the clubs from the north and the midlands which had traditionally dominated the game. Eventually, he was forced to choose between Arsenal and Fulham, plumping for Arsenal because they were still in Division One. Not that they would be for very much longer, finishing bottom of the league in 1913, and reportedly with less then £20 to their name.

His club was in serious difficulty, but, of course, Norris had a bold solution. He wanted Arsenal to move from their home across the river to be closer to the heart of the city. The new site had to be easily accessible by public transport, located in an area which would offer plenty of support and not impinge on any other club. Arsenal eventually found what they were looking for. It was a divinity college plus some acreage close to Gillespie Road Tube Station in

---

* *The Official Illustrated History of Arsenal,* Phil Soar and Martyn Tyler

north London. There was a problem though; one which was wildly out of step with the last part of Norris's guidelines; Tottenham Hotspur played nearby and Arsenal would be moving right into their territory. Despite death threats, and true to his nature, Norris pressed ahead. Spurs, Orient and Chelsea strongly disapproved, while the local press begged fans not to patronise Arsenal. All was in vain. There were no rules at that time to prevent a club from leaving one area for another. Indeed as we witnessed when south London lost another club, Wimbledon, this time to the environs of Milton Keynes, nothing much had changed almost a century later. Arsenal paid £20,000 for a twenty-one year lease of the site which would become Highbury. The last match played at the old Manor Ground in Plumstead took place in April 1913. The club now morphed again, dropping 'Woolwich' from their title. They would be The Arsenal for another dozen years before their name was formally shortened for the last time.

Spurs had been defeated over the move to Highbury, but Norris wasn't finished, not by any means. His next act was a stunning plot aimed directly against Tottenham's welfare. What happened has never been satisfactorily explained, and is open to wide interpretation. It was the factor which truly sealed the poisonous relations between the two sets of fans. Within a year of Arsenal's first game at their new home Archduke Franz Ferdinand of Austria had been shot in Sarajevo and Europe had slid into a catastrophic war. The league played on in 1914/15, but football was hardly a priority and crowds declined sharply. Arsenal at the time were doing well in Division Two and pressing for promotion, something they badly needed in order to service considerable debts caused by the move to and construction of Highbury. They were severely hamstrung by the lack of professional football between 1915 and the close of hostilities in 1918.

Normal football was set to return in September the following year. Tottenham, having finished bottom of the league during the last full season at the beginning of the war had no doubt been delighted that Division One was to be expanded from twenty to twenty-two clubs. It had been expected that Spurs, along with Chelsea, who'd finished a place above them, would now remain in the top league and be joined by the leading two clubs from the Second Division. Norris had other ideas and set out on what

Arsenal themselves later described as "the single most outrageous enterprise ever to be conceived in the history of English football."*

What shouldn't be underestimated is how well established Spurs were at this time. They had been formed by a group of middle-class schoolboys in 1882 under the title, The Hotspur Football Club, though this was soon altered to Tottenham Hotspur. The name is believed to have come from two of the pupils from the St John's school who were fascinated by the exploits of the English knight Sir Henry Percy. An impulsive medieval warrior, Percy fought the Scots and French before rebelling with the Welsh against Henry IV. He was better known as Harry Hotspur.

Strangely the Percy family estate was part of what is now Tottenham, an area which was transformed by the advance of the railways and cheap fares out of central London in the middle of the 19th century. Leafy fields and market gardens on the edge of the city soon became a residential sprawl for commuters. The club, like so many others, had grown out of a cricket section and quickly gained a reputation for entertaining football. The players became part of the local scenery, so much so that, before 1890, they had bought what was then known as the 'Red House' on Tottenham High Road. Today this building, adorned with a golden cockerel and clock, is synonymous with Spurs, being situated just in front of the main entrance to White Hart Lane.

By 1887 Tottenham were getting regular gates of around 4,000 and had reached the semi-finals of the East End Cup. Five years later they were third in the Southern Alliance, their first season in league football. At the turn of the century they won their first ever championship, the Southern League and in 1901, fans around the country were suddenly made aware of their talents. Spurs, still a Southern League club, won the FA Cup, beating Sheffield United in a replayed final. It had been said that half of north London travelled to their semi-final and when the team arrived at Tottenham station with the Cup "they were greeted by fireworks and an enormous crowd of delirious supporters."** It was a remarkable achievement. No non-league club has won a major trophy since.

---

* *The Official Illustrated History of Arsenal,* Phil Soar and Martyn Tyler
** *Spurs: The Illustrated History,* Bob Goodwin

There were no more great successes until the close of the First World War, but Tottenham did gain entry to the Football League in 1908 and were promoted at the end of that season. Their gates were now around 20,000, though their popularity extended far beyond these shores, as tours to both South America and Europe proved. All in all Norris was planning to usurp one of the most respected names in English football.

Arsenal did not share such a steadfast reputation. Fans today tend to feel they are some kind of football royalty, as much a pillar of the established order as Trooping the Colour or tennis at Wimbledon. Highbury helped to reinforce this, with the uniformed commissioner guarding the famous marble halls; but back then Arsenal – because of the move across the river and Norris's earlier schemes – were seen as being a bit, well, unpredictable.

With all this in mind Tottenham officials must have felt they had little to worry about. Surely the authorities would be on their side over Norris's latest gambit, how could they allow Arsenal to be hoisted into the league in their stead? Surely Arsenal had no basis for their claims? If only it had been that simple. Poor Spurs, they simply hadn't figured just how persuasive the Arsenal chairman could be. Norris went to many of his friends and senior figures in the game, outlining Arsenal's case as he saw it. He was a formidable character and a success in his own right away from football. Without doubt many of those he petitioned would have been flattered by his attentions. Leslie Knighton, the Arsenal manager, said of the chairman: "His influence was enormous. [He would] speak to an important person there, suggesting a favour, remind a certain financier who was interested that he had once done him a good turn and been promised something in return."*

Everything on the face of it was against Norris. Arsenal had finished the 1915 season way back in fifth place, far outside the normal promotion spots and when there had been league expansion in the past the lowest teams in Division One were simply re-elected and the highest placed teams in the league below promoted.

Many of those who have tried to uncover the details of the episode suggest that Norris focused on the fact there had clearly

* *The Official Illustrated History of Arsenal*, Phil Soar and Martyn Tyler

been something of a bad smell about the 1915 season. There were allegations of match fixing, some of them proved in the courts, involving Liverpool and Manchester United. It has to be said that these in no way involved Spurs, nor their eventual position at the bottom of the table that year. Norris was developing the idea that the last wartime season, all in all, hadn't been quite normal. Therefore the precedents regarding promotion and relegation simply didn't count, and so places in the new First Division could not be settled along those lines. Sowing these seeds of doubt in the minds of the game's authorities was a mendacious act straight from the pages of Machiavelli. Norris had seen a chink of light, a way through.

It was one thing to cajole, plead, demand and do whatever else was necessary to secure Arsenal's election to the top flight. It was quite another to pull it off. The League met to settle the matter in March 1919. It turned into a thoroughly bizarre affair. Things began smoothly enough, Chelsea were re-elected without a vote taking place and the two clubs which had finished first and second in Division Two – Derby and Preston North End – were admitted. The proceedings then went off the rails. The chairman of the League and of Liverpool, John McKenna, made a dramatic and unexpected speech in which he said Arsenal had the strongest case for taking the final spot in the new-look First Division. McKenna, who was a personal friend of Henry Norris, claimed that Arsenal's service to the League and their long-standing membership should be rewarded. Arsenal had been members fifteen years longer than Spurs. Mind you, Wolves, who'd finished a place above them in fourth, had been founder members, but the Wanderers didn't get a look in.

A vote on which of the seven competing clubs should be given the last place in the First Division was taken. Spurs did well, but not well enough to beat Arsenal who were ten votes ahead. It was an amazing turn of events and Arsenal's official history does not shy away from this, admitting "the arguments used were, of course, complete and utter nonsense. The League is not (and never has been) run on the basis of the most experienced clubs being given the higher places..."*

---

* *The Official Illustrated History of Arsenal*, Phil Soar and Martyn Tyler

At best, it seems Norris had leaned on people, using contacts from his own past which would be of material benefit to Arsenal, as he strove to put the club on a surer financial footing. There is, however, another viewpoint, one which his many opponents have steadfastly stuck to. That is that Norris's case could never, on its own, have carried enough weight to succeed within the upper reaches of the game. For years it was strongly rumoured that he'd gone further, offering large sums of money in bribes to secure Arsenal's promotion. It may even have been that McKenna was in some way compromised by the allegations surrounding his team and Manchester United, which were substantiated in a court of law and thus purchase could be applied to him. Even now these are highly contentious points, ones which are unlikely to be satisfactorily resolved at such a distance from the actual events.

There is also the possibly that something more subtle was going on. John McKenna, like Henry Norris, was a Freemason. Students and opponents of the craft have long claimed it allows men to secretly assist each other in business. The Grand Lodge of England is explicit on this – members are not allowed to use their status for personal gain or advancement.

Personal gain was not quite what Norris required though, his need was entwined with that of the club, these were one and the same. In fact it turns out that Norris was a pretty senior Masonic figure, who rose to the post of Grand Deacon of the United Grand Lodge. It is not difficult to imagine that in his hour of need he approached McKenna, as a brother Mason, to ask for help. If this was the case, McKenna, for a host of reasons, may have found it almost impossible to say no. Whatever the truth of the affair, Spurs were left high and dry. They became, in an instant, a Division Two club. In just six years they had failed to stop Arsenal moving into their own area of London and lost their First Division status to their neighbours. Strangely, in the end it was Spurs, not Arsenal, who paid the heaviest price for the dire financial difficulties brought about by the move to Highbury.

Fired by a sense of injustice they rallied and immediately fought back on the pitch winning the Second Division in record breaking style. In 1921, back in the top league, they finished ahead of Arsenal and won the FA Cup. It was the first time a club from the south had taken the trophy since their own win twenty years previously. Spurs were again, without question, the leading club in north London and would remain so until legendary manager Herbert Chapman arrived at Highbury four years later.

The boot was on the other foot again by 1928. Tottenham had skittered down the league and were relegated amid claims that Arsenal had 'thrown' two games late in the season to ensure their neighbours were sent down. Evidence suggesting there was anything untoward in the results is pretty thin. The league table had been incredibly tight that year and had Arsenal contrived to deliberately lose matches they would have been compromising their own league position.

As for the enigmatic Norris, he came to rather a sticky end in the game. He was forced out of Arsenal in 1928, departing under the black could of scandal involving more allegations of illegal payments. It was revealed that he had been using club funds to have himself chauffeured around London while drinking brandy and smoking cigars. The FA banned him from football for life. Sympathy must have been in very short supply at the other end of the Seven Sisters Road.

Ancient history or not these are the principal reasons for the bad blood between the two clubs who have traditionally been London's biggest. Spurs fans – while not in the main being versed in the fine detail of the story – remain acutely aware of what happened to them at the hands of Arsenal in the early part of the 20th century, and despise the Gunners for it. Even under normal circumstances Arsenal may have struggled to gain acceptance after heading across the river, but their subsequent conduct led to successive generations at White Hart Lane repeating the mantra that Arsenal, neither welcome nor wanted, never have been and never can be, truly a north London club.

Given the history, it will come as no surprise to learn there has always been the capacity for feelings to boil over on the pitch and the terraces, with recorded incidents of gang warfare and knife attacks at derbies going back to the start of the 1920s and, equally, of fighting among players. One encounter which is particularly well remembered for being bad tempered was the second-leg of the 1968 League Cup semi-final. John Radford of Arsenal and Spurs' Cyril Knowles fought, as did Tottenham centre-half Mike England and his Arsenal counterpart Ian Ure. Arsenal won the tie with a late goal. The violence spread to the stands and into nearby streets where there was a stabbing.

This was a prelude to the following decade when both grounds were dangerous places, with fighting in pubs before and after matches and opposition fans trying to 'take' sections of the home terracing. Both sets of supporters explained how the famed North Bank terrace at the Gillespie Road end of the ground was often a target and that the Spurs contingent would infiltrate the terracing, often with no small measure of success, and 'take the North Bank'.

The rivalry was also sharpened during this era by the arrival of skinhead gangs, many of whom had links to the far-right National Front. The NF attached themselves to Arsenal out of their hate for Spurs, which they saw as a Jewish club. For some time the Front campaigned in the streets around Highbury, though the majority of Arsenal fans just weren't interested. For all that, throughout the 1980s it was possible to hear chants at Highbury about gassing Jews and plenty of badges were worn which said – I hate Tottenham Yids.

Times have changed and Arsenal now have lots of supporters – and even a spattering of board members – with Jewish backgrounds. Proof of this was the brouhaha caused by the club's decision to sign a stadium and kit sponsorship deal with Emirates Airlines. Arsenal's Jewish contingent were unhappy that the club was tying itself so visibly to the United Arab Emirates, which has traditionally had poor, or rather non-existent, relations with Israel. Arsenal subsequently entered into a separate agreement to have the Israeli tourist board show electronic video messages around the pitch-side promoting the 'sun and fun' times people could have in the country.

Tottenham supporters of a certain vintage are proud that the club has strong links to the Jewish community. The team was followed by large number of Jews who came to London in the 1940s, settling in places like Stamford Hill. Daniel Wynne the chairman of the Spurs Supporters' Trust, is well aware of the fact. "My dad escaped Nazi Europe. He took me to Spurs when I was just five. You see you can change your wife, family die – unfortunately – friends drift in and out of your life, but the one thing you cannot change is your football team."

Today many fans who go to White Hart Lane are not Jewish, but are happy to be called Yids. Daniel objects to the wholesale use of the word, recalling darker times when it was only a term of abuse. I asked if he was happy that his club was still perceived as Jewish. "Yeah as a Jew it's nice, but to be honest Tottenham will always be Tottenham. If, say, a Russian board came in tomorrow it would still be the same club."

THROUGH ALL OF THESE PERIODS – the Norris-led skirmishes of the early 20th century, war, immigration, segregation and infiltration by the right – I doubt the fixture saw anything to compare with the controversy which engulfed one player, Sol Campbell, when it became known he was leaving Spurs for Arsenal.

Campbell had been a hero at White Hart Lane for a decade, he was the Spurs captain, an international, and for a time, world-class central defender with England. His contract was due to run out at the end of the 2000/01 season and for months it was unclear if he would be moving on or signing a new deal. Most observers believed he would go to a top European club, or possibly Manchester United or Liverpool. Yet Tottenham fans never lost hope that he would stay and the fact that no transfer had been announced by the end of the season gave them further reason to believe. On Tuesday 3rd July, north London and much of the football world was stunned to learn that Campbell had, in fact, moved those four miles down the Seven Sisters Road to Highbury.

It wasn't as if there hadn't been a steady flow of players between the clubs over the years, and even ones which prompted controversy. The first was probably the transfer of the popular Spurs striker, George Hunt, back in 1937. The great Northern Irish goalkeeper, Pat Jennings, made the switch after thirteen years at Spurs, angry that no-one had seen fit to thank him for his services and openly admits now that he signed for Tottenham's greatest rivals on purpose just to annoy the board.

Even Charlie George, a boyhood Arsenal fan and seventies hero of the North Bank, had been prepared to do it, having been told he was surplus to requirements. He was devastated, but needed to find another club. Spurs were interested, but Derby County got there first. George then said there had been "no question" about it. He would have signed for Tottenham.*

Arsenal's celebrated manager, Herbert Chapman, had played for Spurs, while Terry Neill managed both clubs and played for Arsenal. Then there was George Graham. Having been a player at Highbury he subsequently became a highly successful Arsenal manager and, therefore, was never truly accepted during his time at White Hart Lane. He was seen as an Arsenal man to the core and no wonder, Graham is said to have kept his shares and large collection of Arsenal memorabilia, not to mention a garden patio complete with Gunners crest. Poor old George, he just couldn't win, Arsenal fans also saw him as a villain for having gone over to the other side.

The business with Campbell was different. He was a shining light through an era in which Spurs had struggled. The fans were outraged, hanging their former star in effigy close to the Tottenham ground. The fact he was out of contract did not help, as, thanks to the recently-imposed regulations following the Jean-Marc Bosman case, it meant there would be no transfer fee, not a single penny for a player who'd been developed through the youth ranks. To the Spurs fans the whole affair demonstrated how, in their eyes, Arsenal had continually tried to undermine them.

Campbell signed a four year contract which, at the time, made him the highest paid player in British football history. Arsène Wenger said he had signed the Spurs captain because he was "the best."** The best or not, it was a move fraught with danger. The former Arsenal player, Paul Davis had this warning: "He will definitely have to watch where he goes, where he eats and where he socialises because those Tottenham supporters are not going to forgive him and they could possibly turn very nasty."***

No-one expected it to be anything other than nasty when Campbell returned to his former place of work, with his new team. The first derby was held on the 17th of November. Newspapers ran

---

* *The Professor,* Myles Palmer
** *Daily Mirror,* 4 July 2001
*** *The Professor,* Myles Palmer

headlines such as 'SOL TO FACE HATE MOB.'* They were not wrong, the Arsenal team bus was pelted with bottles and beer cans as it squeezed up Bill Nicholson Way and through the gates into the stadium. Ivor Champan, the editor of the Spurs fanzine, *My Eyes Have Seen THE GLORY*, was nearby. "That was a really horrible atmosphere, really horrible. That day I knew when the Arsenal team coach was arriving because of the people rushing up to the main entrance. The police used a Turkish lorry driver, they pulled his juggernaut across the main entrance to protect the coach as it went in."

As the teams came out Spurs fans released two thousand balloons with JUDAS printed on them. One banner simply read John 13:27, another reference to Judas Iscariot, reincarnated as a strapping defender in red and white. As far as the home crowd were concerned Campbell had committed the ultimate act of betrayal. Despite all that, and having to dodge a few missiles during the game, he played superbly in a 1-1 draw.

While he was at Arsenal, Tottenham fans constantly seemed enraged. His transfer made the fixture even more flammable, often leading to scenes reminiscent of the bad old days when there would be fighting in just about every shop doorway along the High Road leading to Tottenham's ground. When Arsenal, with Sol Campbell, won the league there in 2004 there were reports of sticks, bricks and bottles being thrown at away supporters outside and numerous attempted ambushes. The problem is exacerbated by the fact that the fans spill out together into the streets around White Hart Lane after derbies and head for the same trains some distance away from the ground.

Campbell was transferred to Portsmouth in the summer of 2006, not that his departure has improved relations between north London's deadly foes greatly. Steve, a Spurs fan in his late thirties, summed up how they feel about their rivals, saying: "I just don't like them. I wouldn't like to be an away supporter, any away supporter, especially Arsenal. We are found of our own, but we

* *The Professor,* Myles Palmer

don't tolerate away supporters, especially not them. It's a volatile atmosphere. We hate them badly, hate them with a passion."

Tottenham fans are certainly no angels, but the words honour and heritage do seem to be part of their group DNA. These cropped up time and again in conversation. They also conveyed an almost moral sense of the way the game should be played. A motto at the ground spells this out – Winning In Glory, Playing With Style. Spurs supporters have long demanded that the team play in a manner which pays homage to their history and wins the approval of the purist. These feelings stem from the fact that they sensationally redefined the game twice in a decade. For older supporters the side which won the Second then First Division championships in consecutive seasons in 1950 and 1951 was the greatest in the history of the club. They played a style of football so brilliant in its conception that it defines the game even still. Arthur Rowe's 'Push and Run' system was total football twenty years before it emerged from the Netherlands, and drew influence from coaching methods he'd learned in Hungary. Just as the name suggests, players would push the ball to a team-mate before running into space. Long balls and dribbling were substituted for fast short accurate passing and a strong team ethic.

A decade on, a half-back from that era, Bill Nicholson, sent out another Spurs team built on flair and skill. They delighted fans around the country and famously became the first team in the modern era to win the coveted domestic league and cup double.

There's an obvious contrast with Arsenal, a club which has often been perceived as one where functionality takes precedence over artistry. Prior to Arsène Wenger's time in charge, supporters around the country mocked them for their tendency to grind out 1-0 results. Tottenham's support, above all, sought to highlight the difference in styles. For Arsenal winning was enough; while to those watching their rivals, the quality of the play was paramount. Did it entertain, did it thrill?

YET, THOSE DOUR ARSENAL TEAMS were important, not because of the way they played, but for what they achieved. It was on their success that the Arsenal of this new century has been founded. It was George Graham's Arsenal which first strangled Spurs, who despite their famous dash have long been starved of trophies. The winning mentality and high profile of the 'boring Arsenal' of the late 80s and early 90s led directly to the era of Wenger, Henry and ultimately the new stadium.

The Emirates itself, an expensive, visually striking and spacious ground, is the absolute evidence of the club's determination to compete with the very best. Tottenham may be in the same league, but far from the same sphere of influence. While it did not generate the kind of anger brought about by the move north of the river all those years ago, for Spurs fans the very existence of the new stadium taps into all those old negative feelings about legitimacy and confirms the belief that Arsenal are just 'nomads', nothing more than the 'Woolwich Wanderers'.

Their fans may be stunned at the thought, but Tottenham, may also have to do 'an Arsenal' and leave the area which gave them their name, their identity and generations of support. The club's board, too, see increased capacity as a way of not only surviving in the Premiership, but ultimately returning to their former position of dominance. Spurs have been actively examining two contrasting strategies – stay and remodel the ground, or get out, to an entirely new stadium, possibly miles away. Though it's believed the club looked at the new Wembley and the 2012 Olympic Stadium, serious obstacles placed in the way of using either makes their continued presence at White Hart Lane more likely. Quietly Tottenham have been buying up land around the ground.

There are downsides to a revamp in the eyes of some on the Tottenham board though; transport links are relatively poor and the surrounding area is neither as wealthy nor as attractive as they would ideally like. Without doubt any plan to move would be met with unrelenting protests from the majority of fans who would see that as a dilution of Spurs' history and the ultimate defeat over the territory they have reluctantly shared for so long.

A film about the murder of a player at Highbury was made in 1939. It starred the Arsenal players of the day and was called *The Arsenal Stadium Mystery*. On the final day of the 2005/06 season the side was involved in another murder mystery, one which killed Tottenham's hopes of a place in the Champions League.

Arsenal's 'Final Salute' to their stadium was against Wigan, while Spurs had to win against West Ham to ensure fourth place and that final Champions League berth. Tottenham had prepared for the game by staying at the salubrious Marriot Hotel in Canary Wharf. In the small hours of the morning preceding the match ten of their players became ill. Tottenham officials immediately suspected food poisoning, it was rumoured that a large dish of pre-match lasagne had been spiked.

Spurs summoned representatives from the Premier League, demanding that the game be played at a later date. However, as they were technically able to field a team there could be no postponement. The match went ahead as scheduled, but with some players vomiting in the dressing room and clearly under-par on the pitch. They lost 2-1, while Arsenal won 4-2. Martin Jol, apparently not being ironic, said Tottenham were "gutted" by what had happened.*

Tests from official samples taken from the kitchen subsequently showed no poisoning whatsoever. Environmental Health said the illness had probably been caused by a virus. Spurs had to settle for the UEFA Cup while Arsenal, though they lost the final of that season's Champions League, had secured their passage into the elite competition again the following season. Another addition, perhaps, to Tottenham's long list of maltreatment at the hands of their dear neighbours.

* Martin Jol, *BBC website*, 7 May 2006

MANCHESTER:

Not Really Here?

"As a spectacle, the Manchester derby has remained true to the idea of local warfare played out on pitch, terrace and street."

United We Stand, November 2002

IN THE DAMP DARKNESS of the early hours of 9th December 2006 two gangs were making their way through the streets of Manchester. Like the youth movements of the left and right in South American cities under dictatorship, they were concentrating on a message and a slogan, and using the cover of the night to their aid. In a sense too, this was political – City or United. They had come to spread the word, so people would know who 'owned' Manchester, when dawn broke on derby day.

Each group was from the more radical sections of their club's support – LUHG (Love United Hate Glazer) and *Bluewatch*, a City website used mostly by younger fans. The United gang claimed to have caught the City boys defacing 'Red territory' by tearing down a banner near Old Trafford opposing United's majority shareholders – the Glazer family. What followed is unclear, but we can be sure that the same anti-Glazer faction later turned up at City's ground with a 'confiscated' banner which said 'Hate United, Love Glazer'. The United fans posted a video of the offending article being burned outside the ground on the You Tube website. To the tune of City's long-established supporters' anthem *Blue Moon* they smoked and laughed inside their hooded tops as the flames ate through the canvass. I was told this had been done as a warning to keep away from United areas and not to go interfering with anti-Glazer activities.

Ownership, identity and territory are central to this rivalry. Even in this era of world-wide interest in the Premiership supporters of both clubs are determined to show that their team is the one which truly represents Manchester, something which has been a bone of contention in the city for well over half a century.

Manchester United and Manchester City are two of the most famous names in British football, though only United are truly known around the globe. City fans would disagree and yes, they have supporters clubs based overseas, many of them in fact, but really United have made themselves into a global sports name and brand in the way that only a very few elite clubs have been able to. They claim to have in the region of fifty-seven million 'supporters' across five continents. City are not quite in that league, and it's open to question whether they even wish to be, for, importantly, that would be to ignore their own distinct identity.

The basis of today's rivalry can be traced back to the actions of one man in the middle years of the last century. It was Sir Matt Busby who had the vision for what would become the modern Manchester United and he who re-built the club and successive teams after the Second World War. It's an exaggeration – but an understandable one – to say the history of United begins with Busby and is condensed, in the mind's eye, into the catastrophe which befell his first great young team on one of their pioneering trips into Europe. Successive generations of football fans from Manchester and well beyond are still aware of the rudimentary facts of that terrible day of 6 February 1958 in Munich, when a team – The Flowers of Manchester – was lost.

But the division over the incredible achievements of this Scottish miner's son emanates from the fact that Busby had a foot in both camps. He had served Manchester City with distinction as a player, a gifted left-half who also captained Liverpool and Scotland, winning the FA Cup with City in 1934. Until he took charge of United after the Second World War they had been a well-known, but rather provincial northern club. Their fortunes had fluctuated over the years since coming into being in 1878 as Newton Heath, the works team of the Lancashire and Yorkshire Railway. As United they had won championships and the FA Cup during the good years up to the outbreak of the First World War. The 1920s and '30s were poor though, and the club swung up and down between the top two divisions, once almost ending up in the third tier of English football. City at this time were doing well, winning the FA Cup and league championship within three seasons and were certainly the bigger of the clubs between the wars.

City fans of a certain vintage are still prone to call United 'The Rags', a reference to their lowly position in 1945 when Old Trafford had very nearly been bombed to ruins by the Luftwaffe and City had to step in, allowing their rivals to play at Maine Road while the stadium was rebuilt. This was the beginning of Busby's time at United. He hadn't forgotten that he'd been a City man first, and that was why he'd come back to Manchester. "I got this opportunity to as manager of Manchester United. I had a soft spot for Manchester after my City days and it attracted me."* In the first full league season after the war, 1946/47, United challenged for the title, finishing second, just a point shy of champions Liverpool. A year later they won the FA Cup, defeating Stanley Matthews' Blackpool 4-2 in what was acknowledged at the time as one of the greatest finals ever. But this was an ageing team and Busby knew it.

United's large debt, which almost put the club out of business, meant Busby's teams during his 25-year reign, at their core, would be built from members of the youth academy. This also suited him, Busby was a man of action and new ideas who, in contrast with most of his managerial contemporaries, took to the training pitch to mould his men into dynamic, attacking players. His methods worked, the side which won the championship in 1955/56 had an average age of just twenty-two. They came to be known as the Busby Babes.

To win at home was one thing, but the great post-war spirit of European brotherhood and reconciliation was widening football's horizons. Not for the first time the English FA was slow to realise the potential of international competition. Busby was not, and in the face of official opposition, took his side onto the continent. Having lost the semi-final of the European Cup the previous season to the great Real Madrid, in 1957/58 Busby made Europe his absolute priority. The team were doing well at home, but now faced Red Star Belgrade in the quarter-finals of the competition. They won the fist-leg at home before drawing 3-3 in Belgrade to advance

* Matt Busby, *The Hamlyn Illustrated History of Manchester United*, Tyrrell & Meek

to the next round. The following day, the 6th of February 1958, the team flew to Munich. There their plane – a BAE Elizabethan – was due to refuel before going on to Manchester. The Bavarian capital was freezing and had been carpeted with snow that afternoon. The aircraft twice encountered problems and aborted takeoff. On the next attempt there was a massive fuel surge, which caused over acceleration before the power suddenly dropped away. The plane left the runway at high speed, crashed through a fence, crossed a road, struck a house and broke up. Twenty-two people were killed, seven of them players. Two weeks later the brightest star of his generation, Duncan Edwards, also succumbed to his injuries. Matt Busby was left fighting for his life in an oxygen tent.

The BBC interrupted its afternoon schedule to break the news and special editions of the Manchester Evening Chronicle were rushed onto the streets. Where there had been celebration, there suddenly was grief. Football was stunned, as was Britain. In the days which followed tens of thousands attended the funerals, lining the streets of Manchester to pay their respects. Supporters took part in silent tributes at grounds across the country.

Thirteen days after Munich, United took on Sheffield Wednesday in a postponed FA Cup tie at Old Trafford. The United team-sheet in the official programme was left blank in tribute to those who'd perished. Fans, many augmenting their United colours with black, are said to have wept openly during the 3-0 win. The side, captained by Munich survivor Bill Foulkes and managed by Busby's deputy Jimmy Murphy, was packed with reserves and recent signings who hardly knew each other, but they played superbly. A victory had been demanded, and not only by the 60,000 inside the ground. On the cover of the United Review the club's chairman, HP Hardman, wrote that 'an unprecedented blow to British football has touched the hearts of millions and we express our deep gratitude to the many who have sent messages of sympathy and floral tributes. Wherever football is played United is mourned... Although we mourn our dead and grieve for our wounded we believe that great days are not done for us... Manchester United will rise again.'*

---

* *United Review,* 19 February 1958

Hardman was right; ten years later Busby's United lifted the European Cup at Wembley, becoming the first English club to do so. After beating Benfica 4-1 after extra-time, the players ran to their manager and embraced him, a gesture designed to show they truly understood what the victory had meant, to the man and to the club. The sorrow of Munich had weighed on the manager's shoulders for a decade; in other ways it had also been a turning point for United.

Initially, City fans had been as moved by the events in Germany as everyone else. There was no real division on the matter and their support willingly took part in silences and paid their respects. There may have been odd exceptions, and evidence exists to suggest some supporters went out to 'celebrate' the news of the crash because it would put their own team firmly on top locally. In the main the feeling was that those who'd died were lads who'd come from the same kind of (working-class) backgrounds as most football supporters.

Those sentiments changed as time wore on. A section of City's support has long believed the crash was the catalyst for United's mass appeal beyond Manchester – bringing a romantic glory to the club, boosting its image through constant favourable coverage in the national media. Bobby Charlton, himself a survivor, summed this up. "Before Munich it was Manchester's club, afterwards everyone felt that they owned a little bit of it."*

The immediate evidence for this was the overwhelming public demand for United to win the FA Cup after, remarkably, reaching the final post-Munich. This was something felt way beyond Manchester. Bolton Wanderers, spearheaded by England centre-forward Nat Lofthouse, unhappy that their own achievements were being overlooked, duly went out and won the Cup.

In short, the charge made by their rivals is that United built their reputation on the back of the emotional impact caused by the deaths of eight young players. The disaster of Munich propelled United to national acclaim – and crucially – led to a feeling that City's place in the game had been undermined. The side from Maine Road, who'd helped their neighbours when they were homeless, were now generally regarded as the second team in Manchester.

* quoted in *A Strange Kind Of Glory,* Eamonn Dunphy

As far as their fans are concerned, City have never received the credit they deserved for their own achievements. Why? Because of the constant goodwill towards United. When they became English champions in 1968 they were eclipsed by United winning the European Cup a few days later. United did not win the Championship between 1967 and 1993, but yet were always felt to be one of the greatest clubs in the country. During this time City won the Championship, FA Cup, European Cup Winners' Cup and League Cup. In terms of trophies, for that quarter of a century, there is no doubting which club fared better. City's problem was that these victories were sporadic; they never truly dominated the game in the way their neighbours had under both Busby and latterly Sir Alex Ferguson.

The darkest aspect of this frustration is the way the supporters now treat the Munich crash. United are often referred to as 'The Munichs' and at derbies City fans are known for indulging in what's become an infamous chant:

> Who's that lying on the runway
> Who's that lying in the snow
> It's Matt Busby and his boys
> Making all the fucking noise
> Coz' they couldn't get the airplane to go

No City fan I spoke to was prepared to admit ever having sung it themselves. They felt it 'only surfaced' when United went ahead, and was just the way a minority chose to wind up the opposition.

I wanted to find out more about this. The night before the match I took a bus out over the Mancunian Way to Swinton. There I met Alex Channon, a former miner, Labour Party activist and referee. He's now the Chairman of the Manchester City Centenary Supporters Association. Alex is 57 and looks like he has been fit all his life. He stops me as I walk towards his front door, pointing to a square of grass in the middle of the garden. "Do you know what that is? It's the penalty spot from the Platt Lane End at Maine Road."

In his kitchen we drink tea while his wife watches Coronation Street, it's total Manchester. Alex tells me he's watched City for the best part of fifty years. He can remember being at the centre of fights on the terraces before there was segregation and having to hide in back gardens after derby matches to escape United fans. Alex would ideally like to see eleven Mancunians turning out for City each week and is proud that his club still connects with ordinary folk. The Munich chants upset him though. "I hate it. I love the City fans and the atmosphere, but I hate the song, it makes me cringe. I was a kid at the time of the disaster and I think it was like the kind of grief that took over the nation when Princess Diana died, it was of national importance. The people who sing those songs don't grip the meaning of it. It's despicable.

We made a big appeal not to do it last season during the derby at our stadium. But it didn't work, they were still chanting it. The City fans should let it go, it's not a joke. I resent Man United supporters going on about it though. They have sung about [Alf-Inge] Haaland's knee [injured beyond repair by a Roy Keane challenge in 2001] and the death of Marc-Vivien Foe [who collapsed and died playing for Cameroon in a Confederations Cup match against Colombia in June 2003] and when they play Liverpool they sing about Hillsborough and all that. I would say to them, get your own home in order first."

FOOTBALL IN 1968 WAS A game transformed. In the decade since Munich there had emerged completely new expressions of youth culture which eventually led to segregation on the terraces. This ended the era of cross-club support which saw some fans in Manchester go to watch whichever club was playing at home on any given weekend, and gave rise to the phenomenon of what came to be known as 'hooliganism'. By the time United won their next championship, 25 years later, the game had again changed, out of all recognition, with all-seated stadiums and billion pound television contracts. To be outside the Premier League was to be nowhere; and that's where City found themselves by the middle of the 1990s. At the same time United were dominating the league and maximising their off-field potential. City had spent years tearing themselves apart through expensive transfers, repeated changes of management, campaigns against the board and, by May 1998, were struggling even to stay out of what was, in effect, the Third Division. The support turned in on itself and looked to its roots as a source of comfort and pride.

The club which would become Manchester City had been formed amid the poverty of new immigrant communities in the east of the city – in districts such as Gorton and Ardwick. People were flooding in from central and eastern Europe to work in the local industries, living in cramped conditions where problems such as alcoholism and gang violence were commonplace. The Rector of St Mark's Church, Arthur Connell, was much troubled by the situation and pressed his two daughters to help improve things. With typical mid-Victorian zeal they set about their task. Regardless of her sex, Anna focused her energies on the men of the parish, setting up a cricket club. A football team followed in 1880, this was St Mark's (West Gorton), which would later become Ardwick AFC. The club was a success and joined the Football League in 1892. By the time Queen Victoria herself came north to open the Manchester Ship Canal two years later, financial problems were forcing a 'reorganisation'. Those in charge at Ardwick felt this time of great local celebration would also be the moment to cast their net wider and bring in more supporters, while also putting themselves in a better financial position. A new name would be needed to reflect this and, eventually, Manchester City was chosen. Other suggestions were rejected on the grounds that they didn't sound quite inclusive enough; strangely, among them was Manchester United.

As City grew into one of England's leading teams they became more like other clubs, concentrating on football, and the business of being a success. Still, they have always retained more than a passing interest in the welfare of the supporters. The argument is that Old Trafford houses nothing more than a business, while City, according to the club's former Chief Executive Chris Bird, "are still a community based football club that has got strong Manchester roots, that is determined not to become a middle-class football club."*

The contrasts are hard to deny. In 2001 United were worth £1 billion on the stock exchange and were bought in 2005 for nearly £800 million. They are already well established in foreign markets. For instance, three quarters of a million Koreans own United credit cards and the majority of people in China say they know who

---

* quoted in *Manchester United: A Thematic Study,* David L Andrews

United are. Peter Kenyon was Bird's Old Trafford counterpart at the time. This is how he explained the United philosophy: "We've enjoyed quite a lot of success here in England and England is still very important to us. But we knew to grow and keep moving forward, we absolutely had to look beyond our boundaries. So a lot of our strategy is now figuring out ways to bring the experience of Old Trafford to the rest of the world."*

In fact, supporters from the various nations on Earth already make the pilgrimage to Old Trafford. Every time United play at home they pass down Sir Matt Busby Way to gather at the feet of Busby's statue outside the East Stand. He's immortalised there in a paternal pose, smiling gently; one hand resting on his hip, the other clutching a ball. I walked there in the rain, past the badge and scarf sellers, the touts and the women with cracked faces who were blowing smoke from the doorways of the Legends Café. At every turn United display their history, be it through tributes to Busby or commemorations of Munich, such as the clock on the outside of the stadium stopped at 3.04pm, the precise time of the Munich crash. This remembrance of things past is entirely genuine, but it also gives gravitas and legitimacy to the United brand, a powerful draw in itself.

What really struck me about United's home that morning were the dozens of supporters queuing in the drizzle to get into the club's Megastore. Hundreds more were already inside. There, it felt like the January sales had come early, each step was a push past someone else. You could buy almost everything imaginable as long as it carried the United name: replica kits, clothing, footballs, mugs, pens, baby wear and even 'lucky bags'. The musical accompaniment to this was the constant beeping of electronic scanners, a heavenly scene for any marketing manager.

I thought of Busby, high on his plinth just yards away and I couldn't help but wonder what this serious minded and religious man, the coal miner who'd taken part in the general strike of 1926, would have made of it all. Manchester United have moved on substantially since their father figure passed away in 1994. They have taken the Premiership by storm and felt the full benefits of

* quoted in *Manchester United: A Thematic Study,* David I Andrews

football's age of high-finance. Such success also brings risks, attracting newcomers to the game, people who see clubs as a convenient way of making serious money. Even the biggest sporting institutions are not exempt to market forces, and aggressive takeover.

In May 2005, after weeks of speculation, it was confirmed that the American sports tycoon, Malcolm Glazer had won control of the club. The Glazer family had been building their shares over the previous two years before going in for the kill, buying up those owned by the Irish racing magnates, JP McManus and John Magnier. Part of the problem was the Glazers were not arriving with billions to lavish on their new acquisition. The deal had been financed with massive loans and United, having been highly profitable, were plunged into an astounding £600 million debt. The majority of United's support resisted the takeover. They were worried there would be little or no money for new players, and felt it was inevitable that season ticket prices would be continually ramped up to pay off this unwanted, and in their eyes unnecessary, debt. Their angst spilled over into civil disorder the first time Mr Glazer and his sons arrived at Old Trafford. After a sit-down protest, police clashed with a group of around 500 United fans who were chanting 'die Glazer die'.* Barricades were erected and missiles thrown as the demonstrators attempted to ambush the new owners, who had to be rushed away, huddled in the back of a riot van.

Some Old Trafford regulars were so appalled by the takeover they started boycotting matches. To others the Manchester United they loved had ceased to exist. This group felt so disenfranchised they went as far as to start a new club – FC United of Manchester – which really amounts to a breakaway Man United, a non-profit making organisation, playing in semi-professional local leagues.

For those who couldn't find it within themselves to turn their backs on their first love, the Glazer business continues to hum in the background. The issue dominates the pages of United fanzines and internet forums and with good reason. United's annual profits at the start of 2007 were £50 million; the cost of loan charges on their debt was £62 million. There is little chance that the live and

---

* *The Scotsman*, 30 June 2005

highly visible campaign against the American owners will end anytime soon. The back wall of the run-down pub I was staying at displayed a sticker above the pool table. On a white background were red letters: LOVE UNITED, followed by black ones: HATE GLAZER. There were dozens of these on all the main approaches to Old Trafford and the message GLAZER OUT is painted in thick lettering across the red-brick wall of the Old Trafford metro station.

Most City supporters, if they are honest, will have a sneaking admiration for this resistance to Glazer. They are amused by United being owned by Americans, and at the deep financial hole they are in – yet the most caustic laughter they reserve for themselves. As a group City are well known for their black humour. The chant, *We're Not Really Here* is a good example of their self-deprecating tendencies. This has been a response to the considerable ups and downs they have been through. It was first sung when they were outside the Premiership and has continued when struggling in the bottom half of the top league. It has multiple meanings, but can be best summed up as 'we are a big club and should be doing much better'. They long to see their team competing for the greatest prizes at home and abroad as they did through the 1950s to early 1980s.

It's easy to portray City as the local co-operative opposing the great hyper-market of United. The truth is a little less straight-forward. Directors at the City of Manchester Stadium had actively been seeking a buyer over the past few seasons. Immediately after the City AGM, and just days before the derby I was going to watch, their chairman John Wardle said as much. "The board is aware that we need further investment to maintain our challenge in an increas-ingly competitive and high-finance premier league."* News had broken that City were talking to an unnamed party about a package worth in the region of £70 million. The problem was finding the right kind of wealth. Many City fans told me they would be delighted to see money coming into their club, but could not accept anything which compromised their communal values. They were

* *BBC Manchester website*, 7 December 2006

unwilling to tolerate becoming 'another United', or being exposed to a Glazer-esque type of situation. Phil Gatenby, a season ticket holder for over 25 years and now heavily involved with the Safe Standing campaign, sees it like this: "City are a genuine club with a good football in the community section, we have signed up to the Stonewall Agreement [on gay rights], we will have a wind turbine soon, the first green football stadium in the world. At the same time they have to compete with United and the likes of Chelsea, so the club has a serious side and the fans just come to see us play the best we can in the best ground we can. I think the City fans have been superb over the years. We still want to be the biggest club in the country, but the way we play and the club's focus is important. United just want world domination."

A hard truth about the Manchester derby is that what used to be one of the great fixtures of the English football calendar has, for some people, now lost something. United fans feel City aren't keeping their side of the bargain, they are not the threat they once were, are not really there. As a consequence United have turned some of their attention to the likes of Chelsea, Arsenal and, most notably, Liverpool, as their serious rivals. Relations between United and Liverpool have been particularly toxic since the mid 1980s, when tear gas was sprayed over the United team as they arrived at Anfield. Then, in 2006, a small group of Liverpool fans attacked an ambulance which was taking the stricken United player, Alan Smith, to hospital after a hellish leg-break. Add to this Alex Ferguson's stated desire when joining United in 1986 to 'knock Liverpool off their bloody perch' – an ambition more than fulfilled during his highly successful 20-plus years at Old Trafford – and you get a sense of how keenly felt the rivalry between the two most successful clubs in the domestic game has been.

The two cities have never been the best of friends, not at least since the end of the 19th century when Manchester, thirty miles inland, managed to access Liverpool's greatest natural resource – the sea – in building the ship canal. Despite resistance from Merseyside, the canal physically linking the two areas went ahead, helping to alleviate Manchester's problem of being a manufacturing city without a port.

Regular competition in Europe has also meant that United supporters have a wider focus; competing against the likes of Juventus,

AC Milan and Real Madrid, has further diluted the rivalry with City. Reds feel the derby is City's most important fixture, their annual cup final. For these perceptions to change City would have to be making a sustained and realistic challenge for the title.

Meaningless, however, the derby is certainly not. United fans would never accept losing these matches and coming out on top remains a matter of honour which cannot be ignored in Manchester.

Slogans, banners, stunts and ridicule are the currency of these matches and hardcore elements from both City and United have gone to some remarkable, perhaps farcical, lengths to show theirs is the team of Manchester. Put simply, these confrontations – the latest being the spat between the Bluewatch brigade and the anti-Glazer group – are about belonging.

In 2001 a large group of United supporters took to the streets of central Manchester for a birthday party to 'celebrate' the fact that it was twenty-five years since City had won a major trophy, they also painted the away end at Maine Road with a large red '25'. At the final derby at Maine Road, a 3-1 win for City, a fan in the home end enlisted the help of his comrades to unfurl a banner. Only when it was being held aloft did they notice they had been duped, it carried the slogan, MANCHESTER IS RED. Not to be outdone City fans hired a small plane for a derby and flew it above Old Trafford. On seeing it approaching the United fans began to clap and cheer... until they realised the message being trailed behind in *World of Sport* fashion, was unmistakably pro-City: 'Real Club, Real Fans, do you come from Manchester?'

CITY SUPPORTERS HAVE LONG viewed themselves as Manchester's club. Not only do they make the most of the administrative quirk which threw United beyond the city limits into Greater Manchester in the 1970s, they also make much of their rivals' international and UK-wide support: cue all those jokes about disaffected United fans going out and throwing their season tickets into the Thames. It is a message which has not gone unnoticed by the club. In 2005 a series of adverts appeared on buses and billboards around Manchester. On a sky blue background large white letters carried the slogans: 'This is our City', 'Real Manchester', 'Pure Manchester' and 'Greater Manchester'. City went as far as to hire an outside advertising agency for the campaign, which, it was claimed, was not a commercial venture, but rather one designed to poke gentle fun at United and engage with Mancunians of every kind. There's little doubt they also wanted to do more to compete with the United brand and felt the local community was their most obvious outlet.

It's hardly a surprise, but United fans loathe the suggestion that they are not from Manchester. They too have taken steps to promote their Mancunian roots. The more localised sections of the support accept the club has a worldwide fan base. These people, they say, are welcome at matches, but the heart of the club is Manchester people. In recent seasons the idea of a Republik of Mancunia has been heavily promoted among the supporters. A banner devoted to this slogan can regularly be seen across the middle of the West Stand. There are several reasons for the emergence of what can be described as this militant or resurgent United Mancunianism. Part of this is an open hostility to their national team. Again, this directly contrasts with City supporters who are often seen following England – complete with sky blue (rather than red) St George's Cross flags. United fans told me they were sick of hearing their players being booed and abused at England games and prefer to follow United in Europe. The depth of feeling against England is illustrated by one letter to the Red News fanzine during which the writer, Pete Burton, defends Cristiano Ronaldo, the Portuguese winger, who stood accused of contriving to have his club-mate, Wayne Rooney, sent off during the World Cup in 2006. "Ronaldo has been public enemy No.1 for pathetic 'little Ingurlanders' ever since ... the shaven-headed Ingurland brigade have found it very had to accept that for forty years their beloved national team hasn't swept all before them." *

The idea of a Republik also suggests Manchester United is a land apart, something of a free-State (of mind at least). At this club, where Sir Alex Ferguson made the 'them against us' mentality central to the success of his teams, such a notion resonates. It is also a defence mechanism against claims by City to own Manchester and

* *Red News*, Issue 131

what the United fans call ABU's – the 'Anyone But United' faction – who are said to hate the club because of its size and success. Less likely to be articulated, it may also be a response to a United board which seems to have little real connection to the fans.

It may not have been intended, but the idea of a Mancunian Republik fits well with the history of the city and the modern multi-cultural United support. Any causal visitor to Old Trafford on match-day will hear a wide range of accents. Perhaps this is as it should be, since there are many types of United follower, and also many Manchesters.

Since its days as Cottonopolis in the 19th century it has been a liberal and cutting-edge kind of place; the swaggering capital of the north of England to its residents. Here immigrants and natural outsiders can feel comfortable. Its gay quarter is said to be the most vibrant in the UK outside London and the 'curry mile' has over fifty Indian restaurants. Manchester has been home to various artists, has began numerous fashion trends and launched the careers of a host of seminal bands from the Smiths through the Baggy era of the Stone Roses to Oasis.

Today it feels like somewhere at ease with itself, metropolitan and popular. However unpalatable it may be to their rivals, it's inescapably true that United play a large part in this; carrying the name of Manchester around the world while bringing in countless visitors. City fans simply stick to the line that United and their supporters are 'not from Manchester', even though there seems to be little factual basis for this. When, at the beginning of the decade, Manchester Metropolitan University looked at the number of fans with an M (Manchester) postcode they found that United had more season ticket holders within that postcode. But, crucially, City had a higher percentage of season ticket holders when ground capacity was taken into account. That sounds like an honourable draw, if one which explodes as myth the notion that United have no followers in Manchester.

Stuart Parish is in his late twenties and has been going to Old Trafford since he was six. He's a member of the Independent Manchester United Supporters Association and hates the usual stereotypes of United fans. "We have got a lot of working class supporters, maybe not so much nowadays, we've still got a hardcore of about 30,000 or so. You get a lot of middle-class people here too, executives and things like that. Celebrities and hangers-on, anyone who's successful gets that.

If you go into town tonight and you go into the pubs you will just hear United songs all over, whether we win lose or draw. When City win you get the Rusholme end of town and you'll hear a few more, but when United win it's just United all over. It's a myth that City perpetrate because they haven't got any trophies to shout about, so they just go on about 'oh we have got a local fan base' and all that. You are talking to me now and I'm from Manchester."

City's support, in contrast, has managed to remain relatively homogenous, sharing common values and similar backgrounds. They find it easy to sing, literally and figuratively, with one voice. Not so United, and there are consequences. The lack of noise at times at Old Trafford is something which the United manager has remarked upon, most recently on New Year's Day 2007 when a tepid 1-0 victory over Birmingham barely registered with the slumbering 76,000 crowd. Ferguson, in calling for increased volume, was more diplomatic than his former captain, Roy Keane, who felt some of the supporters, particularly those in the corporate areas, were more interested in 'prawn sandwiches' than getting behind the team.

I noticed this even before a ball had been kicked. A few hundred home supporters were waiting for the United players to arrive. When they did, stepping down one by one from their bus, there was a stillness, fans talked in dampened voices, there were few cries of encouragement and not a single member of the first team even so much as acknowledged the crowd. Extraordinary. It would be different when City arrived, I thought; away from home and at this ground of all places the fans would want to unsettle them. Not at all, there was some lethargic booing, nothing more.

A very different scene was unfolding a few hundred meters away. In Sam Platt's pub on the Trafford Wharf Road hundreds of United fans were packed in, upstairs and down, clutching pints and bottles as they sang:

'Kicking a Blue, kicking a Blue
All I want is kicking a Blue'

This was the Stretford End of old; the people who came to bury the Glazers, Shareholders United, LUHG, citizens of the Republik and what used to be known as the ordinary fan. They are the 30 to 40 year-olds who wistfully recall rolling up just before 3pm on a Saturday afternoon and paying a pound to get in. These are the voices the Blues fans are happy to have drowned out. From all directions they are being pushed to the margins, assailed from without as non-Mancunian and ignored from within their own club as an unreconstructed Red rump who cling to the values of football's yesteryear. The supporters themselves will tell you it is they who are the life-blood of the club.

This simple division into Red and Blue is not the only one which has defined the Manchester rivalry. Deep in the background there is the hint of a religious aspect. I'd put it no stronger than that. There have long been perceptions that United have tended to attract more Roman Catholics, without being a Catholic club as such. Certainly Sir Matt Busby would never have allowed that to happen, as a life-long socialist who had grown up amid the religious schism of the west of Scotland, he was vehemently anti-sectarian. Yet there have been suggestions that Busby allowed a 'Catholic' atmosphere to grow while he was in charge. It's also a matter of record that when Newton Heath changed their name in 1902 a proposal to call the new club Manchester Celtic was defeated by only a few votes.

At one time United did draw significant support from Manchester's Irish community, many of whom worked on the ship canal. Also, the club have often had a strong Irish connection on the pitch, though the fact they have consistently fielded players from north and south of the border – the likes of Tony Dunne, Harry Gregg and the outrageously brilliant George Best, during Busby's time – shows that United were only interested in ability, never faith. However, more than one City supporter told me that they could remember asking aging relatives why the family supported the club and being told it was because they were Protestants. I suspect more than anything else this was a reaction to United's Irish support, which by default made City the team of the Protestant working-classes.

None of this ever really made its way, in any meaningful sense, into fans' expressions of themselves. Religion did not and has not coloured the rivalry, though colour itself is an important issue, one which has been taken to almost comical extremes.

The terms 'Blues' and 'Reds' are more than just names, they determine how the fans see their worlds and the use of the two colours tends to be rigid. United fans refuse to wear anything which resembles the blue of City and the feeling is reciprocated; City supporters are known for proclaiming they would 'rather be dead than Red'. There are stories of local supermarkets having to hire a red and a blue Santa so as to ensure no offence is caused. One major United sponsor, realising their products had come to be seen as 'Red', sought, without success, to assure City fans they were a company which wished to be associated with the whole of Manchester. Cleary people do not go to such lengths unless they feel sufficiently moved. All of which confirms that the derby itself, despite United's new rivals at home and abroad, remains important. Over the years there have been remarkable encounters. Some have even taken on their own mythology, and like the best stories, changed a little in the telling over time.

The most iconic of these games took place in the mid-1970s. Snatches of footage still appear every now and again on TV, showing kids in flares with scarves tied to their wrists, sprinting onto the turf at Old Trafford as the players race for the tunnel. What looks like a victorious scene was anything but for the home side, and became known for one player and one extraordinary goal. The pressure had been apparent during the first derby of the 1973/74 season. United stood on the edge of relegation, City were safe. Over 50,000 inside Maine Road on a damp March night, watched a scoreless draw and a much more memorable punch-up between Lou Macari and Mike Doyle. The pair, when they were eventually separated, were sent-off. They refused to go, while in the background, fighting erupted on the terraces. The referee, Clive Thomas, marched the teams from the pitch. It looked as though the game had been abandoned, but minutes later, without Doyle and Macari, they returned. The whole thing was merely the overture to the coming drama.

When the teams met for the second league derby that season, on the 27th April, United's situation had become desperate. They were second bottom and had two games left to play, while the other relegation candidates were finishing their programme that afternoon. A win against City was imperative if United were to retain any hope of staying up. City fans too were desperate for a win, having been relegated in controversial circumstances at Maine Road by United back in 1963. 57,000 people packed Old Trafford to see what would happen. It would not be pretty.

With eight minutes left and the match goalless, a ball was sent in low, bobbling through endless legs across the United penalty area. The next instant someone had back-heeled it past Alex Stepney and into the corner of the net. The City end went berserk while the players leapt on the blonde-haired goalscorer. For him there was no celebration. Denis Law had sealed the fate of the club with which he had been so long and so successfully associated. "I was feeling sick, wondering what I had done. Had I just dumped my beloved Manchester United into the second division? The crowd poured onto the pitch and sheer bedlam ensued. I was totally depressed, wishing desperately that the ball had gone wide and then Tony Book [the City manager] beckoned me off for my own safety."*

With the Stretford End decamped onto the pitch, the final minutes of the game were never actually played, but the result stood. In a sense it did not matter. Law – an icon of the United side which won their first post-Munich FA-Cup, League title and the European Cup – despite the legend which grew up around the goal, did not send United down with the final touch of his domestic career. Other results went against them and the club would have been relegated anyway, for the first time since before outbreak of the Second World War. Denis Law went off to play for Scotland at the World Cup in West Germany; United began to put up steel fences behind the home goal. It truly was the end of an era.

In the years after the war the old stadiums could house crowds anywhere between 60 to almost 80,000, but that did not necessarily satisfy demand for the derbies. On the last day of 1955 United beat City at Old Trafford with the gates locked and 20,000 fans outside. The Babes were on their way to the championship, while City would win the FA Cup at the end of the season. Five years later to the day, United recorded what was then their best ever win over their neighbours, beating City 5-1 at home.

* *The King*, Denis Law

That score-line was repeated at the close of the 1980s, but it was a result which so hurt the United manager, then plain old Alex Ferguson, he went straight to bed afterwards. City, at Maine Road, had humiliated United. It would be their last derby win before being relegated in 1996 and was played out in a feral atmosphere. United fans had invaded the North Stand – a City only area. Fighting soon broke out and the referee was forced to call a halt to proceedings for a time and take the players back into the dressing rooms. Before City slipped out of the Premiership United would have the last laugh, winning 5-0 on the same ground they'd conceded five at in 1989.

The derby drew the biggest English crowd of the season for a rare FA Cup clash in February 1996 which United won at Old Trafford having been a goal behind. They met again at the same venue two months later when the Blues were undone by an audacious goal from Ryan Giggs. The 3-2 defeat that day was arguably the result which sealed City's fate, they were relegated on the final day of the season while United took the championship. For older fans, doubtless it was some kind of recompense for what had happened to them in the 'relegation derby' of 1974.

Since City returned to the Premier League things have been fairly even. There have been a few draws and couple of 3-1 wins for the Blues, one being the last ever derby at Maine Road. There was also a memorable 4-1 win in the first derby at their new stadium in 2004. The match is a different affair though, when United play at home. City had not left Old Trafford victorious since that afternoon in 1974 when Denis Law stuck out a heel.

DESPITE THE STATISTICS, CITY'S support had been confident about their chances. I wondered if their mood had changed since they were nowhere to be seen outside the stadium on the morning of the match. Then, half an hour before kick-off, the United crowd in front of the East Stand parted to the sound of horses hooves. Two large groups of City fans swung around the corner, carrying inflatable bananas, blowing horns and singing:

'Hello, hello, we are the City boys,
Hello, hello, you'll know us by our noise
And if you are United scum

Surrender or you will die,
'Coz we all follow the City.'

The police stood back and watched as stewards burst into life, repeatedly calling for everyone to have their tickets ready for inspection. Within minutes the City fans were inside, their voices ringing round the ground.

I joined them shortly after, though I was in the home end at the top of the East Stand, looking out over the great sweep of what is undeniably a magnificent stadium. The match had been sold out for weeks, and I'd had to buy a ticket from the official United website. It was priced at three times its face value, on the dubious basis that the corporate hospitality 'package' included a 'free' match programme and five pound voucher for the Megastore.

The teams walked out to the strains of the Stone Roses' *This is the One*, while the PA announcer shrieked 'this is the Manchester derbyeeee!' His style would have been better suited to a boxing match. I was worried – being made to feel you are attending a special occasion usually means one thing – its not.

It didn't take long for the derby to bite though. Almost immediately City's Joey Barton smashed into Ronaldo sending him through the air and over the touchline. This turned up the volume and the insults considerably from both sides. Ronaldo may have been flattened, but he was still effective. Within six minutes Wayne Rooney had latched onto a cross from the Portuguese winger and, with the City defenders flailing and air-kicking, finished easily. The pattern was set, the majority of the crowd settled back in their seats. Much of the time, and despite the setback, the 3,000 City supporters below me made more noise than the towering United sections. But, waiving their inflatables and boxed into the corner of the South Stand, they seemed like a collection of naughty children, wailing as they were ignored by stoical parents.

As the break approached, Louis Saha made the most of more defensive dithering by converting another cross. United fans got up, celebrated, and then left their seats as the cry came drifting up for the away end:

'Time for Prawn Sandwiches, Time for Prawn Sandwiches.'

The United fans responded by mocking City's years without a trophy:

'Thirty-one years, thirty-one years...'

During half-time, an Irish team came on to parade a trophy they'd won apparently for the umpteenth time. The fans were asked to show their 'appreciation', but few took much notice. Nor did they when a group of children were marched out to take penalties. The whole thing had something to do with United's main sponsor, AIG. Predictably each of the kids trundled their kicks towards goal and each time they managed to creep in. The best part of this rigmarole was when the PA guy described Lou Macari – who was taking charge of the competition – as one of United's 'ex-legends'. It is one thing to be a legend in your own lifetime, but quite another to become an 'ex-legend'.

When City's Hatem Trabelsi lashed in a goal with his left-foot from twenty yards the away fans seemed surprised, almost as if something had happened which they hadn't expected. They waved their bananas while singing: 'We're not really here.' Actually, they were, and their team was in with a chance again.

It was not to be, as City pushed forward looking for the equaliser United stole the ball, breaking away for their third, this time from Ronaldo; though the motif of the goal was more appalling defending. City had made, but failed to take, chances throughout the match. The final act was the pitiful sending off of their Italian striker Bernardo Corradi, who received a second yellow card for blatant diving.

By that time the mood had turned sour below me, the inflatables had been put away, though the majority of the City support stayed until the finish, chanting 'United, United not for sale', 'USA, USA' and 'Fuck off back to London'. As for the Munich song, well I was told later by United fans they had heard it. I didn't myself, but clearly saw Blues fans closest to the home end standing up and stretching out their arms, pretending to be aeroplanes.

Outside the ground a chill wind was being whipped up from the quays. United fans were criss-crossing Sir Matt Busby Way while, in the midst of this, the City buses began to slip past. Fans in the first few just kept their heads down or looked straight ahead, they couldn't be bothered with gloating Reds. That didn't stop the United fans laughing, and in turn, City responding with hand gestures; some thumped the windows of their coaches, and one or two made their feelings clear by dropping their trousers. Two United fans at the bottom of the street were waving goodbye and singing a version of the Inspiral Carpets song:

> "This is how it feels to be City,
> this is how it feels to be small,
> this is how it feels when your team wins nothing at all."

On the way back to the Metro I walked past a woman with two young girls. They couldn't have been much older then twelve and were as drunk as their elder chaperone. City songs were being sung as they weaved across the pavement, including one with unprintable lyrics about the Neville brothers and their mother. The few remaining United fans around didn't seem to care. They were now nine points ahead of their newest rivals Chelsea at the top of the table, and City had been put in their place once more. Tonight Manchester would again be painted red, metaphorically and perhaps literally. More slogans commemorating United's triumph and City's defiance, were already being planned; the boys of Bluewatch and LUHG would be back on the cold streets.

United and City would meet again in the final throes of the season at the City of Manchester stadium. United's 1-0 win took them to within touching distance of the title, an achievement which would be secured 24 hours later when other results went in their favour. United, despite all the doom-laden portents regarding the Glazers, were on top again. This time, having hauled themselves clear of relegation, City did not stand still. By the beginning of the following season the club had finally found their saviour, one with deep pockets and an intriguing reputation to match. Whether the former Prime Minster of Thailand, Thaksin Shinawatra, was 'the right kind' of money the fans had demanded, was quite another matter. Thaksin was wanted on corruption charges in his homeland and had been linked to allegations of police brutality and even 'disappearances' while in high office.

The billionaire was welcomed by some supporters, others told me they were near suicidal about it. It did after all place City firmly in the hands of foreign owners, much like their neighbours. It wasn't just the new owner's background which filled them with dread, there was also the choice of manager – the former England coach Sven-Göran Eriksson – and the fact that Thaksin had once been pictured holding a United shirt standing next to Sir Alex Ferguson. What could not be denied was that he had the financial means to set City on a course designed to truly have them competing again with the biggest clubs in England and Europe. Let's not kid ourselves, City aren't interested in beating Barcelona and AC Milan. No, it is United they want, and privately every City fan must have wondered whether or not this was the moment when a real, sustained, challenge to their rivals' position of dominance would at last begin. A sweet, and well-deserved, victory – the first for nearly 34 years – at Old Trafford in February 2008, on the day of the commemoration of the 50th anniversary of the Munich Air Disaster, seemed to add grist to that particular mill. Perhaps they would have to get used to thinking of themselves as more than just, in their eyes at least, the genuine club of Manchester. Only time would tell.

LIVERPOOL:

Fiery Across The Mersey

"To me as a Merseysider, it's just the best club game
in the world. The best to win, the worst to lose.
I'm inconsolable if we lose ..."

Peter Reid – *Everton v Liverpool, the Great Derbies,*
Brian Barwick and Gerald Sinstadt

THE FORMER BRITISH Prime Minister, Harold Macmillan, is
remembered for the saying – "events dear boy, events" – a
comment on how they tended to come along without warning. The
morning of the 205th Merseyside derby I woke to discover that
overnight a policeman had been killed during rioting at the Sicilian
derby between Palermo and Catania. European football was
shaken. Later that day a ferry collided with a cargo ship in the
Mersey and almost sank with three hundred people on board. Yet,
by the middle of the afternoon, 3rd February 2007, neither of these
events were a priority. Across the city the airwaves would be
buzzing with the sound of fury, a madness sparked by the use of
just two words – "small club".

It's not difficult to be infused with the sense that anything and
everything is possible in Liverpool. There's an old joke told by local
comedians about how there are five countries in the United
Kingdom: England, Scotland, Wales, Northern Ireland, and
Merseyside. The reason for this, so people tell you, is that it sees
itself as a place apart. Liverpool is both the most romanticised and
most clichéd city in Britain, something to which its football teams
have hugely helped to contribute.

Examples of the way the city's reputation goes before it are not
difficult to find. Outside Lime Street railway station, which was
billing itself as the Gateway to the Bright New Liverpool, I spotted
one of Mr Macmillan's successors as Conservative Party leader,

Michael Howard. Howard has been a Liverpool fan since the days of Billy Liddell in the 1950s. He was there to deliver a speech and was going to the match the next day. "I love Liverpool" he said. "I fought my first two general elections here, a long time ago when I was a very young man, and I've always loved the city. The people of Liverpool have a wonderful sense of humour. I always say the difference between Liverpool and London is that if you get into a lift in London, nobody will say anything to each other and if you get into a lift in Liverpool you will come out laughing."

Ah yes, the famous cheeky Scouser. There may very well be a distinct Liverpudlian sense of humour, but it has to fight for house room with a host of other images. Liverpool is friendly, witty and emotional. It is the loveable working-class home of The Beatles, *Brookside* and the *Boys from the Blackstuff*; identifiably a community which has proudly struggled through adversity. Then there are the others, ones which paint Merseyside as a haven for political subversives, petty criminals, jobless scroungers and scallies trying to make a fast buck. Perhaps each of these things, both good and bad, says something about the history of the place.

It's not called Merseyside by accident. The river has been everything to the city and it continues to flow through the lives of those who live here, day by day, as it has for generations. Once, though, it was a great power, ushering in transient workers and immigrants from around the UK and the world beyond, importing cotton and other materials for the textile factories of the north-west. It made Liverpool the entrepot for industrial England. Tens of thousands of men, the majority of whom were unskilled and casually employed, worked both sides of the river in its heyday. As a port, its height was probably the first two decades of the twentieth century. Over the following years, as competition stiffened and the textile market moved elsewhere, Liverpool fell into a slow, long-term decline, and the work and the people just ebbed away.

Things were seriously on the slide by the end of the 1960s and at the turn of the 80s the industrial policies of Margaret Thatcher's Conservative government, or rather lack of them, simply accelerated this demise. Of course, there can be no pride in decay, and little in poverty, though on Merseyside there was some means of escape. It was found in the Blues and Reds of Everton and Liverpool.

LIVERPOOL DID NOT IMMEDIATELY fall in love with football, though once it was established at the very end of the nineteenth century, both Everton and Liverpool soon became leading clubs in their own right, winning the championship and also, in Everton's case, the FA Cup by 1914.

The clubs have almost always been in the top division, though not necessarily at the same time. The really great era of Merseyside derbies began when Liverpool returned to Division One in 1962 after a ten year absence. There was an immense appetite for the matches; in fact the demand was so great their FA Cup fifth round tie of 1967 was beamed live from Everton's Goodison Park back to Anfield on giant screens. 40,000 people saw the match remotely at Liverpool's ground, making the combined attendance 105,000, and this a time long before football was a regular event on television – *Match of the Day* was a mere two and a half years old. The match was sold out in just three hours – one hundred people were injured in the rush to buy tickets. One fan even swapped his car for a ticket. Thankfully for him Everton won 1-0.

On Merseyside, when it comes to football, things have tended to be done rather differently. In the same season as the big-screen derby the old Charity Shield match was also played at Goodison. The teams came out together with Ray Wilson of Everton and Liverpool's Roger Hunt parading the World Cup they had won as team-mates with England that summer. Then, together, the sides showed off their winnings from the previous year, Everton had the FA Cup and Liverpool the league championship. It is hard to imagine a similar gesture in another major footballing city.

In the difficult years to come, the clubs were points of stability in a changing world. To have Liverpool and Everton doing well at home and abroad lifted the spirits and kept the name of the city in the headlines. Between them, from 1977 to 1990 they won 11 league titles, 3 FA Cups, 4 League Cups, 4 European Cups and 1 Cup Winners Cup. It remains the case today that the clubs' fortunes can strongly affect the mood of the city, and on a practical level they contribute by employing almost five thousand people between them; bringing around three quarters of a million visitors to the area every season.

This cross-city bonhomie led to the derby being given the title, the 'friendly rivalry'. Bill Kenwright, the current Everton chairman, has a fairly typical recollection of what match days were like. "My dad was a Liverpudlian, but I've been an Evertonian since I was a kid. The family was always very football, though. We always used to meet at my Gran's on a Saturday, all the uncles and the nephews and go to Liverpool or Everton."* The image is of Blues and Reds coming and going from the match together, having been mixed harmoniously on the terraces. We are repeatedly told how the fans come from the same streets, even the same families, and that it's considered normal to have both blue and red scarves in the hallways of homes across Merseyside.

The warmth of such tales have tended to suggest the supporters were typically good natured. It is an image developed by those early editions of *Match of the Day*, featuring the new phenomenon of mass community singing, on Liverpool's Kop in particular. However, this does not reflect the realties of football; Liverpool and Everton supporters have long been as potentially combustible as they were cuddly.

IN THE 1960S, OPPOSITION fans visiting Liverpool were warned to be on their guard, with numerous incidents of mass muggings in the streets adjacent to the r960sailway station. During the same era the national press advised shopkeepers to close for the day when Everton came to town. A minority of the Liverpool support made 'going on the rob' a regular addition to their many European adventures during the late 1970s and into the following decade. The ransacking of continental designer shops makes these fans seem relatively harmless at this distance, yet the truth is that long before one hellish night of violence in Brussels changed things forever, it was not unheard of for Reds to stand and literally fight their ground. As far back as 1966 they were involved in widespread and prolonged fighting with Celtic fans during a UEFA Cup tie.

In the same year, Evertonians mauled one of their most successful managers. Harry Catterick, who'd brought the championship and FA Cup to the club, had decided to drop the much-loved star

---

* *Everton v Liverpool, the Great Derbies, Brian* Barwick and Gerald Sinstadt

player – Alex 'Golden Vision' Young – from the team to play away at Blackpool. Everton lost and the manager was attacked by protesting supporters as he tried to board the team bus. In what was seen as a gentler age it was an extraordinary incident. Catterick was relatively safe, he was on the right side. Not so the Millwall fans who found themselves in the Gwladys Street end of Goodison back in 1973. Eleven of them left the terracing with stab wounds, including one 17 year-old who had his lung punctured.

As for the derby, this idea of sunny comradeship has been over-played somewhat, but is not without a few kernels of truth. The pinnacle of the game's 'friendship' was reached almost at the same moment which led directly to today's more embittered version. In March 1984, Merseyside was much in need of a boost. Unemployment was at eye watering levels and the local authority budget had become a battleground between the Militant controlled Labour council and the national Tory government. Against this backdrop and that of a national miners strike, Liverpool and Everton met for the first time at Wembley. 100,000 people watched the final of the League Cup at the old stadium. There was no need of segregation inside the ground and pubs opened as normal to provide entertainment before kick-off. The match ended goalless and is best remembered for its aftermath. Without prompting the two sets of players began to trot around the pitch, some with red and blue scarves tied together. Then from the stands came the joyous and unifying chorus, again and again – 'Merseyside, Merseyside.'

In May of the following year Liverpool went to Brussels for the final of the European Cup. A match which should have been all about Platini, Boniek, Dalglish and Rush – as Liverpool, the holders and four-time winners, took on the Italian champions Juventus – turned instead into a sickening orgy of death at the crumbling Heysel stadium in the Belgian capital. There had been minor problems between the fans in the hours preceding the match, but nothing to indicate what was to follow. Prior to the kick-off, broken bits of terracing became missiles which were thrown back and forth between fans behind one of the goals. Liverpool supporters then tore down the wire mesh fence separating them and charged the opposing fans with the intention of removing the Italians from what they saw as the Liverpool 'end'.

The Juve fans panicked, and were pushed back into a small area close to the corner flag, where the perimeter wall collapsed. 39 people, mainly Italians, were killed and 500 injured. Live television carried the pictures of the agonised, stricken faces of supporters desperately pleading to be one of those hauled from the asphyxiating prison of limp and bleeding bodies.

While a section of the Liverpool support had a well-earned reputation for petty theft, they had not been associated with the kind of outright hooliganism attached to some other English clubs. One factor which is believed to have contributed to their aggression that evening was that a large number of celebrating Kopites had been attacked by gangs of Roma fans after the final at their own Olympic Stadium the previous year.

That some of its own people had caused such destruction stunned Merseyside. Under the resulting avalanche of opprobrium from all quarters of the British establishment the city retreated into its defensive shell. Even more than usual it turned its back away from England. There was an understandable need for mutual support and initially the majority of Everton fans shared in this sense of unity. Days after the tragedy and with the active support of the Thatcher Government, all English clubs, not just Liverpool, were indefinitely banned from European competition. Everton, the reigning league champions, were punished particularly harshly for something which they had no hand in. Having behaved impeccably during their own victory in the final of the Cup Winners Cup just two weeks before Heysel, their supporters could do nothing to prevent the loss of their club's place in the Champions Cup the next season.

Within a few years the best Everton side in a generation had been broken up and the manager, Howard Kendall, left to coach on the continent, admitting that he missed the European nights. Liverpool retained their position as the leading English side, while Everton moved largely between the mediocre and the awful, something not lost on their fans.

THE PLAY WAS RAGING ON through the early afternoon at Anfield while great gusts of fog spiralled over the back of the Kop and into the stadium, blocking the weak winter sun. The players faded away through the mist, their shirt sponsors and designer kits with them, until they were only reds and blues and could have been actors in this fixture from some long-gone era. My reverie was shattered by the Everton fans around me who poisoned the skies with their cries of 'murderers, murderers'. This was shocking because they were as good as accusing their friends, cousins, siblings and even parents of having blood on their hands over Heysel. It was staggeringly callous, but didn't end there.

The Kop sang: 'Justice for the 96'

In return, Everton mocked this with: 'Justice for the 39'

It's hardly surprising that memories of Heysel have been superseded in the minds of Liverpool supporters. The second catastrophe surrounding the club was different, this time their own people were the victims. So horrific were the events of the 15th of April 1989 that a single word is now used when referring to what happened – Hillsborough.

Hard though it may be to contemplate; on a mild and bright day, that of the FA Cup semi-final, 96 Liverpool supporters were crushed or trampled to death at Sheffield Wednesday's ground. They had been crammed into high-fenced pens with no means of escape. A dangerous situation turned deadly when police decided to let thousands of extra fans into the most overcrowded areas. To compound this, during a crucial period in which lives could have been saved, the South Yorkshire force thought they were dealing with an episode of hooliganism and failed to act.

Liverpool fans, for almost twenty years have continued to surround themselves with memories of Hillsborough. Inside Anfield I saw banners relating to the disaster while outside, both before and after the match, fans were being given, and wearing in their thousands, yellow and white stickers highlighting the ongoing campaign demanding 'Justice for the 96'. It's not difficult to understand why these feelings are still so acute. The police clung to their original story of drunken fans forcing their way into the ground. The line was gobbled up by the media at large and trumpeted viciously across the *The Sun* newspaper in particular. No-one in authority that day, nor since, has truly put their hands up and said 'sorry, we got it wrong' despite much damning evidence.

Some people, who are not from the city, feel that, twenty years on, the fans should stop grieving and get on with their lives. It has often been said that Liverpool has an excessive, overly sentimental attachment to death. I've heard plenty of jokes along these lines, like the one about a pigeon being run over by Scousers on the way to Anfield and a minute's silence being held at the game in memory of the dead bird.

The accusation made by *The Spectator* magazine in 2004, after local man Ken Bigley was kidnapped and then murdered by Islamic militants in Iraq, was that Liverpudlians were happy, even enjoyed, wallowing in death as part of its victim status. The editor, Boris Johnson, also a member of the Tory front-bench, was sent to the city by a furious Michael Howard to apologise in person. The article failed utterly to understand that the city views death in a far more emotional and celtic way than the rest of England. The roots of this lie in Liverpool's Irish hinterland and very real community spirit.

What happened at Hillsborough touched, in some way, almost every local family. The absolute, inescapable, bottom line in all of this is that people died, dozens of them, simply because they'd gone to watch a football match. Sure, it happened almost two decades ago, but that does not mean the hurt evaporates, not for the families and friends and not for the supporters. It's like asking the people of New York to forget the terrorist attacks of 11th September 2001; its not going to happen.

One fan, 'Mick R', was in a relatively safe area of Hillsborough that day. He was eighteen at the time and, even now, struggles to come to terms with it all. "As the years have passed, the tears have gradually reduced. I've listened to the self-pity jibes, and shrugged them off. What do they know? I reacted to the Hillsborough disaster in the only way I knew how. Yet always I felt guilty. I wasn't involved with the crush. I didn't know anybody who died. Why should I be crying? What the hell was wrong with me?

I wept nearly all day on the 15th April 2005. In 2006 I decided I wouldn't let myself be weak. I would be strong, and I would be strong from now on. I didn't want anybody to accuse me of wallowing in self-pity. I didn't want to accuse myself any longer of being upset about something that didn't 'directly' affect me, if you know where I'm coming from ... there would be no more standing at my bedroom window at 3.06pm on April 15th, watching the trees blowing in the wind, tears dripping from my chin. There would be no more sitting on the Kop on April 15th, red eyes covered by sunglasses."*

The morning after the disaster, as Anfield opened its gates to the first of three quarters of a million mourners, the fourteen ton bell of the old Anglican cathedral rung out across the city, peeling not for the death of a monarch as in the past, but for the sufferings of ordinary families and to mark the greatest tragedy anyone alive on Merseyside could recall.

Liverpool would not compete for almost a month. Fittingly, perhaps, their first match was a derby at Goodison. Everton fans were involved in countless small demonstrations of support, though the most memorable was a chain of scarves, red and blue tied together, which stretched around their ground that day. The Liverpool support responded with an unequivocal message to their rivals and to the football world beyond: 'The Kop thanks you. We never walked alone.'

The scale of the tragedy at Hillsborough and the resulting treatment of the Liverpool fans by sections of the media, meant that only years later could Evertonians vent their anger over what had happened to them as a result of Heysel. Supporters on both sides now firmly believe this is why the atmosphere at the derby is not what it once was.

The Labour MP, Peter Kilfoyle, is a life-long Evertonian, with Goodison Park in his constituency. We met in the Palace of Westminster where he marched me along thickly carpeted corridors to a tea bar. A veteran of numerous political fights, he looks like a retired boxer in a double-breasted suit. He talks in quick thrusts, as though jabbing at the argument. "I remember about four years ago taking my sons to a derby game at Goodison and I felt a change in the Everton supporters I was amongst, not only the attitude, the language, the real bitterness they exhibited towards the Liverpool supporters. Although they were segregated, you know. I was just appalled by it, maybe I was just in among a bad crowd at that time but it was very alien to me and I was probably more conscious of it because my two sons are Liverpool supporters. It never used to be

* *TTWAR*, Issue 75

like that, I think it has changed for the worse. It wasn't in the actual chanting, it was just individual blokes who were hurling abuse. One fellow comes to mind, he had his young son alongside him and he's effing and blinding about Liverpudlians and making the most bloody ridiculous allegations about them."

Kilfoyle is right, fans used to be able to mix and display their colours and openly back their team without fear of reproach. To a degree this still happens, Reds can sit among Blues and vice versa, but it is no longer guaranteed to be trouble free.

"There's a lot of nastiness towards us now," says Arian Killen from the Anfield Museum. "You go to Goodison Park and it's extremely volatile. I was in the Upper Bullens and when we scored I got threatened, I got told to sit down. When we scored the second goal I even did it more. I was on my own and I was surrounded by Evertonians, but there were clumps of Liverpudlians around me and there were quite a few fisticuffs, some were escorted out."

Killen stresses that he's now talking about the actions of a minority before adding: "I know some people who went to the toilet at half-time and had to be taken out of the ground because they had been surrounded by Evertonians. The police said, you either go now, or we will arrest you and escort you out of the stadium for your own safety. There's been a lot more bitterness in recent years. They even shout 'murderers' at us at every derby game. I have been to every derby game, home and away, since 1957 and I have to say, it's got a lot worse."

There were around 4,000 Evertonians packed into the lower section of the Anfield Road end, behind the goal, me amongst them. Most of the Everton fans had arrived just a few minutes before kick-off. I could picture them marching together across Stanley Park. The accents were invariably Scouse and they all seemed to know each other. I had the feeling they would be wondering who the hell I was. My seat was next to half a dozen empty rows which were intended to act as a buffer between the home and away ends. During the match insults, were traded ferociously and constantly over this no-man's land. At the final whistle, one Everton fan in his late twenties clambered onto a seat and, spittle flying, began to shout murderers directly at individual Liverpool fans a matter of feet away. One home fan, just as angry, demanded matters be settled in the street outside.

I was surprised that all the supporters were allowed to leave at the same time but, once outside, Everton's low chants about the family of the Liverpool captain, Steven Gerrard, faded into silence. It looked as though things would just get back to normal with people content to live and let live.

Not always the case I'm afraid. Early afternoon kick-offs, although they stop fans drinking very much before the games, do leave the rest of the day free to be spent in bars. There's often trouble 'in town' after the derbies now. This tends to happen sporadically and does not involve the majority of supporters, but in recent seasons there have been a significant number of arrests along the main routes back into the city. In a way, dispute rather than fraternity, is much more in keeping with the history of the clubs.

THE COMBINATION OF MUSCULAR Christianity and the search for a winter alternative to cricket, as so often the case, brought the first major club of Merseyside into being. In 1878 the Methodist chapel of St Domingo's on Breckfield Road North started their club, just one of many springing up in the area. They would not last long, not in that guise at any rate. A year later, to reflect the involvement of the wider community, they became Everton FC, based in Everton village.

They first played on nearby Stanley Park, but quickly moved into an area next to the Anfield Road, where terraces were erected and thousands regularly paid to watch. Everton were a success at Anfield before Liverpool even existed. The men who ran the best clubs at this time may well have been football fans, however they were almost always businessmen too, not people who'd naturally let a good money making opportunity slide past. The then Everton president, John Houlding, fitted the mould precisely. A hotelier, brewer and local politician, he'd used his contacts to secure the Anfield site. The club rented the land and began playing there in 1884, winning their first title in 1890/91, the third season of the Football League. It soon became a serious asset, hosting an international match within a few years. Houlding was in the unusual position of being a leading official at Everton and collecting the rent for the landlord. Not only that, he also owned part of the land adjoining Anfield. While this looks like a conflict of interest, there were no great difficulties until notice arrived of a substantial rent increase from £100 to £250 per year. The idea of raising the price came either from Houlding or the landlord; no matter, Everton were far from amused. They were urged by Houlding to buy the football ground outright, since in the long run it would make financial sense. This seemed like a reasonable suggestion, but the problem was the club would pay while he would profit. He also expected Everton to use his company to do this and wanted them to buy his acreage nearby as part of the deal to boot. Things came to a head in October 1891 when the Everton members rejected the new terms and Houlding, in a move unique in football, demanded that his own club leave the premises. As Everton prepared to move to Goodison, on the other side of Stanley Park, Houlding was voted out of office. He was left with an excellent stadium, but no team. Players he could buy, but a greater worry was keeping the popular Everton name, which was claimed by both sides. Eventually, the FA ruled that the majority who'd left Anfield were the real Everton. 'King John of Everton' as had been known, would have to find an original name for his new club.

In March 1892 the other great power of Merseyside football was christened under the grand title, the Liverpool Football Club and Athletic Grounds Company Limited – Liverpool FC for short. The choice of name, taken from a local rugby club, was deliberate – Liverpool were soon playing in the city's own colours of red and had incorporated the local emblem, the Liver Bird, into their crest. Their first team, the Team of the Macs, so called because they arrived en masse from Scotland, would have to bide their time to get a crack at Everton. Liverpool's initial application to join the Football League was rejected after, in all probability, the team now playing across the park opposed their inclusion. They started out in the local Lancashire League, a move which restricted their attractiveness, while Everton went from strength to strength. It was an attempt to strangle the new outfit almost at birth.

What came to be known as 'The Split' not only created the rivalry, it has also allowed Everton fans to portray Liverpool as upstarts and impostors. What it did not do, though, was to hinder the development of either side in the longer term. When the first derby was played, at Goodison in the autumn of 1894, 44,000 fans turned out to watch Everton win 3-0 in front of various local dignitaries. The return match, a 2-2 draw, brought 30,000 people to Anfield, a figure which demonstrated that Liverpool now had their own following.

Perhaps the schism which brought Liverpool into being was simply unavoidable. Houlding seemed to be the cuckoo in the Everton nest all along, his professional life had long jarred with the ideals of his fellow directors who clung to Everton's Methodist principles. Like other Protestant reformers Methodists had long been advocates of the Temperance movement, believing that abstinence was the way to cure many of society's ills, especially those rooted in poverty. Alcohol got in the way of God and led husbands to beat their wives or spend their weekly wage in the pub.

Houlding had the players change at his hotel before games, and so affording them ample opportunity to socialise there afterwards. He also regularly convened board meetings at these premises next to Anfield. In this sense he was already making money from the club on a regular basis. Had Everton bought Anfield he would have been free to sell beer, his own beer, on match days at the ground. This was considered a step too far. Someone who has seen the minutes of the meeting which confirmed The Split told me that while rent had been central to the debate, the issue of beer being sold also caused a rumpus. This was confirmed by Houlding himself when he said it had been the "teetotal fanaticism" of the Everton Methodists which led to the breakdown in relations.*

The importance of religion in Liverpool should not be underplayed. Even today any vantage point across the city reveals the peaks of the two cathedrals dominating the skyline. These gigantic structures, one Church of England, the other Roman Catholic, face each other on Hope Street. Religion once permeated much of Liverpool life, and in an area so shaped by immigration this has not always made things easy. By 1850 Liverpool had an Irish population of around 100,000. These people were just a fraction of the millions who left the mother country at the time fleeing hunger following the terrible potato famine caused by the airborne phytophthora infestans fungus in 1845. They flocked to the west coast of the UK and, if they could afford it, to the United States, bringing with them

---

* quoted in Williams, *Passing Rhythms*

their own traditions, culture and religion. Arriving in such numbers, they were not entirely welcomed by the indigenous community. In a city where employment was famously casual, the established labour force worried that they would be squeezed out by the Irishmen, who, having escaped desperate circumstances at home, were prepared to work for very little.

This prompted a response along religious lines. Protestantism began to organise through Conservative Working Men's Associations and Unionist clubs, while the numbers of the local Orange Order (an openly pro-Protestant society which Catholics cannot join) began to swell. There had also already been an influx of Protestants from Ulster who came to work on the ships. So visible a presence were they that the annual 12th of July march to commemorate the Battle of the Boyne was called 'Carpenters Day'.

It was these Irish immigrants, possibly from both traditions, which gave the city its celtic feel and particular emotions; but the tensions between the communities also led to a divided city. Though far from uniform, it was nevertheless possible to point to clearly demarked Protestant and Catholic areas right up until the 1960s, with education often also delivered according to religion.

Local politics were also caught up in this, as Peter Kilfoyle explained. "You used to have Protestant Working Men's Associations and a lot of working-class Protestants, at that time, put their energies into these. They combined with the Conservative and Unionist candidates so that, up until 1964, I think out of nine seats in Liverpool, maybe seven of them, six at least, were [electing] Conservative and Unionist candidates.

The working-class vote was split on sectarian grounds and it was a positive effort by forward-thinking working men and women in the city who said: 'hang on. This is bananas. What separates us is less than what unites us' and there was a conscious effort to break down that religious sectarianism in the politics. The Conservative and Unionists wanted to keep it that way because on the basis of that sectarianism and dividing the working-class, they won the parliamentary seats. We were very conscious of changing it in the other direction, because there was a natural constituency for Labour if we could pull all these people together, and we did."

The only Irish nationalist MP ever elected to Parliament on the British mainland, TP O'Connor in 1885, represented a Liverpool constituency. On the other side of the coin the Liverpool Protestant Party was formed in 1909 and remarkably continued to fight elections right up until 1974.

Liverpool was the club which came to be identified with the Protestant community, principally because important figures in its early life – namely Houlding and John McKenna (the same McKenna who helped Arsenal into the First Division instead of Tottenham, incidentally) – had ties to the Orange Order and to Freemasonry. Yet this did not lead to a club made in their own image. Even though the first team they ever fielded was stuffed with Scots, many of them were in fact Scots Irish, Catholics from Glasgow.

Various claims have also been made for Everton as a 'Catholic' club. This is surprising given that they have no obvious links to that faith. What Everton did have, though, in the middle of the twentieth century, was a whole raft of Irish players, something which drew the local Irish/Catholic community to Goodison. It has also been suggested that Toffee was used as an early nickname for the Irish in Liverpool and could explain the reasons for Everton being known as the Toffeemen.

Everton's alleged Catholicism seems unlikely, though some fans did say that it had been possible to see priests in what was the shareholders' stand many years ago. The comedian Arthur Askey – in his autobiography – says there was a tale about Liverpool beating Everton. "Pat says to Mike, aye there'll be some sad hearts in the Vatican tonight."* The overriding point about all of this is that neither club has ever been a vehicle for religious segregation. Players were not signed on the basis of their background and, for the fans, religion played no part in determining which team to follow. This meant that in reality both Everton and Liverpool were football clubs and nothing besides.

The former Chairman of Liverpool, John Smith, understood the importance of this in moulding the atmosphere of the city. "Liverpool could have gone the same way as Belfast, or Glasgow over religion, but when you've got streets, offices and shops, even families divided down the middle – red or blue – they haven't the

* *The Old Firm*, Bill Murray

time or the energy for other divisions."* Indeed, it has always been a simple case of red or blue, Blues or Reds, and messages of support have rarely been in short supply.

OUTSIDE GOODISON PARK YOU will find EFC daubed on walls, a club crest lovingly painted on a nearby home, but also, in thick black graffiti – ROONEY DIE. The most prominent slogan among these is Everton's claim to be The People's Club. It dates back to the day in 2002 when David Moyes took over as manager saying: "I am joining the people's football club. The majority of people you meet on the street are Everton fans. It is a fantastic opportunity, something you dream about. I said yes right away as it is such a big club."** Others have suggested the Scot was prompted to say this as a PR stunt. No matter, it was wonderfully put and something which has now been officially adopted.

At least it would have had a large white banner along the Park End Stand not fallen into disrepair, its letters now restricted to the less striking proclamation: 'EVERTON   EOPL   '. It hadn't changed the spirit of the message, however.

I was keen to have another look inside, since it had been years since my last visit. Three different club officials told me I would be able to get in, something hard to imagine at most Premiership grounds. Sure enough a security guard agreed that it was fine as long as I stood well back from the pitch. Though still an expansive stadium, beautifully crafted by that master of early twentieth century stadium design Archibald Leitch, in the gloaming I felt sorry for the Grand Old Lady, some of the blue had faded, making her seem cold and a little careworn.

I wasn't the only one being treated to Evertonian hospitality. The Winslow pub, opposite the main stand, is one of those spartan, untouched, inner-city watering holes in which football fans have always gathered. The afternoon before the match it housed a sprinkling of men silently watching the horse racing. There was a yellowed picture of recently-deceased former Everton captain of the 1960s, Brian Labone, on the wall and a child of about five was sitting alone behind the bar.

---

* *The Old Firm*, Bill Murray
** *BBC website*, 15 March 2002

A fellow drinker leaned across to ask if I had a spare ticket. He did this in what sounded, to my untrained ear, like a distinctly German accent. It turned out that Johann and his friend Marcus were from Liechtenstein and, being mad about British football, had come over for the game. They really knew their stuff, French League, German, Dutch, but Liverpool against Everton, now that was worth seeing they said.

Yet, this was the kind of place in which, in some cities, I would have worried about their short-term health. Not in Liverpool. Here men with their accents can talk drunkenly and loudly and no-one seems to mind. As I left, they were being shepherded into the night, off towards another pub and the promise of tickets by a kindly stranger and his daughter in a pink Everton hat. Perhaps this really is the club of the people.

This image of Everton suggests authenticity, an institution welded to the area. Indeed, the streets around the ground are heavy with Everton history. True, the old Toffeeshops have gone, but the tower pictured on the club crest still stands nearby. The fact that attendances dropped to their lowest level in seventy years at Goodison during the economic depression of the 1980s, while remaining steady at Anfield, suggests Everton really are a locally supported club.

The author of several books about their rivals, Paul Tomkins, thinks that is a gross oversimplification, however. "Evertonians are mostly from Merseyside and North Wales. Anfield on match day is a much richer mix. Evertonians sing 'spot the Scouser on the Kop'. Anyone going to Anfield will see thousands and thousands of Scousers, obviously, but also hear accents from all over the UK as well as fans from the Far East and fair few Scandinavians. A hell of a lot travel from Ireland for the games too. Everton is a club of Liverpool. Liverpool is a club of the world (which, of course, includes Liverpool)."

It may be going too far, but Evertonians are also keen to portray Liverpool as now nothing more than a soulless corporate brand. However, it is staggering to think that the club which their great manager, Bill Shankly, felt demonstrated a form of socialism in the bond between the team and the fans is now owned by a firm which has its head office in Texas, but is registered and owned by companies in the American State of Delaware and the Cayman Islands.

The alternative to the £450 million deal reached in the spring of 2007 with the American businessmen George Gillett and Tom Hicks had been for Liverpool to throw in their lot with the ruling family of the Dubai. The club, which had been owned and run by the Moores family for decades, had courted these suitors and others over a period of years knowing serious financial investment was required, not only for future playing staff, but more especially if a new stadium was to be built. On both sides of the divide, whether to go or stay in their hallowed, but cramped, stadia became something of a running sore and yet another issue to have raised the ire of Evertonians in particular.

Both clubs came to the conclusion, early in the new century, that their grounds either needed major refurbishment or they had to move out. They came up with separate ideas to address this. In 2000 Everton declared they wished to relocate to King's Dock. Three years later the plan was dead in the Liverpool waterfront, the cash could not be raised.

Liverpool submitted plans to move just a few hundred yards into Stanley Park. At this point, and at the prompting of the local council, an idea first mooted in the early 1990s was revived; talks were restarted about sharing the Stanley Park development. The concept was simple, to get the most out of a single asset. However, Liverpool wanted to own the ground outright, while Everton demanded a joint stake. In 2005 the Liverpool board, knowing that they didn't need the involvement of another party, finally said no.

Liverpool got the go-ahead from the council the following year. Yet, even still, with the plans finalised and the funding of the £280 million project in place, there was an attempt to bring Everton back into the deal. In March 2007 the council again asked Liverpool to consider joint use of the ground with their neighbours. Again the answer was no. The reason for asking was that Everton were, quite literally, on their way out.

Late in 2006 Everton announced, to the fury of their supporters, that they were seriously exploring the possibility of moving to a site in Kirby, four miles outside Liverpool. The stadium, backed by the supermarket Tesco and Knowsley Council, would be located close to the M57. Amid angry scenes at the club's AGM one shareholder said it "would represent the start of the erosion of our fanbase. It would be the equivalent of us hoisting the white flag to Liverpool

FC that they can 'have the city'."* Liverpool fans were delighted, immediately re-naming Everton The People's Supermarket.

The friction caused by the stadium issue, just as with the The Split in the late nineteenth century, is very real. Evertonians complain that Liverpool too easily get their way with the council while they, on the other hand, remain stuck in a decaying stadium. The real problem, though, is that Everton's financial situation is a straightjacket on their ambitions. The club announced a pre-tax loss of almost £11 million at the end of 2006.

Peter Kilfoye feels the two boards have let the fans down and is not surprised there have been problems. "I think part of the rivalry is at the top level of the clubs. This showed over any question of a shared stadium. These are competing businesses, let's make no mistake about it. People think of them as some kind of offshoots of the same sporting phenomenon, and that's true in the sense that they both play football, but they are certainly rival businesses.

When Peter Robinson, for example, was Chief Executive of Liverpool and Peter Johnson had taken over Everton. I remember having a meeting with the two of them and it was, you know, there was a hostility there which I personally don't understand. I think mature, intelligent people even in such a competitive sport as football can sit down and talk about areas of mutual interest in a cooperative way. That didn't strike me at the time as being the way in which they responded to each other. It was barely disguised hostility and that hasn't changed much."

THE FEELING AMONG EVERTONIANS that Liverpool, because of their success and selling power, tend to have their path smoothed somewhat doesn't end with the local authorities. In 2005 Everton finished fourth in the Premiership, higher than their rivals, and occupying the final Champions League place for the coming season. The problem was that Liverpool then went on to win that very trophy on a memorable night in Istanbul.

The new European champions hadn't qualified for the following season's tournament, but now demanded they be allowed to defend

* *The Independent*, 12 December 2006

their crown. Such a suggestion seemed to seriously threaten Everton's own participation given that the precedent for this had seen Real Zaragoza relegated to the UEFA Cup in place of the stardust of Real Madrid, five seasons earlier when the same situation had arisen in Spain. It looked as though Liverpool were again about to put a spoke in the wheels of Everton's European ambitions.

In the end the FA asked UEFA if five English teams could be entered into the competition. No country had ever been allowed such a large allocation and UEFA would have to break their own rules if they agreed. For a time it did not look good at Goodison.

Then, in early June 2005, supporters on Merseyside got what they wanted, a place of their own in the Champions League as UEFA's executive committee let Liverpool back in, though with a number of caveats attached. Peace reigned, though the Everton manager, David Moyes, outlined exactly what had been at stake. "If Liverpool had got [into the competition] ahead of Everton there would have been uproar, it would have been a disgrace and could have caused a lot of problems in our city."*

Moyes had a point. The FA were well aware of the situation they faced and took the only possible route open to them, desperately wishing not to be seen to have favoured either club. It was a wise and ultimately successful strategy, one which avoided making an enemy of heavyweights who had done so much to shape the great traditions of the English game.

LIVERPOOL FANS HAVE LONG talked about 'The Liverpool Way'. This was more than a loose method of playing, it was a system, very definite and highly effective which emerged under Shankly but was passed down the managerial chain to Bob Paisley and then Joe Fagan. The idea was that each player fitted into a rigid and highly disciplined approach based on two touches, control then pass. The whole thing depended on collective responsibility and hard work. It was the template for the greatest period in the history of the club, but an anathema to Everton. There the emphasis has

* David Moyes, *BBC website*, 9 May 2005

long been on the artistry of individuals who could thrill and amaze; players of the calibre of Tommy Lawton, Alex Young, or the incomparable Ralph 'Dixie' Dean. Dean himself knew there were differences even in his day. "Everton have always been noted for going on the pitch to play football. We got called 'The School of Science' quite rightly. The other lot, the Reds ... well, they were a gang of butchers."*

Dean's era, the 1920s and 30s, was indeed marked by teams called the School of Science, though various Everton sides have earned the name, most notably in the '60s and early '70s with the 'Holy Trinity' of Kendall, Ball and Harvey commanding midfield, and then Kendall's own dynamic and successful team of the mid-1980s. It's thought the idiom School of Science was first used in the 1920s after a Derby County player said Everton "always manage to serve up football of the highest scientific order."**

Despite this scholarly approach, there remains a touch of the Pagan ritual at the ground. Even today fans are treated to the sight of the Toffee Lady perambulating the side of the pitch handing out boiled sweets. Each week another teenage Evertonian is picked to perform the task. The sweets themselves are known as Everton Mints and their black and white stripes reflect an early strip worn by the team.

Traditions are important at Goodison. While most clubs today have adopted a piece of music which is played when the team comes out onto the pitch for a home game, this is nothing new at Goodison. There the distinctive and punchy 'Johnny Todd' theme to Z-Cars, the BBC police drama of the 1960's, has long been associated with their own boys in blue. The show was gritty for its time and was set in an unidentified area of Merseyside known as Newtown. Strangely much of it was filmed in what could be Everton's new home, Kirby. A reinterpretation of an old local folk tune this has become so much an established part of the Goodison experience that when a new theme was introduced in the mid-90s it was met with widespread revulsion by the fans. Within weeks *Z-Cars* was back.

* *Everton, The School of Science,* James Corbett
** *Toffee Web*

In late August 2007 the tune rang out before a Champions League tie at Anfield in tribute to 11 year-old Everton supporter, Rhys Jones. Rhys died after being shot three times in the neck by a teenager in broad daylight while on his way home from football training. This bewildering turn of events had left the city in mourning once more. Perhaps this confirms that, although the derby now displays an aggression like that in other cities, Merseyside's particular emotion still has the power to unite. Liverpool's solidarity with Everton extended to a minute's applause for the dead boy. The players also wore black arm bands in his honour.

The most easily identifiable custom among those who go to Anfield, of course, is the singing of *You'll Never Walk Alone*. This has been associated with the club since the early '60s when the local band Gerry and the Pacemakers had a number one with what had been an old music hall number. Slow and emotional, its flavour is both supportive and defiant:

Walk On, Walk On
With Hope in Your Hearts
And You'll Never Walk Alone
You'll Never Walk Alone

It is not the kind of sentiment one might expect to hear from a football crowd and demonstrates the independent spirit which has long been in place at Liverpool. Perhaps the best example of this was when, in the early 1950s, before the era of mass singing truly took off, the Kop showed it would not be forced to recite something not recognised as its own. Arthur Kagan and his brass band had become famous for conducting at FA Cup finals. When he tried the same thing at Anfield, the supporters began singing an entirely different song.

The Kop has always been unusual, rarely booing returning ex-players and always applauding visiting goalkeepers. Then there are the banners. It was during the team's European successes of the 1970s and '80s that the Kop began to import an almost continental attitude with large-scale banners, some highly colourful, but most homemade. They bore cuttingly sarcastic messages, often with a play on words, such as: 'For those of you watching in Blue and White, this is what the European Cup looks like.'

Its capacity was cut severely when seats were introduced and with the terracing went much of the atmosphere, according to Kop die-hards. There is now a campaign to Reclaim the Kop and a bona fide singing section. It is an attempt, prompted by the fans and backed by the board, to recreate some of the essence of the old ways. The banners and slogans are still around, though now they tend to be part of a more choreographed entertainment. I watched, at the start of the derby, as flags on long slim bendy poles were twirled in figures of eight by individual fans standing well away from their fellow supporters. It was all very safe, very measured, and utterly unlike days of yore when thousands crammed onto that huge bank of terracing in what became a rite of passage. Then a long, thin, red and white banner was marched around the front of the stand, clearly a dig at Everton's claims to represent the populous: 'One City, One Club, One Name – Liverpool'.

To be truthful, the match itself was dire. Everton's defence dominated, Liverpool quickly ran out of ideas and lumped balls into the box. We were treated to a half-time rendition of *In My Liverpool Home* and the away fans in front of me really did pass around the Everton Mints. On the pitch there was a single moment of brightness in each half. In the first Craig Bellamy had the ball in the net only to be ruled offside. Then Andy Johnson scuffed a sitter which would have put the visitors ahead.

The goalless draw was far better for Everton and extinguished the last embers of Liverpool's more imagined than real challenge for the title. The Everton fans taunted Liverpudlians with cries of 'We're the pride of Merseyside', having taken four points from a possible six against their rivals that season.

As the ground emptied they sang 'Fuck Off back to Norway', a mocking reference to the Scandinavian element among the home support. I doubt this would make it into any publicity material for the event which is said to be the "rocket fuel" propelling Liverpool's economy – the European Capital of Culture 2008.* What would hundreds of thousands of potential visitors make of being told to 'eff off' home? We can only hope that something would be lost in translation. These things do seem to happen on Merseyside. Apparently.

---

* *Liverpool 08 website*

The two managers, Rafa Benitez and David Moyes, had grown increasingly angry and impatient as the match wore on. They had rubbed along together on the touchline for the majority of the game, following the play while staring straight ahead, as if the other simply wasn't there. The illusion wasn't to last.

Later, inside the Anfield boardroom, the Everton representatives were informed that a rather delicate situation had arisen as a result of the Liverpool manager's post-match press conference. They were angry and indignant in the presence of their hosts, it was little wonder. Benitez had, on television, radio and to the press generally, repeatedly described Everton as a small club. "I look at the match and I'm really disappointed because one team wanted to win the game and the other didn't want to lose it. Everton had eight or nine players behind the ball and defended narrow and deep, but when you play against a small club, that's what they do."*

Incendiary stuff. David Moyes was diplomatic when asked about the remarks by a salivating press pack, but his words carried a sting. "Everton are one of the big clubs in England. We are, at this present time, smaller than Liverpool but, if Rafa had been managing Everton I think he'd have tried to do a similar job today. It would just be nice for these managers to show a bit of humility, wouldn't it."** The Toffees' Chief Executive, Keith Wyness, dismissed the Liverpool manager, saying the Spaniard was "in a minority of one in believing Everton is, in any respect, a small football club."***

Benitez's English is not the finished article, but still, his words were mischievous at best and at worst dangerous. Evertonians were furious. On the website *When Skies are Grey*, Tony from Old Swan wrote: "We have contested more seasons in the top flight of English football than any other; not bad for a 'small club'." A fan on the BBC's 606 site described the Liverpool manager as a "petulant bully", while another said Liverpool's insecurity about not winning the league meant they "can't help but have a dig at Everton."*

* *The Guardian, 5 February 2007*
** *The Guardian, 5 February 2007*
*** *The Guardian, 5 February 2007*

Across the same forums Reds were not slow to bite back. One asked how it could be that just one comment had sent "every single poster on here off their rocker? I thought you don't care what we say. But you are a big club, though. I mean, just look at what happened when you got fourth place, your manager was on Sky Sports News sipping champagne hailing the achievement."**

I WAS LEAVING BEHIND a city in turmoil. As my train inched and swayed its way out of Lime Street that afternoon, investigations were already underway into what had happened to the ferry which so nearly sank only hours previously, while in Italy all league matches had been postponed after the violence of the night before. Merseyside cared not. For days in newspaper columns, during phone-ins, in bars and on the street the often ugly debate continued. The friendly derby really had become nothing more than a memory.

In the middle of May 2007 the final Premiership table showed both clubs had done well, though not nearly as well as they would have wished. Liverpool finished third, some distance behind champions Manchester United and second-placed Chelsea. Everton qualified for Europe by finishing a perfectly respectable sixth, ten points shy of their neighbours across the park. It's probably best not to ask if that margin was large, or small.

* *The Guardian, 5 February 2007*

** *The Guardian, 5 February 2007*

GLASGOW:

Prisoners Of History

"It's more than just a football team they're playing for.
They're playing for a cause and a people."

Tommy Burns – *Celtic Minded*, Joseph M Bradley

FIRST THERE WAS the noise, like some guttural thunder bubbling up without warning, then my legs swayed with the movement of the building itself, left and right. I looked up to see the television screen crease into fuzzy white noise, before going blank. Seconds later, with the power restored, the pictures showed how Charlie Adam of Rangers had slung a free-kick under the Celtic wall to put his team into a two goal lead. I was standing, pie in hand, on the concourse of the Club Deck, the highest point inside Ibrox. A few feet away over 40,000 people were screaming in delight.

It was Saturday the 5th May 2007, the final Old Firm match of what had been, for the home side, an abominable season. Celtic were champions, and had won the league without ever being troubled by the club with which they have dominated Scottish football for longer than any living soul can remember. Rangers had been so poor they'd let their manager go during his first season, something unheard for them. Paul Le Guen lasted just seven months and left after a period of rancour between himself and some of the players which was punctuated by a series of results comparable to the worst in Rangers' long, and, mostly, glittering history.

Today, though, those in blue would see their rivals off the premises with smiles on their faces. Rangers fans around me talked eagerly of next season, of rebuilding work, of their returning manager Walter Smith (controversially tempted away from the Scotland job) being able to get the better of Celtic as he had done for most of the 1990s. It all suggested brighter days around the corner for Rangers. They would be welcome.

This mood of change was entirely in keeping with the times. Scotland had just elected a new national Executive, or Government. The Scottish National Party had beaten Labour at the polls two days previously in a cliff-hanger of an election. At the match, the Celtic fans made use of the electoral bunting. VOTE GREEN was just one of the many messages they had for the Rangers support as they entered the ground, the two sides being separated by a three-deep wall of police and crush barriers.

Prior to the arrival of the players, Rangers had played the theme from the Dambusters and bag-piping medleys. The songs being sung around me fitted right in, they included God Save the Queen and Rule Britannia. The fans were enjoying themselves, but also showing considerable restraint. It could have been the Last Night of the Proms, but for the additions of rather more opaque numbers like *Derry's Walls* and *The Sash*. The Celtic end had anthems which were equally unusual. They sung *The Fields of Athenry* and *The Soldiers Song*.

The teams came out to an honour guard of large Union Jacks and Scottish saltires. There were British symbols of all kinds around the three ends of the ground containing the home support, including a splattering of Red Hands of Ulster; the away end was dominated by green, and the green white and orange of the Irish tri-colour.

My seat was almost at the very back of the top tier of the main stand. As soon as I arrived I was confronted by the sight of a figure jumping up from his seat and shouting to a nearby policeman. There followed a prolonged bout of pointing down towards the Celtic support to our left. When he came back I asked him what the problem had been. He said "they" were flying "the Starry Plough" which he described as the flag of the INLA (the defunct Irish National Liberation Army). He'd asked for it to be removed, because "what is good for the goose is good for the gander." Sure enough, within five minutes the same officer came back, nodding his head and the giving the thumbs up.

For those who understand the history of the two clubs much of this will sound entirely familiar, very much in keeping with the sharpest divide of all the rivalries covered in this book, and very probably around the world. But, I'm afraid the commonly held idea that Celtic and Rangers merely represent two different and competing branches of Christianity is, although in part true, also deeply simplistic. There's much much more to this story than Rangers as Protestants and Celtic as Catholics. To go no further is to ignore the many subtleties, exceptions and contradictions which reach deep into the Scottish psyche. The context and the key to understanding both the 'old' and the 'new' Scotland is knowing that the country, although a small part of northern Europe, has been touched profoundly by some of the most remarkable events in the history of that continent.

An Gorta Mor or the great Irish famine of the mid 19th century was caused by a blight or fungus which came from the new world. The crops of many countries were hit, none more so than in Ireland, where potatoes were all but wiped out. Those living on the land tended to be smallholders with tiny plots, which they rented from aristocratic British absentee landowners. They worked the fields to pay the rent and survived in the main by feeding their families on potatoes which grew easily in poor soil. The crop had been unpredictable in the years leading up to the famine and known to fail completely in some areas. For that reason alone London can be forgiven for not initially understanding the extent of the problem which enveloped the country. However, the overall response by the administrative and de facto feudal overlords has remained a source of deep anger and controversy. In broad terms Ireland was given no relief from starvation because to do so would interfere with the free-market economics in vogue at that time; threatening the profits of the British landowners.

Throughout the famine, which lasted five, long, bitter years, Ireland exported grain, livestock and other commodities such as butter in massive quantities across the water. Put simply these were 'money crops', those the farmers produced for their masters, unlike the 'subsistence crop' of potatoes which they consumed at home. Despite the famine, Ireland was more than capable of feeding herself had London permitted.

Numbers are difficult, but historians believe that anything between half a million and two million people died during this period and at least three hundred thousand others migrated to Britain alone. Fully a third of these refugees came to one country, Scotland. In the years after the famine through to the early part of the following century they continued to come, mainly to Glasgow and the surrounding districts of the industrialised central belt. By that time their numbers had trebled. It was immigration on a massive scale, and to a country which had little love of these Irish men, women and children. They were unskilled and terribly poor, living in the most rundown parts of Glasgow and Lanarkshire. Even in a city which still gloried in the title – Second City of the Empire – there were economic reasons why they were not wanted; principally the fear that – just as in Liverpool – desperate to work and stereotypically seen as only being capable of carrying out manual labour, they would undercut and take 'Protestant' (working-class) jobs in heavy industry.

Hand in hand with this went another reason for a campaign of what today we would have no hesitation in calling racism by elements of the popular press and even parts of the establishment. It would have been bad enough that these immigrants came from a community which was seen as radical within the British Isles – constantly agitating over the cause of Irish nationalism – but in Scotland they were alien and distrusted because they were, in the vast majority, Roman Catholic. The Protestant Reformation of the sixteenth century took on particular characteristics in Scotland. The leader of the movement there, John Knox, had been a disciple of Calvin, one of the architects of Protestantism. Knox studied under Calvin in Geneva and, when the time came, applied a doctrine similar to his teacher's strict observance of the word of God as it appeared in the Bible. The power of Knox's sermons had been known to unleash violent mobs which destroyed religious images; smashing altars and relics. Austerity prevailed and church walls were whitewashed so that God's glory would not be obscured by the bright colours of Catholicism. In 1560 the Scots Parliament abolished the authority of the Pope and outlawed mass. Scotland officially became a Protestant country, one in which only a handful of Catholics would remain.

The zeal of the Scottish Reformation was matched in few other European counties. The anti-Catholic fervour of the times remained long after the battle to disestablish the Church of Rome had been won. If evidence were needed for this, Glasgow in the late 18th century had more anti-Catholic societies than there were people of that religion residing within the city. It was against this complex background of religious fundamentalism, poverty, immigration and imperial and industrial might that Celtic Football Club was formed. In late November 1887, after months of debate, the decision was taken to press ahead with the idea of setting up a football club in the east end of Glasgow. Discussions about forming the club had been dominated by priests, but every section of the Catholic community had played its part, including local school-masters, small businessmen, politicians and well known agitators for Irish reform. They aimed to send out a team which would make the Irish of the city proud. Part of the thinking behind this was a concern among religious leaders that young Catholics would lose their religion by mixing freely with Protestants. This new football team would ensure that a significant part of their limited leisure time would be spent entirely among their own kind. Celtic were not the first team in Scotland to be formed by Irish Catholics for Irish Catholics, but they would soon be the most important.

There was another, much more pressing reason, one which the club has long preferred to hold-up as the factor behind its emer-gence. Celtic was to be a charitable organisation, providing relief in the form of food and clothing for the poor of the area. Specifically the poor in mind were the children of the three Catholic parishes of the east end. Clearly then, in this very narrow sense Celtic were sectarian, but only because they emerged from a particular commu-nity and their raison d'etre was to improve the lot of those people, practically and spiritually. Quickly, they became a beacon of Irish success and an institution through which these immigrants would be able to freely express the norms of their cultural background. What Celtic were not, even in the earliest days, was in any way exclusive about who could play for them. A motion put before the board in 1895 that only three Protestants at one time should be in the team was roundly rejected and then thrown out again two years later. The matter had forever been settled; there were no 'right' and 'wrong' types of player, ability was all that mattered.

Celtic's first game could only have been against one team. The match, at Celtic Park in May 1888, saw the fledgling 'Irishmen' beat Rangers 5-2. Unlike Celtic, the team which came into existence playing on the public pitches of Glasgow Green in 1872 had one simple reason for their creation, a love of Association football, a game which a handful of young rowers had watched after mooring their boat on the banks of the Clyde. Hard work and ambition saw Rangers (as with Liverpool the name was taken from an English rugby side) rise quickly to prominence; the club already had its own ground just two years after formation. They contested the Scottish Cup final twice before the decade was out and even managed an appearance in the FA Cup semi-final in the 1880s. They were joint champions of the first ever Scottish League and regularly won it outright during the years which immediately followed.

That initial match against Celtic was a friendly and very much played in that spirit, with both sides having supper together and then an evening of 'the happiest character'.* So convivial were their relations they continued to hold post-match social evenings and would invite each other to watch English teams play at their grounds. Needless to say the warmth of this companionship was not to last. The reason was simple, Celtic weren't prepared to accept their place in the established scheme of things. They had made an impact on Scottish football from the off, reaching the Cup final in their inaugural season. Three years after that Celtic hammered the dominant amateur team, Queen's Park, 5-1 to win the competition. The Bhoys, as they had become known, were Scottish champions four times in six seasons between 1893 and 1898, pulling in large crowds whenever they played, on both sides of the border.

With another Irish immigrant side, Hibernian from Edinburgh, also doing well, the question began to be asked, in the press and elsewhere, 'where is the team to take on the Irish?' A Scottish solution was needed, a home grown tartan team to which the people could rally. Rangers emerged as that club after it became clear that the considerable power of the first aristocrats of the game, Queen's Park, was on the wane. The Spiders had been such a strong outfit that they didn't concede a single goal in their first ten years. The problem was they were wedded to their amateur status and remain so to this day. That would be little good in a game which, with Celtic prime among those clamouring for serious reform, was moving inexorably towards professionalism.

Rangers and Celtic, with their frequent meetings, multiple trophy successes and record-breaking attendances also realised there was serious money to be made from the popularity of football. Slowly they became the Old Firm, not a term of endearment,

* *Celtic, A Century With Honour*, Brian Wilson

but rather one reflecting their commercial pulling power. Consequently the relationship changed and Rangers, in taking on the mantle of the Scottish or Protestant challengers, could not afford to be seen as being too close to their main rivals. The same was true of Celtic. From this time Rangers received both the tacit and direct support of mainstream Scottish society, a position which would remain unaltered for decades. Towards the end of the 1890s they were fully equipped to become a serious force. They had one of the best stadiums in football with the team, the support and therefore the finances to match. Glasgow's Lord Provost, at the opening of the new Ibrox Park in 1899 described Rangers as a club "par excellence" who no doubt would continue to be the best in the land.* Indeed they would, alongside Celtic at any rate. Together they won more than thirty major trophies in the next twenty years.

By that time Rangers would have secured their status as the champions of the native population in adopting a clear practice of not playing Catholics. This was a trend which developed slowly at the club, but became important, at least for financial reasons; sectarianism was good for business and with the majority of the community to choose from it did Rangers no harm on the pitch. It has long been claimed that the arrival of the Belfast-based shipbuilders, Harland and Wolff, in Glasgow in 1912, was the catalyst for the hardening of Rangers' stance. The focus has tended to be on the aggressive anti-Catholic sentiment of the employees at the parent yard, who had made their workplace all but a Protestant-only zone. Whether the migration to Govan of a relatively small number of Ulstermen was alone enough to determine the policy of the biggest football club in the land is debatable, though the attitudes of these workers may have helped to radicalise the Rangers support at large. Certainly the newcomers relished the chance to rally to the cause of the local, and singularly Protestant, club.

What may be of more importance is that Rangers were in no position to reject such support, the club sorely required as much revenue as could be mustered. The reason for this was the financial fall-out from the Ibrox disaster of 1902. Twenty-five people were killed and hundreds injured when terracing gave way during a

---

* *The Old Firm*, Bill Murray

Scotland v England match, sending spectators down through a hole at the top of the stand. Desperate to avoid further catastrophe, piecemeal improvements to the ground were carried out between 1902 and 1917 and major rebuilding work followed in the coming years. Harland and Wolff were on hand to help. The company, rather than the workers, privately lent the club £90,000 with the caveat, it has long been alleged, that Rangers must not sign Catholics. Whatever the truth, Celtic's first manager, Willie Maley, reflecting on the matter as an old man, admitted that he felt this was the point when religion fully began to define Rangers and their relationship with Celtic. Yet, while the Belfast shipbuilders no doubt played a part, there actually seems to have been a number of interlocking reasons why Rangers chose to exclude not only Catholic players, but Catholic employees per se. In the same year that Harland and Wolff came to Glasgow the first Rangers president, James Henderson, passed away. He had been a notably respected man, famed for his philanthropic works across the communities. He was succeeded by John Ure Primrose. Primrose was strongly anti home-rule in Ireland, his charity work never extended into the Catholic areas of Glasgow and he now openly tied his club to the cause of Freemasonry. Then there were the overwhelmingly patriotic feelings which accompanied Britain's fight with Germany in the Great War. Scots rallied to the cause and public opinion was firmly with those fighting in the trenches. The Catholic population was treated with further suspicion after the 1916 Easter Rising in Dublin, especially when it became known that Irish Republicans had agreed to Germany's offer of guns and ammunition to help in their struggle against the Crown.

While the war effort continued and in the years immediately thereafter such attitudes did not necessarily hamper Catholics in any practical sense. So long as there was work they could live and eat. This changed during the depression between the two world wars. In this era of mass unemployment, Scots with native-sounding names were given preference by the Protestants who, from top to bottom, ran every major company on the west coast. Throughout this time Celtic remained firmly Irish and Catholic in outlook. Yes, the club continued to play Protestants, and did so in significant numbers, but those in charge were Catholic and retained strong ties to their own religion and to the old country. Much of the literature which came out of Celtic Park was Catholic in tone and open air masses and other celebrations were frequently held at the ground. Priests (though it must be said, clergymen of any denomination) were admitted free of charge at home games right through to the modern era. In no way was the present official view – that Celtic is a Scottish club proud of its Irish origins – applicable. Not only did the team undertake various trips back to that country, but at their St Patrick's Day dinner of 1936, nearly half a century after their formation, the toasts were to 'the memory of St Patrick' and 'our homeland'. The words of the Irish Free State's national anthem, the *Soldier's Song* were even printed on the menu.

These were the established patterns of behaviour for the Old Firm over the next fifty or so years, Celtic, while operating an open-door policy, retained strong spiritual and political ties to the country their founders had come from and their support still identified with. Rangers, however, were Protestant to the point of exclusion, identifiably the team of the people and the establishment, representative of the majority unionist outlook, as traditional and as normal as the Boys Brigade and Sunday School.

THESE IDENTITIES AND COMPETING world views became, and to some extent remain, a fault-line running through much of Scottish culture. Just ten years after their first encounter Old Firm matches were already being scarred by regular violence. Gang fights, brawls, pitch invasions, bouts of missile throwing, attacks on players and even full-scale riots were all part and parcel of these encounters through various eras. Neither the dread of Nazism in the '30s and '40s nor the austerity which followed tempered things greatly. Scotland, however, did not remain entirely untouched by the liberalising attitudes of the 1960s which slowly loosened the grip of the Church. Also by this time the descendents of the Irish immigrants were no longer ghettoised and the longstanding discrimination against them in employment was beginning to fade. This coincided with the period of Celtic's greatest and most sustained success, achieved under the guidance of their first Protestant manager, Jock Stein. Under the Portuguese sun, Stein's men, the Lisbon Lions, carried out a thrilling destruction of Inter Milan's detested ultra-defensive Catenaccio system in the European Cup final of 1967. The effect was pronounced and a famous victory was celebrated throughout Scotland and beyond. Celtic were the first Scottish, British and indeed, northern European side to win the competition. Perhaps this was the moment the club, with four Protestants in the team, first truly connected in a meaningful way with Scots of all backgrounds. Celtic had always had non-Catholic, fans but from Stein's time, and through to the present day, those numbers rose to something like a quarter or more of people calling themselves Celtic supporters. No longer were they restricted in minds of the majority to being just a Catholic or an Irish football club.

It's often forgotten that Rangers, too, were an extremely good side at the time, narrowly losing the final of the Cup Winners' Cup just a week after Celtic's historic victory. For all that, the warning on the Rangers club badge – Ready – beneath the Rampant Lion, never seemed so inappropriate. They were far from prepared for the modern era, finding it easier to back away from change. This lion was cowering not roaring. Evermore Scots were coming to the conclusion that there was something fundamentally wrong, even un-Scottish, about the way Rangers decided who was fit to wear their colours. The storm began to break over their heads when, in 1969, their fans invaded the pitch at St James' Park in Newcastle after defeat in the latter stages of the UEFA Cup. For the first time the press openly linked the violence to the club's sectarian stance.

Some hoped Rangers would tackle the issue in the wake of the second Ibrox disaster; sixty-six people having been killed when a stairway collapsed during the closing stages of an Old Firm match in 1971. But no, their silence continued. The following season Rangers beat Dynamo Moscow in Barcelona to lift the European Cup Winners' Cup. Several times their fans streamed onto the pitch in what was, in all likelihood, intended to be an exuberant celebration. The Spanish riot police did not see it that way, and on the Nou Camp pitch, with batons in hand, they fought the many thousands of supporters from Scotland. Rangers were handed a one-year ban from European competition. Further serious disturbances, at a friendly match in Birmingham in 1976, buffeted Rangers into action. This time an official declaration was issued saying "Rangers Football Club divorces themselves completely from religion and sectarian bias in every aspect on the field of play and on the terracings." The board, it went on, were "determined to end Rangers image as a sectarian club."* Crucially Rangers said they would sign a Catholic if one could be found who was good enough.

A decade later, when the former Liverpool captain and midfielder, Graeme Souness, arrived from Italy to become player-manager no suitably gifted Catholic footballer had been unearthed.

Souness had spent his entire professional career away from Scotland, in England and on the continent. A supremely confident man, as a footballer he had won just about everything going. He came to Rangers when they were on a low, caught in a seemingly never ending cycle of mediocrity, well behind Celtic, Aberdeen and even Dundee United. His team won the League Championship and League Cup in his first season and from that point on the words 'Souness' and 'Revolution' were inseparable. Major singings such as the England captain, Terry Butcher, and goalkeeper, Chris Woods arrived, reversing the traffic of players down the generations. Scottish football was being transformed, and Rangers once again had the whip hand.

Graeme Souness may be many things: socially sophisticated, a lover of designer suits, an avowed Thatcherite and a notoriously unyielding personality. A bigot, however, he was not. He had married a Catholic woman, something which would not have been tolerated at Ibrox in the past. "No other experience in nearly forty years as a professional player and manager has created a scar comparable with that left by the treatment I received at Rangers."** That was the view of Sir Alex Ferguson, who as a player had done the same thing and strongly believed he'd been hounded out of the club he loved for doing so.

Rangers' new young owner, Sir David Murray, had made it clear there was no ban on signing Catholics; had Souness at any time been told otherwise its hard to imagine him either coming to or remaining at Rangers. Nevertheless, when push came to shove, there was eye-popping astonishment at the choice of the first player from that faith to knowingly come to Ibrox in modern times.

The news leaked out on the morning of the 10th July 1989. Maurice Johnston was going to play for Rangers. A striker of

* *Graeme Souness,* Sandy Jamieson
** *Alex Ferguson,* Managing My Life

considerable repute, Johnston had twice made the sign of the cross in front of the Rangers support while with Celtic. He had since been transferred to Nantes, in France, but was now coming home. Two months earlier, wearing a Celtic shirt at Parkhead, he told reporters how he was delighted to have re-signed for the club he'd supported since childhood.

When he then turned up in the Blue Room at Ibrox, many people actually refused to believe what they were seeing. It's no exaggeration to say that this was one of the biggest news stories of the century in Scotland, one which would have repercussions both on and off the field of play for years to come. How he came to sign for Rangers having apparently already gone back to Celtic is a story which has only emerged in fragments. Where and when Rangers and Souness first became involved is not at all clear. What we can say for sure is that the paperwork which would have registered Johnston as a Celtic player beyond all doubt was not completed on the day he appeared before the press at Celtic Park.

As a midfield enforcer Peter Grant had been a central force in Celtic's drive to the league and cup double of the club's centenary season, a year before the Johnston contrversy. We met at Norwich City's training ground during the short spell in which he managed he club. Grant has a clear recollection of what his friend, Johnston, said to him during this period. "I remember it as if it was yesterday. Mo had actually been to the Cup final, sitting with me when we went to play Rangers. And I remember sitting on the bus going to the game and Mo went, 'I've not signed the contract yet.' So we played the Cup final and we won. Then I went away with Scotland." Johnston's mere presence at the Scottish Cup final against Rangers, on the 20th May, was credited with giving Celtic the lift needed to win the trophy before attention turned to the national team's games against England and Chile.

It was at this point, with the Scotland squad gathering almost immediately after Celtic's win at Hampden, that Grant learned Johnston was never going to sign that contract, but would still be playing his football in Glasgow. "I remember we were down at one of the coastal places and Mo and Coisty [the Rangers striker Ally McCoist] were winding me up saying 'ah Granty I am going to be nut-megging you next year'. Mo's saying that, and I'm like, what are you talking about, you mug? He says, 'yeah, I'm going to go with Rangers'. I'm like, 'what!!' And Coisty is like, 'no, really he's going to come.' It was true."

This suggests Johnston knew he was going to Ibrox long before the official explanation about the timing of the move offered by Souness. The then Rangers manager has consistently maintained that he made no approach for the player until his relationship with Celtic had broken down at the beginning of July, though, after losing the Cup final, he did tell his players not to worry, he had something up his sleeve which would shatter their rivals.

In the short-term Rangers fans were far from pleased, but in fact only a handful turned up at Ibrox to protest, burning scarves, delivering a wreath and ripping up season tickets. It had always been expected that when the club did rid itself of this particular 'tradition' Celtic supporters would have welcomed it as progress. The circumstances simply did not allow that to happen. In the resulting hurricane of media discussion and pub debate it was lost on many that Souness had staged a coup. He was getting an excellent player at a more than reasonable price. It was also a move which would keep Celtic very much on the back foot for the majority of the following decade, something which had been all too clear to Grant. "It was a massive blow to us because Rangers were ahead, their stadium was nearly finished and all their finances could go on the best players. Ours couldn't. We lost Mo, and that was a big blow not just to the players, but to the support. And I genuinely feel that was a big, big part of our downfall during that period.

I was gutted, absolutely gutted, because I was friendly with Mo. I thought he was a wonderful striker, really, really was. I genuinely thought he would have helped us with the league that year and for the next couple of years. You thought, that's one of our best players going to play for our rivals and they have already got a big percentage of the best players anyway. If we cannot afford them, we should never lose them to Rangers."

What then had been the reason for Johnson turning his back on Celtic? "You hear so many stories about how they were willing to pay Mo's tax. That's what he wanted in his contract. They were willing to pay the tax and Celtic weren't willing to pay the tax. And I still think to myself, if that was the case it's very, very disappointing for us.

I still get on very well with Mo, but it did become strained because he had to live in Edinburgh, had to live away out of [Glasgow], he didn't really have a life away from that side of things and I just think, all things taken into it, was it worth it? To look back now, it was a fantastic signing for Rangers, brilliant, great credit to Graeme Souness. Rangers raised the bar, probably put Scottish football back on the map, gave it the kick in the backside it needed. But unfortunately we lost one of our best players, and I genuinely believe Rangers would never have won nine [championships] in a row [equalling Celtic's record from the 1960s] if he had been playing with us."

Did Grant feel Johnston had been aware he was making history in committing himself to play for the other half of the Old Firm? "I genuinely believe that he made a financial decision, that's the reason he went. I don't think Mo was going to think well, 'I am going to unite or destroy'. I'm sure there was a lot of Rangers fans who never, ever went back and would probably never accept him. Yet again, it comes back to the Celtic Rangers divide. I used to say, 'he's not one of us, he never goes to mass'. I'd say to him, 'wee man, don't you ever say you are a Catholic, you have never been inside the bloody chapel'. I was determined to say, 'no Rangers have not signed one, make sure you sign one like me that goes to mass week in week out'. Laughing like, you know."

Perhaps there is something more than friendly banter between players in these remarks, though. Rangers were signing a Catholic only in the loosest sense. Johnston came from what is termed in Scotland a 'mixed', religious marriage. Not only that, as Grant states, he did not worship, and his father was known to be an ardent Rangers supporter.

Grant also thinks the fact that Johnston had committed himself to Celtic and then gone back on his word was bad enough, but to end up across the city intensified the situation a hundred fold. "It was a massive decision. Had he come back from Nantes, direct to Rangers, would it have been such a problem? I'm not so sure. It takes a brave one to do it. Mo did it, and was successful at it. Whether he will always be revered in the Rangers history, I'm not so sure. The history books will probably look back and you will see his name, but not many pictures. That's what Celtic and Rangers is about, the feeling that, if you are betrayed that's it, you are finished.

But if you give the punters a hundred per cent, they will give you a hundred per cent back."

The picture painted in most quarters was that Johnston, in signing for Rangers, ended completely and forever the religious apartheid the club had clung to for so long. It would be churlish to say this did not move Rangers forward immensely, of course it did. What it failed to do, however, was change things out of all recognition down the Copland Rd.

Johnston scored more than 50 goals in 110 appearances for Rangers and was so successfully assimilated he was known to sing the old Orange battle anthem, *The Sash*, on occasion. Despite all that, and scoring the winner in Old Firm matches, he was gone within two years. He became about the tenth Roman Catholic to join the club since its formation 117 years previously. That would be a blunt enough statistic were it not also the case that some of them didn't even manage a game for the first team. Yet, in one sense he was in the majority; with hardly an exception they had all been Catholics from Scotland.

After 1989, the matter of religion ceased to be discussed when a player arrived at the club. Since then Rangers fans have accepted without question, for example, an Italian Catholic captain in Lorenzo Amoruso and a French defender, Basil Boli, who said the Pope was his hero. But it would be almost another decade before a Scottish Catholic pulled on the royal blue jersey again, when Neil McCann joined from Hearts. It has to be said that the only real problems which McCann faced came from Celtic supporters who couldn't accept that he had gone to play at Ibrox. So for Rangers the anti-Catholic dam had burst, but in a very particular way. They were signing, and continue to sign, plenty of Catholics from all over the world, but rarely from Scotland, and, it seems, never from Ireland, north or south of the border.

Part of the problem was that supporters on both sides remained pretty entrenched in their views, so much that perhaps it has not been entirely easy for Rangers to sign people closer to home who know the club has traditionally been antagonistic towards them. These things do not change overnight, though Rangers have had plenty of time to make such a breakthrough.

I asked one Celtic season ticket holder, Gerry Hart, if he felt young Scottish and Northern Irish Catholics could now play for

Rangers. "I think it would be possible, but I don't think his background would be brought to the surface, it would be hidden as much as possible. There was a story that Christopher Burke signed for Rangers and he had to become Chris. They didn't want to tag him with having a Catholic sounding name. He's a Celtic supporter from a Catholic background.

Rangers have signed Italian Catholics, again that wasn't brought to the fore either, that was hidden by the club as well. They weren't allowed to bless themselves on the park [this is no longer the case] they had to do it in the tunnel. So I don't know, maybe a Northern Irish Catholic will sign for Rangers, but it won't be displayed."

THE SCOTLAND INTERNATIONAL, Paul Hartley, grew up in a family thoroughly in the Celtic tradition. Interestingly, both Old Firm clubs were after him during the transfer window which closed in January 2007. In fact he seemed to be just hours from signing for Rangers until Celtic came in with an offer. Hartley said being wanted by Rangers had been "a massive compliment" and he would have played for them with Walter Smith in charge.* Clearly he felt that neither Rangers' history, nor the attitude of some of their supporters, was in any way an obstacle to moving there.

A counter to Hartley's attitude is the experience of Celtic's former captain, Neil Lennon. Although a brash character, he had a torrid time during his seven years in Scotland. Not only at Ibrox, but at many other stadiums, Lennon was abused on a regular basis. His personality may have played a part, but one suspects it was not the only reason. While in Glasgow he had been forced to end his Northern Ireland career because some people simply could not accept a Catholic Celtic player as the captain of their international team.

Then there is the case of Aiden McGeady. The Celtic winger, born and brought up in Scotland, has chosen to play for Ireland, the land of his grandparents. The decision has caused McGeady no end of grief. "Obviously there are grounds like Ibrox and Tynecastle where you get every insult under the sun, but it's a decision I chose

---

* *Daily Record*, 1 February 2007

to make. I've stood by it, but I'll get a lot of stick as well. There are still grounds I go to where, when the ball goes out for a throw-in and I go to pick it up, sometimes I feel like putting my hands over my ears with some of the stick. But that's what happens."*

McGeady is viewed as a traitor, refusing to play for Scotland at a time when they were doing poorly. There's much more to this than football, though. The player actually feels Irish, regardless of where he was raised. The point made by McGeady's supporters is that no-one would dare question the right of, for example, Scots-Italians or Scots-Indians to say they have a stronger affinity to these countries than to Scotland, but that is not the case for the Scots-Irish.

Some make the point that the Irish are the largest minority in Scotland, but often an invisible one. It may be closer to the truth to say this actually demonstrates just how far the Irish in Scotland have come. It could also be that the Scottish population at large still don't fully realise how important Ireland remains to some sections of that community.

The Old Firm has always had something of an Irish backdrop. Large numbers of fans regularly travel to their games from both sides of the Irish border. So obvious was the influence of the teams that very often throughout the 1980s and into the middle of the next decade any sectarian disturbance filmed by television cameras on the streets of Belfast would be likely to show the replica kits of either Rangers or Celtic dominating the mob. This is hardly surprising since so much of the paraphernalia of the Old Firm tends to concentrate both on the recent and more historic conflicts in Ireland. During my own trip to Ibrox I could have bought a mountain of unofficial Rangers merchandise: flags and scarves which featured the word 'Ulster', or the slogan 'Our Wee Country' and even one showing King William of Orange on his white horse at the Battle of the Boyne. There were also badges, new ones according to the vendor, expressing support for banned paramilitary groups.

Celtic Park is not greatly different. It's no trouble to buy the Irish national flag and various others of a similar ilk, there are also

* *Scotland On Sunday,* 26 August 2007

tapes of rebel songs and even, on sale in the official car-park, the openly Republican fanzine *Tiocfaidh Ar La* ('our day will come') which has long raised money for Republicans over the water. The sympathies of the Celtic support have always been broadly with the formation of an Irish Republic which includes the six counties of Northern Ireland. That being said, support for the Provisional IRA of recent times has never been anything like as strong as that felt for the IRA of the war of independence. The fans' political orientation has also tended to be left of centre, reflecting the backing that the Catholic community at large has long given to the Labour Party in Scotland.

Historically Rangers supporters have been a curious mix. Feeling instinctively British and pro-Union, many would also be Labour voters and trade unionists. What we can probably say is that while the majority are not Conservative voters, they have tended to have the largest minority of Tories at any of the senior clubs in Scotland. Three Conservative Prime Ministers – Churchill, Macmillan and Thatcher – have all been to Ibrox. The general perception is that Rangers fans are loyalist and conservative, either with or without capital letters. The feeling and outlook has been one of consistent loyalty to the Crown. Both King George V and VI made official visits to Ibrox and the reining monarch is toasted from 'the loving cup' at the beginning of each year. Under Souness the team would hang a picture of the Queen in the dressing room when they went to Celtic Park, extending an Ibrox tradition. It's said that England captain Terry Butcher even donated a picture of Queen Elizabeth for the Rangers players to touch on the way out of the tunnel at home matches.

There is, of course, nothing in the least bit unsavoury, sectarian or illegal about venerating the British head of state. In almost any other context across the UK such an act would provoke little or no public outcry. It's reasonable that this should also be the case at the home of Rangers, especially since these gestures have almost always been carried out in private. Yet, it seems, some Rangers players and senior staff have, on occasion, taken things to rather more controversial levels, ones which have hardly been likely to foster peace and harmony.

It is alleged that at least one player, while celebrating the winning of the league championship in 1994 wore a T-shirt which displayed the slogan – 'Hang All IRA Terrorists'. The Rangers and Scotland goalkeeper, Andy Goram, wore a black armband during the Old Firm match of January 1998. He said it was in memory of his auntie, who had passed away three months earlier. On the streets the punters claimed to know different, openly saying that it was actually worn as a mark of respect for the UVF leader, Billy Wright, who had been killed in the infamous Maze Prison at Lisburn, just outside Belfast.

Celtic fans may feel they are able to smirk at all of this from the safe distance of the moral high ground, but their players have not been entirely blameless in the past either. Peter Grant didn't specify, but he told me that certain old numbers had been trotted out during his time. "I remember singing songs when I was at Celtic Park. I didn't even know what they meant, but Celtic sang them, we sang them. I look back now and I think, I was singing that. I never even knew what they meant. Maybe it is different now, because you learn a lot younger. It was a tribal call, that's what it was. It wasn't because I didn't like him, or I didn't like the Pope or I didn't like the Queen. It wasn't the case, it was just a fact that those were our songs and as it was part of your tribe."

When it comes to acts of Old Firm lunacy and the singing of controversial songs there is one clear winner. In 1999, Donald Findlay was vice-Chairman of Rangers and still is the leading QC in Scotland; in other words a man of considerable professional talent. Findlay lost his position at the club when, in the wake of their treble-clinching victory over Celtic in the Scottish Cup final he was filmed at a Rangers social club, microphone in hand, doing his best rendition of a number of songs including *The Sash* and the *Billy Boys*. Unfortunately for him the latter in particular has been a source of some discomfort to Rangers, since it seems to advocate the killing of Catholics. To some this may sound harmless; would the words of a song prompt anybody to act literally? In the context of the Old Firm anything is possible. A 16 year-old boy in a Celtic top was killed near Hampden shortly after Rangers' victory. Another fan, leaving Parkhead, died when his throat was cut in 1996.

Findlay himself was unfortunate. He was at a private function, and therefore it's highly unlikely he had set out to offend. He had no idea he was being filmed and was doing what the overwhelming majority of Rangers fans have done for years. On the other hand, perhaps someone in such a senior position should have known better. Footage of that night, sold to the press by a Rangers supporter, became front-page news and caused Findlay no end of grief. He felt he had let himself down, but more importantly, he'd let down the club he loved.

He agreed to see me towards the conclusion of one of the biggest murder trials in Scotland for years. A Polish student, Angelika Kluk, had been raped and brutally killed, her body stowed under the floorboards of a Catholic church. I discovered him, dressed in a dark pin-striped suit, puffing away on his pipe, leaning back against a side door to the High Court at the top of the Royal Mile in Edinburgh. Looking back, did he have any regrets about the cause of his downfall? "Regrets? Certainly that I had failed to take on board as I did, that society's attitude was changing, and I should have done. I mean, I of all people should have had the sense and the experience to realise that society's attitude was changing.

I still get on very well with Rangers fans across the board, but I always have because that's what I am. I'm a blue nose punter. It was just that I was lucky enough to get to the very highest echelons of Rangers Football Club, but I'm still a Rangers fan. I get on no better and no worse with Celtic fans than I ever did, ninety-five per cent of people know it's a football rivalry. In the morning you get Paddy's Market beside the High Court [in Glasgow], where there are lots of Celtic fans. And if Celtic win I always make a point of saying: 'right on you go, come on, get it over with'. And if Rangers win I'm like: 'where are you hiding the day lads'. And that's how it should be.

Despite what the media have written over the years, nobody once has been prepared to take up the challenge that I have offered them, and that was to produce one single human being that I had ever prejudiced in any way, because of religion, or colour or anything else." Yet the implication was clear from the press reports at the time of his impromptu cabaret; Findlay was a bigot, he'd been caught singing anti-Catholic songs, hadn't he? What did he now think of those songs and should Rangers fans be allowed to sing, for example, *The Sash* and the *Billy Boys*?

"I think that is the most difficult area. For me, I don't think there's anything wrong with *The Sash*. If you take the actual words of the song, they are standing up for something and representing something, a tradition, a history. What I think nowadays is that there are words – just as calling a black man 'a darkie' is not acceptable – there are words in songs which are socially just not acceptable and I think these just have to go. History is changing, time is moving on. Can you go to a Rangers against Celtic match and sing 'We are up to our knees in Fenian blood' – no. Not any more. Can you sing *The Sash*, absolutely, why not?

I think even at football matches now, a lot of people, a huge portion of a Rangers crowd would quite happily join in, tap along, or whatever, to *The Sash*, but if you hear that bit of the *Billy Boys* they would say, 'oh for fuck's sake guys, come on, give it a rest'. That's social attitudes changing."

There does seem to be a credible argument that the songs are different. *The Sash* is merely triumphalist and celebrates the victory of (Protestant) William of Orange in 1690, over James II, who was trying to reinstate Catholicism in Britain. This is how it goes:

> For it is old and it is beautiful
> And its colours they are fine
> They were worn at Derry, Aughrim,
> Enniskillen and the Boyne
> Sure my father wore it as a youth
> In the bygone days of yore
> And it's on the 12th I love to wear
> The Sash my father wore

It's straightforwardly praising the victory of one side in battle, in exactly the same way as the Scottish national anthem, *The Flower of Scotland* speaks of standing against proud Edward's army and sending them homewards to think again. The *Billy Boys*, on the other hand, and specifically 'that bit', to which Findlay refers is blatantly anti-Catholic:

> Hello, Hello, we are the Billy Boys
> Hello, Hello, you'll know us by our noise
> We are up to our knees in Fenian blood
> Surrender or you'll die
> For we are the Brigton, Derry Boys

Traditionally, Fenians opposed British rule in Ireland, supporting instead the cause of Irish independence. While some Protestants were Fenians, overwhelmingly it referred to Catholics and became an abusive term directed towards them. Certainly in this context the word means Catholic. When I heard it being used at Ibrox, which to be fair wasn't all that often, it was always affixed with 'bastard' and prefixed by 'dirty'. There was also some grumblings about 'tattie-howkers', a reference to the potato famine, which I felt was much more offensive.

Even these remarks show that Rangers are a club which is changing and has, to some extent, already changed. Just a few years ago, terms like the F-word would have been freely used in the stands. Yet this also highlights the continuing differences between the club and its fans. Those in charge have long been convinced of the need to jettison some of the historical baggage, while many of the supporters were not so keen and have only recently modified their ways as a result of unprecedented pressure from various quarters.

A battle is being fought at this moment for the soul of Rangers FC. There's an almost constant drip of stories in the media about songs associated with the support, especially the Billy Boys and others relating to Ireland. Some fans believe these are very much part of their particular identity, and have helped to make the club special, something out of the ordinary. There is little room for debate though, since Rangers seem to be on the point of severe sanction by European football's governing body – UEFA – having twice been fined in as many years. Their woes began during an away tie against the Spanish side Villarreal in March 2006. Then the fans sung discriminatory songs against Catholics and a supporter broke the window of the home team's bus. They were then cleared of giving Nazi salutes during a match in Israel, before fighting erupted during a badly-policed UEFA Cup clash against Osasuna in Pamplona in March 2007. Disorder would be bad enough, but UEFA are now in serious mode regarding issues of race. It emerged that Rangers fans, after the match but while still in the Reyno de Navarro stadium, had again indulged in sectarian singing. The case against them wasn't all that difficult to prove, the evidence was posted all over the internet.

During the post-Souness years, while dominating Celtic and going on their famous run of nine consecutive league titles, Tina

Turner's *Simply the Best* would be blasted out at Ibrox. The song came to define the Rangers of that time as the never-ending champions. The problem was the fans had tailored the anthem to suit. By some strange coincidence, one imagines, the song was also played in Pamplona. While Tina takes a breather after singing the first line of the second verse – 'in your heart I see the star of every night and every day', the Rangers fans, clearly audible, roar:

'Fuck your Pope and your IRA'

Simply the Best no longer gets an airing at Rangers home matches. Good for the club for scrapping it? Well yes, though the cynic might conclude it was only done with the sword of Damocles hanging above their heads, not before. To the fans, they have made it clear, one more offence may result in either the partial or complete closure of Ibrox for European ties. Walter Smith, makes no bones about Rangers predicament: "Something, somewhere has to change. The club are trying everything to get the message across and I think the vast majority of Rangers supporters are taking that on board. I think the club is doing as much as it can do and will continue to do it ... I've said it before and I will say it again. It has to stop.

We have had a reaction from an awful lot of Rangers supporters. But there's still a minority who continue to sing the [offending] songs and that minority are putting the club's current situation in danger and the future of it. I don't think you can exaggerate that. I firmly believe that's what they are doing at the present moment."*

It is little wonder the tone of the statements on this subject are so doom-laden; the forces ranged against Rangers are considerable. While UEFA monitor foreign fields, at home the Scottish Government has been doing the same. In 2005 the then Labour First Minister, Jack McConnell, mounted what the press termed as nothing less than a 'war on bigotry'. Summits were called, involving the clubs, churches and local councils. Legislation was passed to strengthen the hand of the police in dealing with sectarian abuse and violence; the issue became a defining theme of McConnell's time in

* The *Scotsman*, 7 August 2007

office. The intentions were good, and Scotland's leading politician himself made it clear that the problem was one for society at large, not just the Old Firm. Results were harder to come by and not always predictable.

McConnell and his team commissioned a report into sectarianism and racism in Scottish football. This was carried out by the Director of Football Studies at Glasgow University, Professor Bert Moorhouse. It exploded in the faces of ministers at Holyrood. The finding picked up by the press was that Strathclyde Police officers, those who support one or other of the clubs, might actually be contributing to the problem by taunting rival fans and turning a blind eye to the sectarian actions of their own side. The police rejected this, saying the document was no more academic than the average football phone-in. The story only came to light after the report was obtained by a newspaper under the Freedom of Information Act. The media believed the document had been suppressed and delayed. Professor Moorhouse agreed, saying it should have been out months earlier. The Government denied it had in any way tried to suppress the report.

From various conversations, I've discovered that the journalist in question had to repeatedly ask for the document, even though he'd officially requested it under the FOI act. Also, the version which was eventually released contained many passages which had been blanked out by civil servants. I've been told the reason for this was not so much to do with the police, but rather, because fans from other clubs agreed that the 'sectarian' problem was not equally shared between the Old Firm.

The general feeling was that while Celtic had cleaned up their act, as it were, Rangers weren't making any real efforts to reform and really paying no more than lip-service to tackling their problems. Because of this there was more hostility towards Rangers than Celtic. This was not what ministers had been expecting and with an election on the horizon it's not difficult to imagine they might conclude that it was unnecessary to trouble the electorate with such matters. The perception that Labour had taken sides in the Old Firm divide would hardly be likely to play well at the ballot box.

The Scottish Premier League has no such concerns and has issued new regulations to deal with discriminatory chanting, including the possibility of clubs being fined and or having points docked. On the first day of the 2007/08 season Rangers again found their name in the mire for alleged sectarian chanting during the match at Inverness Caledonian Thistle. One English-based fan who was at the match told me the singing had amounted to *"Derry's Wall's, The Sash* and a few UVF numbers, nothing really."

The issue remains a thorn in the club's side, though Rangers themselves can hardly be accused of inactivity, even suggesting they would consider banning their own fans from away grounds until they fall into line. Their logic is sound: campaign for change, get supporters to confront the gravity of the situation and encourage them to self-police. This is related to a series of initiatives stretching back to the mid 1990s – some taken in tandem with Celtic – aimed at eradicating sectarianism. Whatever the club has been accused of in the past, no-one in authority at Rangers is now pretending that burying heads in the sand will suffice.

The latest campaign – *Follow with Pride* – takes over from the much-detested *Pride Over Prejudice*, which many felt was an invitation to the media to again chip away at Rangers. Signs of that campaign were hard to avoid at Ibrox. The slogan was repeatedly stretched across the internal TV screens and accompanied elsewhere by promptings to Show Racism the Red Card.

Admittedly part of the problem, both for Celtic and Rangers has been in defining what is and what is not sectarian. Which songs, which flags, which words and which gestures should and could be banned? It has proved to be something of a minefield for all concerned, so much so that Rangers decided to issue fans with a list of approved songs and lyrics in the form of the Wee Blue Book.

The whole sectarianism question particularly infuriates the Rangers support, who overwhelmingly feel that they alone are the targets of these campaigns. The songs issue, it's said, is symptomatic of a trend which is threatening the archetypal Rangers fan almost out of existence. A broad sweep of supporters, not necessarily confirmed die-hard bigots, would argue that they sing the songs which reflect the historic values of the community at large. The sleeve notes on the back of a Rangers LP released in the early 1970s – *Glory! Glory! Glasgow Rangers!* – are typical of how things used to be: "The songs which are sung on the terraces at Ibrox echo the triumphs of the past and encourage hope in their future. They are the tunes of glory, melodies that ring with romance, lyrics that spell out the glittering parade of their triumphs. They are the songs of the people because Rangers are of the people. These are the songs the people sing."

Well, not any longer; at least in the minds of the lawmakers of Scotland. The Rangers support, especially those of a certain vintage, wonder how a club which once represented the natural order of things has, as they would see it, become so pushed to the margins. They feel that Ibrox is the only place in the country where heritage is a dirty word. None of this has much to do with Celtic, nor with Catholicism, and everything to do with finding a settled modern Rangers identity. Most of the fans desire what might be summed up as a pro-Protestant and generally conservative approach, one which is not in any way anti-Catholic. That, though, is not an easy trick to pull off, since the club was defined for so long not just by what it stood for, but perhaps even more, by what it would have nothing to do with.

ACROSS THE ROAD FROM THE Ibrox underground station, I met Mark Dingwall, the founder of the Rangers fanzine, *Follow Follow*. Dingwall is clearly something of a celebrity among the fans. As we talked, a steady stream of people introduced themselves. He firmly told one young supporter, dressed head-to-foot in red, white and blue, that he had been banned from the fanzine's website: "Am no, no me, honest," came the response as he smiled his way into the pub behind us.

Mark says the controversy surrounding the songs has produced strong feelings among the support. "Rangers have been caught in this campaign for the Disney-fication of football where essentially anything, at any time, can be deemed offensive and because the club has been on the retreat for so long, once the campaign to get rid of the *Billy Boys* started up, the club wasn't prepared to defend itself in any meaningful manner. As if no other club in the world has similar songs. I think among Rangers fans there's a great deal of resentment – you know –'why are we being picked on?' Let's have a look at every other club's songs, let's see if UEFA are going to apply things fairly. So I think a lot of people have rebelled against that because they think, well, why us?"

People indeed, are rebelling. At every approach to the ground the home support was offered a small cardboard leaflet from the

Rangers Supporters Trust, a grassroots organisation run by fans. One side advertised the summer GersPride conference, the other showed a list of demands including that the Rangers Chairman make a statement sanctioning the phrase 'We are the People' and backing the flying of the Union Flag. There was also a picture of that flag and another of the Rangers support beneath. Beside these, in bold black letters were three one-word questions:

Sectarian?
Offensive?
Criminal?

Yes, the flyer went on, according to some prominent sports-writers, 'Journalists with an agenda, demonising the Rangers support with their bigotry, one-sided reporting and lies – and doing this without fear of sanction or penalty from the club. Join the Trust now and help us stop the discriminatory and unfair criticism of our support and club.'

Irritation over the way Rangers are portrayed in the media was a point which came up time and again among the fans I spoke to. There was, they said, a constant connection between the word sectarian and Rangers, something entirely misrepresentative, according to Dingwall. "I have no doubt there are some people in the club who would like to pretend that it just happens to come from Glasgow, and just happens to play in blue. They would like it to be, you know, a large Scottish Macclesfield, and deny its history and its roots because, they really don't fancy the struggle to face up to the caricature that's presented in the media, very often.

I started the fanzine nearly twenty years ago because I didn't recognise myself, my friends, my experience as a Rangers fan in the mainstream media, and I don't think much has changed. If you look at the coverage that there's been over the last couple of years of Rangers and Rangers fans I think people would be absolutely stunned to find that crowds at Ibrox – 50,000 people – there was less than one conviction every two home games for any sort of criminal offence. I think if you went by what is said in the media you would be expecting a cross between a Nuremberg Rally and a lynch mob. So the reality of what it is to be a Rangers fan amongst non football-goers? Well I think they would have a very poor view of Rangers fans that would have no link with reality."

Dingwall also thinks the idea of Scotland as a country riddled with sectarianism has little basis in fact. "In Glasgow there are a huge percentage of mixed marriages, I think throughout Scotland according to the last census 28 per cent of marriages are mixed between religion and races. So, Scottish society is not a sectarian battleground. There may be pockets of discrimination in terms of the education service, in terms of not being able to find a Protestant Lord Provost in Glasgow for thirty years, but essentially Scotland doesn't have a sectarian problem anything like Northern Ireland where people are geographically separated in housing and where people have been murdering one another on a very regular basis. You know, people say Rangers and Celtic are the tip of the sectarian iceberg in Scotland. I think the tip is all there really is."

It's a good point. Glasgow is not a divided city, it only sounds like one in the context of the Old Firm. People are able to go about their lives without the slightest concern for any religious divide. Catholics and Protestant now live and work side by side in what is an overwhelmingly friendly place. Old Firm matches do tend to reaffirm ancient enmities; but may not be the only factor. An education system which places Protestant and Catholic into different schools is also cited as a cause from time to time. This is an argument about assimilation, and one which Catholics in particular have tended to reject on the basis that their schools, just as much as Celtic, have been critical in maintaining their cultural identity. It is certainly the case that Celtic and their fans have a modern sense of themselves which has generally been more palatable than that of their Old Firm counterparts. The club has never really had a problem regarding the religion of players, and the support prides itself on its anti-fascist and anti-racism stance. Yet, here too, questions are being asked about the songs.

Much of this is bound up in the way the various authorities are circling the Rangers wagons. Concerns have been growing among the directors that simply by being the other half of the Old Firm the club may be next to be scrutinised. UEFA has now redefined its rules to outlaw what they describe as any 'extremist ideological propaganda'. This is enough to make Rangers fans foam at the mouth. The reason – Celtic have plenty of songs about the IRA and major republican figures down the years. *The Boys of the Old Brigade*, *Sean South*, and others venerating individuals such as the hunger striker, Bobby Sands, get regular outings away from Celtic Park. Should vocal support for a proscribed organisation, and one as high profile as the IRA, catch Celtic in UEFA's nets? There's no simple answer to the question. The club say they have never remotely been threatened with European sanctions or been told that they are being investigated. On the contrary UEFA and FIFA have given Celtic fans special awards for good conduct.

The difficulty seems to be where to draw the line. Celtic's Chief Executive, Peter Lawwell, wants police and stewards to root out offenders, but knows himself that some songs about Ireland are wrongly being identified as problematic. "A proportion of our fans celebrate those roots and links by singing Irish ballads. In no way could these ballads be described as sectarian, but I think in some quarters it is misinterpreted as sectarian. It's not sectarian behaviour. There is a difference there. We are a proud Scottish club, but with strong Irish connections. It's a fact and we don't want to hide it."*

The ballads Lawwell is talking about are those such as *The Fields of Athenry*, which is primarily a love song set against the background of famine. It speaks of a couple having dreams and songs to sing, as well as stealing corn, so the young might see the morn. It's clearly not a song about the activities of an armed group, though at times Celtic fans also discolour it with additional lyrics about Sinn Fein and the IRA; the work of a few according to Lawwell. "There is, however, a very small proportion of our away support who offensively chant songs that are contrary to what the club stands for. It embarrasses the club, it is unacceptable and we have a very firm plan to stamp it out."** These plans have already sparked a section of the support into campaigning against what they believe to be an assault on their history and identity.

SINCE THE REBUILDING OF Celtic Park was completed towards the end of the 1990s, pride in the new stadium has slowly been replaced by wistful talk of the old days, the constant singing

* The *Scotsman*, 26 October 2006
** The *Scotsman*, 26 October 2006

and a deserved reputation as a football ground of no little character. The more committed sections of the support got together in 2005 naming themselves the Jungle Bhoys. One of their members, Suzanne Walker, is convinced it was a necessary step. "The JBs were formed as a non-political group to help spark colour and a better atmosphere at Celtic Park. Since the Jungle [terracing opposite the main stand] was pulled down, the atmosphere has died rather and we try to help change that by beginning songs and doing displays and so on."

They have been successful, but some of their members felt the group was a little too close to the club and wished to take the fans in a different direction. In time they split, to form the Green Brigade – Celtic's ultras. The two factions no longer see eye-to-eye, both vying to shape the support. The Green Brigade freely admit they are ultras, though perhaps a little different in their aims to the hooligan groups associated with the term around Europe. They are certainly left-wing; advocating the establishment of a Scottish socialist republic and a united Ireland along the same lines. They say they are against violence and any form of prejudice while giving a voice to supporters who disagree with what they feel is the 'anti-Republican stance' taken by the club. As a consequence they are determined to keep singing songs long associated with Celtic because, 'political expression is not a crime'.*

The group also believe a corporate agenda is taking over, while at the same time aspects of the club's past are being airbrushed away. These frustrations have started to come out in the stands, with banners like: 'If being Irish means we're guilty then we're guilty one and all'. There's also a demand in song, to *Let the People Sing*, a phrase which would be understood by many of the faithful over at Ibrox.

Let the people sing their stories and their songs
And the music of their native land
Their lullabies and battle cries and songs of hope and joy
So join us hand in hand
All across this ancient land

* *Tal fanzine*, Issue 41

Throughout the test of time
It was music that kept their spirits free
Those songs of yours and mine

The Green Brigade and like-minded individuals are now coming into regular conflict with Celtic. Fans singing *The Soldiers Song* have been ejected for sectarian singing and others have been removed at away games over similar incidents. There have also been rows about the flying of Irish flags. These fans want the club to engage in debate over the issue. No dice. The Celtic chairman, Brian Quinn told the club's AGM of 2006 that "wherever you draw the guidelines you will find opinion split. It's a task which is very difficult to address. I think people know which songs are offensive."*

I also attended an Old Firm match at Celtic's ground that year. There were large Irish flags both inside and outside the stadium; others carried the colours of the Basque Country and the Palestinian territories. One supported the anti-fascist German club from Hamburg, St Pauli, and several more were dedicated to former players. These were choreographed to ripple across the fans and others flapped on large poles; it all looked very stylistic, almost European in feel. Supporters next to me banged an Irish bodhran drum and constantly sang *Oh the Rangers are Shite, The Soldiers Song* and *This Land is Our Land.*

There are others who feel Celtic's association with radical politics is misguided. The former Chelsea, Everton and Scotland winger, Pat Nevin, grew up as a Celtic supporter, often standing in the Jungle to watch his team. Nevin is known to have been active in the anti-Apartheid movement and the Labour Party. He's now turned his back on Celtic. The reason: "Bigotry has driven me away. I cannot reconcile that."

In an interview in 2002 he was asked if he felt Rangers had more of a problem with sectarianism than Celtic. "No," he said. "I think they both have the same problem. The vast majority of other fans in

---

* The *Scotsman*, 26 October 2006

Scotland, and beyond Scotland and Ireland look at the situation with the Old Firm and say 'get on with the football!'"*

Suzanne Walker agrees. "The Green Brigade wants republicanism and the football to be linked, but we felt that wasn't the way things should go because times have changed and I think that heavy politics stuff can put a lot of non-Republicans off supporting the club."

Perhaps the beliefs of the Green Brigade and those like them are really only representative of a tiny minority at Celtic. Alternatively they may be on the road to galvanising a larger number of their fellow supporters who agree that the Irish part of their identity cannot be allowed to wither on the vine. If so, the club has got a fight on its hands. It could yet prove to be a bumpy ride. Not that travelling with the Old Firm and attending their matches has ever been anything other than a bone-shaking experience. The games themselves have always proved to be occasions to rouse the passions, and then some. The matches I attended were relatively peaceful, yet still made front-page headlines.

At Celtic Park Neil Lennon got involved in a shouting match with a supporter as he left the field. Lennon hurled a water bottle, full-force, into the Rangers dug-out. It was empty at the time (the technical area, not the bottle). This detail didn't matter to *The Daily Record* which screeched: 'Lenny Loses It!'**

Then at Ibrox, as Lennon left the Rangers pitch for the final time in his career, the Celtic 'keeper Artur Boruc plucked a green Champions flag from the Celtic support behind him, dashing away up the pitch, swishing it behind the head of the Rangers captain, Barry Ferguson. The flag was offered to Lennon, who declined, knowing full well that the mere sight it in his hands was likely to start a riot.

Boruc should really have known better, despite his Polish background. In 2006 the player was formally cautioned by Scottish prosecutors for making the sign of the cross in front of the Rangers fans. The news sparked a debate which touched most quarters of public life: churches, police, press, even senior ministers at

---

* Pat Nevin, in *The Alternative View*, 12 November 2002
** *Daily Record*, 12 March 2007

Holyrood and Westminster. Amid the furore, it hadn't been noticed that Boruc had got himself into trouble for making more hand gestures towards the away support than any priest would approve of.

These were relatively minor examples of the kind of incidents which have long defined the rivalry. In 1999 more than a hundred people were arrested after Rangers won the league at Celtic Park. It was as shameful a backdrop to a match in Scotland as had been seen in many a long year. The most striking image of that afternoon was of the referee, Hugh Dallas, on one knee, blood streaming from a wound in his forehead caused by one of many coins thrown in his direction. One fan threw himself from the upper tier of a stand in an effort to get his hands on the official who also had the windows of his home smashed that night. At the final whistle, celebrating Rangers players were next to be pelted with projectiles for mimicking Celtic's huddle, while outside the ground one man was stabbed. To all of that add three red cards and you have an occasion memorable for all the wrong reasons.

This pales into insignificance compared to the Scottish Cup Final of 1980. After Celtic's 1-0 win a full-scale riot took place inside Hampden. Hundreds of fans, many throwing bottles, fought running battles across the turf of the national stadium while mounted police charged their flanks. The whole episode was broadcast live on television. The clashes, which were also going on outside the ground, ended with 100 people injured, including four police officers. Fifty people were treated in hospital, some having been seriously hurt, and over 200 were arrested. The clubs were each fined £20,000 and the Scottish Criminal Justice Act was promptly passed, banning alcohol inside grounds.

1980 became a watershed for the rivalry and for the whole of Scottish football. Yet still fans around the world talk in awe of the Old Firm, of how they would love to go to a match to experience the 'special atmosphere'. They don't do so because of the quality of play, but for the intense hatred bound up in the fixture. It's akin to a safari holiday, or taking part in extreme mountain sports, there is an enticing danger attached to the experience. Some hope that in the future fans at Old Firm matches will simply be watching two of the best teams around, stripped of their ancient tribal affiliations. The focus, it is said, would then be solely on two great sporting icons.

Perhaps there's much to be gained from such a scenario, but also a great deal to be lost, not all of it bad, and certainly much of it quite unique. The fans sense this is the way the wind is blowing, they just don't want to be in its path quite yet.

THE CELTIC SUPPORT DRIFTED away together, still singing, their flags twirling in the breeze. The Rangers fans I stood with just watched, smiling in silence; all but one, who shouted a promise that there would be some heads 'kicked-in' later. There followed a great deal of hand-shaking, mine included, before saying goodbye. They were so happy they'd forgotten to take one of their own flags with them – a fifty foot Union Jack which had been passed over our heads at half-time. It was now dumped on the back of my seat, crumpled, dusty and lifeless. I pointed it out to the police and headed for the underground – the Clockwork Orange (the name is nothing to do with the sympathies of the Rangers support – it is painted orange and runs around the city in a circular fashion).

No-one can hear you underground and boy didn't the Rangers fans know it. There, shuttling back towards the centre of Glasgow, in cramped compartments, they thumped the metal frames of the train and sang all the old songs, heartily, the way they always had. They may well be songs of hate, but they didn't really feel like it, at that moment they were songs of celebration too, regardless of the words. On buses elsewhere in another part of Glasgow men and women in green and white would have been doing much the same.

EDINBURGH:
The Dancers And The Harp

"I don't think he realised the intensity between the
Hearts and Hibs fans, the rivalry and for want of
a better word, the hatred."

Mickey Weir, *That Was the Team that Was*,
BBC Scotland 2nd February 2007

"LEGALLY VICTIMIZE THEM, the known troublemakers. I
want you to get in their faces." Superintendent Keith Chamberlain
of Lothian and Borders Police was in no mood for trouble with the
opening match of the season – Hearts against Hibs – only two
hours away. He was speaking to more than a dozen of his most
senior officers, gathered in the control room at Hearts' Tynecastle
Stadium.

I had been given access to the police operation for the derby, in
order to discover what it takes to manage a match between the two
great teams of the Scottish capital. The answer was constant prepa-
ration and vigilance. Not to put too fine a point on it, there is a
strain of hostility here which has been known to get seriously out
of hand.

Chamberlain, the match commander, is a strong looking man in
his forties with salt and pepper hair. He knows only too well the
possible pitfalls of this fixture. As a young constable he had been
beaten unconscious in the old shed opposite the main stand as he
made his way down through that black hole of a terracing. His
advice to his officers – there is "a well-documented and historic
rivalry between the sides" – which he urged them not to forget.
Intelligence suggested the Hibs boys were meeting in this bar,
Hearts in another. The information was good, he said, he knew the
source himself. "The guys have all been in the pubs". These were

undercover officers and moles. Forward Intelligence Teams were also being sent out to harass those believed to be most likely to cause trouble; they would be constantly filmed and photographed.

Even though there were no leads about plans for serious disorder, it was understandable that contingencies had been made, just in case. Groups of casuals have long been attached to both clubs and caused major problems throughout the 1980s. Hibs' Capital City Service and the Casual Soccer Firm, attached to Hearts, have never really gone away and have been undergoing something of a resurgence. In 2002 police used dogs and CS spray to subdue rival gangs after a derby at Easter Road. The same year, a group of Hearts supporters were attacked and seriously assaulted by casuals as they left their bus minutes before the start of a derby. Lothian and Borders police have now set up a special task force to hunt down the leaders of these gangs. There have been early morning raids across the city and frequent arrests. The new unit seems to have come into being after scores of hooligans fought running battles at the end of a drawn match at Easter Road in October 2006.

Back in the control room there was a discussion about the availability of the magical sounding creature, the Iron Horse (which turned out be a large portable fence used to screen fans from each other) and the rather more mundane Section 60, a document which would be signed if officers required further stop and search powers. The final message to the troops was "stay alive, be alert, switch-on." No-one demurred.

Shortly afterwards Chamberlain was dealing with his first problem of the night. The Hibs team bus had broken down en route to the ground. Thankfully it was in a relatively tame area of the city. Immediately, though, motorcycle outriders were sent to escort the players and the replacement bus to Tynecastle. The order was given to get them there as soon as possible. If the Superintendent was determined to keep things on course, it was understandable. For the first time, the number of officers at the derby had been cut. The idea was simple, stewards working for Hearts would be responsible in the first instance for controlling supporters – police would only act if disorder occurred. It was a risk, calculated of course, but one which would literally pay-off if it worked. Fewer cops would cost Hearts less money, while freeing them up for duties elsewhere.

The question of resources was topical. The match was taking place 24 hours after the start of the 2007 Edinburgh Festival and should have been played two days earlier. It had been put back to Monday 6th August because of the need for high numbers of officers at the annual cavalcade, the traditional opening of the three week event. Edinburgh was awash with acts of every description. It was difficult to avoid performers in luminous costumes who were leaping around on street corners, to say nothing of the endless flamethrowers, jugglers and musicians.

With half an hour to go before kick-off I wondered if the punters had chosen the Festival over the football. I needn't have worried. Within minutes, the stadium had filled up. The automated counter in the corner of the control room steadied at 16,436. Chamberlain was using binoculars to look through the triple-glazed windows, scrutinising the Hibernian support and sometimes the faces of the Hearts fans closer to hand. Above us, half a dozen of his officers monitored CCTV screens and fed information across various radio frequencies.

As Hearts kicked-off their fans sang: 'Oh when the Hearts go marching in'. A single touch from each from the strikers took the ball back to Michael Stewart, who immediately tried to lob the keeper, without success. It would have been an outlandish opening – the Hibs goalie was making his debut, while Stewart had very much been the focus of attention having returned to Hearts from Hibernian during the summer for a second spell at the club.

Within seconds, Hibs were racing up their left wing, flashing a cross in towards the six-yard box. There, another debutant, Michael Kerr, stooped, poked out his head and nodded the ball into the net before picking himself up and running away, punching the air in front of the Hearts fans who were blasted by the noise from the opposite end. The Hibs contingent went into overdrive with supporters clawing at each other in celebration, a moving jigsaw of humanity propelled by a single emotion. Two minutes showed on the clock.

As predicted, trouble erupted. Some Hibs fans, delighted by the early goal and continuing their unbridled celebrations, were able to make it through a gate at the side of the pitch, dancing in front of the home supporters. In the other corner they ran through the 'sterile' area – a section of the Roseburn Stand which was empty because of a partial boycott by Hibs, angry at having to pay £33 apiece for a ticket. It was meant to be a buffer zone, but at that moment opposing fans were just feet from each other.

Chamberlain didn't like what he was seeing one little bit. There was to be no repeat. The stewards, he said, must do better and the area had to be taped off. But as the play restarted, Hibs fans continued their cavorting on the stairways. "There's people bouncing about in the aisles and basically just taking the piss," he muttered darkly. His men were sent in to help the stewards move fans back into their seats." The next time it happens the culprits are to be removed from the stadium," Chamberlain decreed. No sooner had he issued the warning then there was another outbreak. "That guy in the yellow jumper" he shouted, "he's just ejected himself."

The play became a scrap for control of the midfield with Hibs looking the more skilful. The away end was bouncing again by half-time. As the whistle went Hearts were booed from the field. The season was 45 minutes old.

During the second-half I stood inches from the corner flag, in the company of two policemen and a steward, who paced languidly up and down the touchline. Outside the control room, in the late summer air, the noise of the fans was that much greater, its initial impact seeming to slap the face. Tynecastle is that kind of ground, the stands hang over the players. It's all very compact, it feels as though there's hardly room to sweat.

Slowly Hearts began to edge into things. Their fans sang: 'This is my story, this is my song, follow the Hearts and you can't go wrong'…

… and then…..'JAM TARTS, JAM TARTS'….

With twenty minutes left, a Hibs player was brought down on the edge of the box. Around me supporters stood up, veins straining in fury. The same thing happened again two minutes later and someone shouted: "Fuck Off, Hearts. This is fucking dreadful." In turn the Hibs fans began celebrating, sensing that the win was close. Mainly they seemed to be men in their teens through to early thirties, with more families represented among the home contingent.

Hearts continued to pour forward, forcing McCann of Hibs to clear the ball, arcing it through the cloudless night onto the roof of the main stand. It all became too much for one shaven-headed fan who threw his scarf onto the pitch before turning to walk out in disgust. He was then barracked for his actions, raising two fingers to his critics as he left. Oblivious to the row the steward next to me dashed onto the pitch to retrieve the scarf while the play was at the other end.

'Oh To, Oh To Be, Oh To Be a – Hi-Bee.'

The Hearts fans were desperate now: "Fucking get fighting you bunch of ..." That wish was granted immediately. The ball went out of play feet away with two players scrabbling around on the ground trying to get their hands on it. Hearts won the wrestle and before the referee had time to say otherwise the play was on the move again. Hearts went on to do everything but score; they had corners, won free-kicks, took long-range shots and even got through, one-on-one with the keeper, only to be flagged offside. Until this time the Hibs manager, John Collins, has been standing motionless next to the dug out in a dark suit, hands in his pockets, absolutely the picture of relaxation. Now even he had become consumed by anxiety, fidgeting away on the touchline.

Another Hearts scarf floated down to the pitch just before the final-whistle. When the end came, moments later, they were booed for the second time, louder and longer, while Hibs celebrated as though the league itself had been won. Many were naked from the waist up, swinging their green and white tops above their heads.

'Easy, Easy, Easy…'
'And now you're gonna believe us, we're going to win the league.'

THE FEELING AMONG THE police was mainly one of contentment. There had only been a handful of arrests, a quiet derby by the standards of these things. As I headed off into the night, they were preparing for the second part of their operation, dealing with the fall-out from the match. Around the corner from the ground, next to Robertson's Bar, I discovered a man in his twenties smashing his fists repeatedly against a metal shop-front. It was noisy and must have been hellishly sore. He then held his head in his hands and shouted ... 'Bastards!' A couple of Hibs fans at the nearby bus stop shrank back, sensing a possible confrontation. A moment later the police were on the scene, checking for bleeding and leading the seemingly berserk Hearts supporter away while his friend continued to play chicken with the cars on Gorgie Road.

Everything I had seen and heard showed this derby has plenty of fire, even when it is the first match of the season, played on a Monday night at the end of summer. This is nothing new, but animosity between the fans seems to have grown over the last quarter century. There are various reasons for this, such as the introduction of segregation which stopped families and friends standing together no matter who they followed. But one episode in particular has cast a long shadow over the fixture. It was a poisonous affair which took place in the summer of 1990. What happened then raised the prospect of ultimate defeat for one side over the other.

It began amid a chaotic press conference on the 4th of June. The man with the plan – Hearts chairman Wallace Mercer – was shouting at his advisers as he arrived, pushing through the pack of TV cameras and photographers, "get them out."[*] Mercer, a property tycoon and an abrasive figure at the best of times, had expected his briefing at a top hotel to be for selected journalists only. Fat chance, the whole of the Scottish press corps had descended. His anxiety, while understandable, was perhaps also an indication that he had underestimated the public reaction to the story. The idea was as simple as it was outrageous. Mercer was buying Hibs in order to merge them with his own club and create a single Edinburgh team to take on the Old Firm. It was described as a once in a lifetime opportunity to release Scottish football from Glasgow's grip.

If the official bid, costing a total of £13 million, succeeded Hibs would be out of business, without either a stadium or a squad. What was presented as a merger was actually a takeover. Mercer remained sanguine, saying he saw "no reason why there should not be one major club in Edinburgh. We live in an ever-changing world. It should not come as a shock to put together teams who have been competitors for 100 years."[**]

[*] Wallace Mercer, *The Scotsman*, 5 June 1990
[**] Wallace Mercer, *The Scotsman*, 7 June 1990

The news led the BBC's national TV bulletin. Moira Stewart informed the watching millions that Hearts planned to "wipe Hibs from the footballing map."* Down at Easter Road hundreds of fans had gathered, some in tears, demanding an explanation and wondering how such a thing could have happened. The answer was easy, Hibs had been sleepwalking towards oblivion.

Three years before Mercer made his move, the club had been bought by David Duff (a lawyer with business interests in the leisure industry) for a sum of just short of £900,000. Duff, the chairman at the time of the Hearts bid, had borrowed the bulk of the money needed to finance the package. He struck a deal with an English businessman, David Rowland, who would receive almost 30 per cent of Hibs shares for his backing. A year later, in 1988, Hibs floated on the stock-market. They were just one of three British clubs to do this at the time, the others being Millwall and Spurs. Fans rushed to buy a slice of what was being touted as their 'new tomorrow.' In fact it was this sale which opened the gate for the Hearts chairman, who was all too aware that the club across the city had run up debts of around £6 million. Hibs were being dragged down by the failure of much of Rowland's business empire in which they were entangled and Mercer struck an irrevocable agreement to buy the entirety of the Hibs stock held by Rowland. Although the board at Easter Road rejected the approach for their club, Mercer was now in a position to go for the jugular.

Without doubt Hibs' financial problems had given him the opportunity, but I suspect he was provoked by something which had happened closer to home. He'd learned, through bitter experience, how difficult it was to overcome the Old Firm and truly believed the chances of doing so would be vastly improved if Hearts, or whatever the new club might be called, were the only senior side in Edinburgh. On the final day of the 1986 season Hearts had needed only a draw away against Dundee to win the league title, their first Championship in two and half decades. But they went down to two late goals, while Celtic were beating St Mirren 5-0, giving them the trophy on goal difference instead. The

* *BBC Scotland*, 2 February 2007

following week Hearts lost the Scottish Cup final 3-0 to Alex Ferguson's Aberdeen and the team which had played magnificently throughout that season was, quite cruelly, left with nothing. Mercer may well have vowed then never to let such a thing happen again, no matter the cost or the scale of the changes needed to ensure this.

The Hibs fans were far from willing to be swept aside, immediately springing into action; determined not to let their club fall into the clutches of the man they called 'Wallet Mercenary'. The Hands Off Hibs campaign became the focal point, and while Edinburgh should have been following the, admittedly dismal, performances of the national team at the Italia 90 World Cup, rallies were held, stickers and posters printed and T-shirts made. They ended up in every corner of Scotland.

Though the Hibs fans had the support of their counterparts at almost every club in the land, it must also be stressed that many Hearts supporters also helped – fearing the loss of their own name and the possible sale of their ground in favour of a green-field development. Mercer, albeit with the complicity of the board, was as good as isolated, unable even to rely upon his own star employees. The Hearts striker, John Robertson, appeared to great cheers at a large Hands Off Hibs demo. Robertson had grown up as a Hibernian fan, but became one of the quintessential goal-getters in Hearts' history, known as the Hammer of Hibs, due to the frequency of his derby strikes. At the time he admitted the Hearts squad were keen to see their rivals survive. "We can only lend our support. We want the derby matches to continue. We are not in contradiction with our chairman. He has a view about the future of Edinburgh football and he respects ours."*

In the end, Mercer, who'd had his life threatened and his property vandalised, saw his bid fall at least ten per cent short of the required number of shares. It was withdrawn in early July, the battle was over, the people had won; Hibs were free. There was more to it, of course. Heavyweight figures like the former chairman, Kenny Waugh and the Kwik-Fit entrepreneur, Sir Tom Farmer, had helped considerably. The latter then went on to re-shape the club, overhauling its long-term finances.

---

* John Robertson, in *The Scotsman*, 7 June 1990

The news sent fans out onto the streets of Leith in celebration. It was pure emotion and triggered a new relationship with the local community, which had been flagging in recent years. Only when it appeared that they were going to the wall had people fully appreciated the importance of Hibernian in their everyday lives, especially in that part of the city.

Hearts won the first derby of the following season 3-0 at Easter Road. During the game banners appeared in the home crowd celebrating the defeat of the Hearts chairman, who was wise enough not to attend. It was a tense occasion and predictions of trouble were well founded. Furious Hibs fans attacked the Hearts players as they celebrated their opening goal. It was all the police could do to stop a riot. John Robertson didn't help this time, scoring twice.

We will probably never know exactly why Wallace Mercer chose to try to create an Edinburgh super-club. Some believe his vanity got the better of him, others feel he was a visionary obstructed by Luddites and still more say the whole thing was just another business deal for a man who could fathom only the balance sheet, never emotion. When he died, in 2006 aged 59, he was still the great bogeyman of capital-city football. The Hibs fans never forgot or forgave, even in death. Just days after he'd passed away, Hearts paid tribute with a minute of applause at Tynecastle. There had been little chance of getting through a traditional silence without disruption – Hibs being the opponents – before, during and after the match they sang: 'Tell all the Hearts you know, Wallace Mercer is dead and we're no'. They turned their backs during the applause, while the manager, Tony Mowbray, was later forced to deny his players had slighted Mercer's memory by standing with arms linked together rather than joining the clapping.

SIXTEEN YEARS AFTER THE collapse of his takeover plan, it remained a deeply divisive issue. Had Mercer succeeded, the second oldest derby in British football would have been killed stone-dead after 112 years of almost constant competition, a rivalry which had seen the clubs emerge from the same back streets to win the greatest prizes in the Scottish game.

Edinburgh's Old Town in the early 1870s was well named. It had become a crude squash of tenements and alleyways. Here, between the castle and royal palace of Holyrood, but a million miles from both, Hearts were born in 1873, though the accepted date of their formation is a year later. The team which came out of the South Back of the Canongate took their name from what had been one of the city's most infamous landmarks, the Heart of Midlothian. This was how the old tollbooth at the top of the High Street, next to St Giles Cathedral, was known. It had been the meeting place for the Scottish Parliament, the High Court and the local council. It also had a sinister reputation, acquired from its other function as the town's jail and site of several hangings. It was demolished in 1817, but immortalised by Sir Walter Scott in his novel of the same title. Today it is considered good luck to spit on the heart-shaped crest which marks the spot where the building once stood.

The men who formed Hearts spent much of their free time at nearby refreshment rooms, which housed the original Hearts – the Heart of Midlothian Dancing Society. The title may have sounded fairly grand, but really these were a just a group of working-class friends fortunate enough to have a local base for their social gatherings. While careering around to music with young ladies in the evenings had its appeal, the Hearts boys, like so many other young men of the time, had also become fascinated by Association football and extended their activities into that arena. Soon they would forever leave their dancing days behind.

Two years after their formation Hearts had joined the Scottish Football Association and helped to set-up its Edinburgh equivalent. Already their identity was being formed, officially registering their colours as 'marone' or maroon. By 1878, they had bagged their first trophy, the Edinburgh Cup. In the final, which took five matches to reach a conclusion, they overcame a new and altogether unwelcome footballing force.

St Mary's Street in the Cowgate is less than a quarter of a mile from the spot where Hearts had first seen the light of day. It was the home of the Catholic Young Men's Society, with links to the nearby St Patrick's church. Here, in Little Ireland, as the area was known, more than 25,000 Irish immigrants were living in pretty dire conditions by the middle of the 19th century. Their team, of course, was Hibernian. The title was no accident. It came from Hibernia, the old Roman name for Ireland. Hibs intended being exactly that, a team for the Irish; exclusively so at the beginning. The CYMS was, by its very nature, an all-Catholic organisation. Hibs was the first club in Scotland to be identifiably Irish and Catholic, visibly wrapping itself in motifs which celebrated these roots. The harp, the ancient symbol of Ireland, was taken as the crest, and may even have appeared on the team's earliest strips. The motto, Erin Go Bragh, was adopted. It translates as Ireland For Ever.

The men of Hibernian were keen to play; but others weren't keen to play them. Frankly, their ethnicity was a problem. Just as in Glasgow, the Irish were not the most popular minority. Both the national and local FA's objected to their membership on the grounds that Hibs were not Scottish enough, in fact not Scottish at all, but Irish. At first the football authorities in Edinburgh decreed that none of their members should have anything to do with Hibernian, who were having trouble even finding opponents for friendly matches. However, there was one club which had the courage to take them on.

Heart of Midlothian played their neighbours for the first time on Christmas Day 1875, winning 1-0. In this act of sporting solidarity Hearts could hardly have known they'd been the hand-maidens to an enduring and tempestuous relationship. Yet, for two years, the clubs were on good terms, attitudes only hardened when they were thrown together in successive cup ties. These showed that Hearts' pre-eminence was under threat from the very team they had brought in from the cold.

In 1877, the first time Hibs were allowed to take part in the Scottish Cup, they were drawn to play Hearts and beat them in a replay. There was fighting in the stands as the Hibs players and supporters celebrated. The following year they contested what became an epic final of the Edinburgh Cup. In a series of matches lasting from early February to the end of April, there were fights, protests and, when Hearts eventually won the trophy, their captain was chased through the streets by an angry mob. Relations would never really improve; certainly that early camaraderie was dead and buried. Hibs won the Edinburgh Cup in 1879, beating Hearts in the final. They took it again the next season. Then, with Hibs on their way to a third local cup success on the trot Hearts tried, and only just failed, to have them expelled from the Edinburgh FA, claiming their fans were badly behaved and the team too physical. After this, things settled down and both sides went on to prosper, though never to the extent of the Old Firm. Between them they had taken fewer than twenty major trophies by the start of the 1960s. Despite being the capital city of Scotland, Edinburgh's disadvantage lay in being half the size of Glasgow. It was also a city where football had serious competition from rugby union, firmly the game of the middle-classes and those who aspired to join them. Here, as in most other places, football was the preserve of the working-class. It's fair to say both clubs, in general, drew their support from that strata of society. Hibs came to be seen as the Leith team, part of north-eastern Edinburgh which sweeps down to the Firth of Forth and the docks from the city centre. It was once an independent settlement and has always retained something of a sense of apartness. Hearts were firmly anchored in Gorgie, a district in the west of the city which has traditionally been both industrial and residential.

The mistake which is often made by fans of other clubs, and especially those outside Scotland, is in believing these teams to be nothing more than the Old Firm in miniature. Their identities do overlap with those of Celtic and Rangers, but not to any great extent. Of the two perhaps Hibernian have most cause to anger at being dubbed the 'little Celtic', not only because of their own Irish roots and the fact they pre-date the Glasgow side. In a sense this is true, since the early successes of the Irish team from eastern Scotland gave their fellow immigrants in Glasgow the inspiration to set up their own club.

After Hibernian's Scottish Cup victory of 1887, a celebration was held for them in the east end of Glasgow. Before returning to Edinburgh one senior official urged those at the gathering "to go and do likewise" in their own city. Celtic took that advice a little more literally than had been intended. Having built their ground from scratch they went out and actively sought the best players to grace it, knowing full well where to find them. By the time Hibs returned the following season, five of their players were in Celtic colours and more were on the way. The result of this raid was a serious dip in Hibs' fortunes and attendances. Three years later the club, which had been one of the best known and most popular in Britain, went bust. Even now something of a bad feeling remains about all of this among the support at Easter Road.

Hibs re-emerged a year later, but with a changed outlook. In order to guarantee survival they would no longer restrict themselves to playing only Catholics, effectively binning their sectarian policy. The club now makes the entirely spurious claim that on being formed they 'immediately became fully integrated into the Edinburgh community'.* It's much more realistic to say that, over time, Hibs sought to disassociate themselves with their Irish Catholic past.

Even after their resurrection following the formation of Celtic, it was clear the anti-Irish or anti-Catholic sentiment of the day would continue to dog them. Hibs complained to a local newspaper about what they saw as constantly unfavourable coverage. Then, when they won the Second Division, at least two clubs successfully lobbied against their promotion. In the early part of the 20th century, while in the throes of erecting a new stadium, a court order was obtained by the British Railway Company claiming some of the land was needed for a rail link. Hibs were forced to abandon the project; the extension to the railway was never built. Easter Road was improved substantially in the mid-1920s, but with dire timing. Heavily in debt from the renovations, Hibs soon faced the prospect of bankruptcy caused by worsening economic depression. Their investors, fearing the worst, campaigned for a greater say. This was granted at the beginning of the following decade, loosening the control a small number of Irish families had always had over the club. This ushered in the era of one of the most contentious figures in Hibs' history, Harry Swan. The first non-Catholic to join the board, he became chairman shortly after, a position he would not relinquish for almost thirty years. During that time he would oversee a number of measures which brought him into direct conflict with the more traditional sections of the support. The least problematic of these was a change to the Hibernian strip in the late 1930s when white sleeves were added in Arsenal-esque fashion to the green jersey. This was quickly accepted, something which would not have happened with the all-red strip which was said to have been mooted in the late '40s. Hibs, I am told, went as far as to construct a mock-up of this.

* Official Hibernian website

Changing their historic colours would have been unpalatable enough for the fans, but there were also suggestions around this time that Hibs were toying with the idea of a new name. Such a radical step is not entirely without precedent for a club of their background. Dundee Hibernian had morphed into Dundee United in the 1920s. What Swan certainly did was end the practice of clergymen being allowed free into matches. His critics alleged these reforms, when taken as a whole, showed an anti-Catholic bias. The complaints increased in volume when, in 1952, as President of the SFA, he was central to an unsuccessful demand that Celtic remove the Irish tri-colour from their ground. Swan will also be remembered for the controversial changes which took place in 1955. Work had been carried out to improve the general look of Easter Road. When this was finished, the mural showing a harp, at the main entrance had gone, never to be replaced. Some have suggested it was painted over, but in fact the wall it appeared on was demolished to make room inside the ground. Regardless, the disappearance of the symbol which had been associated with the club from the outset was particularly unpopular. Those close to the Hibs chairman consistently and strongly maintained he was no bigot, but merely a man of progress intent on modernisation. Swan had famously said "give me ten years and I will make Hibs great."* If aspects of their Irish connections were dismantled along the way and the team's appeal widened then so be it, there were plenty of good reasons for doing so. Both before and after the Second World War there were large-scale violent protests against Catholicism in Edinburgh. It was in this climate that Swan was acting.

The politician and broadcaster, Lloyd Quinnan, has been a Hibs fan since boyhood. An SNP member of the first Scottish Parliament, he still lives in Leith, the area in which he grew up. Over a cup of coffee at a local pavement café he explained the social significance of his team's Irish connections. "There always was a sense that the history of the club went back to the Catholic men's society at St Patrick's, but in reality it was something before that as

---

* *Hibernian, The Complete Story,* John R Mackay

well. But I think, when John Cormack and the Protestant Action party was formed, its most powerful base, in reality, was in Edinburgh and not in Glasgow. The biggest anti-Catholic riot of the 20th century was here in Edinburgh."

Cormack, who was a highly visible and energetic city councillor for twenty years, could often be seen campaigning behind the slogan 'No Popery'. He was an anti-Catholic extremist in word and deed, having been radicalised by his time serving with the British army during the Irish War of Independence. After his expulsion from the Edinburgh Protestant Society on the grounds that he'd made physical threats against Catholics he founded Protestant Action. At its height the party had a membership of around four thousand. This was in 1935 when there were vicious clashes in the city. The first was in June of that year when police fought demonstrators furious that the Prime Minister of Australia, a Catholic, was being given the freedom of the city.

The violence and scale of the protests were far greater a month later during Scotland's first ever Catholic Congress, which was being held in the Morningside district, more famed for ladies taking tea in fur coats. Buses carrying women and children were stoned as they made their way through a baying mob numbering into the thousands. In the end police, fearing serious sectarian violence, carried out a full-scale baton charge.

"I know that a lot of people from a Catholic, Irish background changed their names", Quinnan admits. "There was a desire to not let this explode. There has been a lot of mythology about Harry Swan; that Swan was a Freemason, which apparently is not true, that he was anti-Catholic and he tried desperately to move the club away from all that. But no management, as we know from Rangers and Celtic, can make that change, it's more organic. I have realised from speaking to older folk, people wanted to tone that Irish, that Catholic thing down, because they didn't want the football to get caught up in what was happening on a political level."

Concentrating on the game was a wise move since these were golden days for Hibs. From the late forties to the middle of the next decade they had a successful side spearheaded by the Famous Five of Smith, Johnstone, Reilly, Turnbull and Ormond. Also, whatever people thought of Swan, he proved to be remarkably perceptive, strongly advocating European competition and beginning his club's long association with that arena.

The harp did eventually return, being incorporated into a new crest in 2000 alongside a depiction of Edinburgh castle and a ship, representing Leith. For the first time the name of the city was also used with the words – Hibernian Edinburgh – encircling the crest. There may also have been a hint of compromise in this; the harp is actually dominated by local and more identifiably Scottish symbols. Harry Swan would not have objected.

Hearts fans, on the other hand, complained that the new badge was nothing more than a gimmick, designed to exploit the fact that their title referred not to the city itself but to Midlothian. If they were being thin-skinned perhaps it was understandable.

Since the Baltic banker, Vladimir Romonov, took charge in 2005, there have been constant taunts that Hearts are now nothing more than an outpost of Lithuanian football. Their squad has been flooded with imports from that country to the extent that Scottish players have sometimes seemed to be in a minority. Unsettling times for many at a club which is highly traditional and has a strongly developed sense of its history and place in the game.

David Speed is the official Hearts historian. His own links to the team go back to the club's earliest days. David, who was carried into the ground as a child, told me this was not unusual. "There is a big family tradition at Tynecastle. Hearts supporters regard it as 'Edinburgh's club', 'Edina's darlings'. I notice that Hibs have put Edinburgh on their badge because they struggle for identity, as far as I am concerned, as an Edinburgh club. We consider ourselves to be the city's club. When they put Edinburgh on their badge, I thought, 'well, that's a wee bit petty.' I'll come right to the point here, we consider ourselves the superior club and it's supported by the fact that we have won more honours. The Hearts have won 44 per cent of the derby games to Hibs' 26 per cent. We have beaten them more times at both Tynecastle and Easter Road." In fact Hearts even went on an unbeaten run of 22 derby matches beginning in the late 1980s.

"So we do consider ourselves to be a wee bit special," continued Speed. "We do see the Hearts as a cut above the rest. I can imagine every Hibs fan cringing at me saying that, but that's how we feel. We are Edinburgh's club and the number one club in the city."

David also says the fans have certain standards which have always been important. "My father works in the fish market in Edinburgh and he's been in that trade all his life. He's eighty and he still works to this day. When he gets home from work he has a shower and puts his best clothes on and goes up to Tynecastle. He's a working-class guy, but would never dream of not tidying himself up to go to see the Hearts playing. There are some parts of Britain where people used to go to the games in their working clothes, not in my experience at Tynecastle.

My dad started going in the late 1920s and, even after the war when the guys worked until twelve o'clock, it was a bit of a pain getting away home, getting changed and up to Tynecastle, but they did it. They wouldn't have been seen dead there in their dirty gear. It's very unusual. Again we do see ourselves as a football club being a wee bit more classy."

David is right in as much as Hearts have long been viewed as the establishment club in what is the city of the establishment. To the great Scottish poet, Hugh MacDiarmid, Edinburgh was a 'mad god's dream' and to others 'the Athens of the north'. Really, though, at its heart is finance and institutions such as the legal system and the established church. Edinburgh thrives on power, and has long been undeniably wealthy.

While Hearts fans willingly accept their role as part of the established elite, their rivals see this as a negative. Lloyd Quinnan told me how for him. "The real difference is that Hearts are the team of the rich.," he said. "That's what I have grown up with, crystallized for us by the fact that the posh boys from George Watson's [a leading private school] wore maroon and white scarves, so they didn't have to buy another one when they went to Tynecastle on a Saturday.

Also the board of Hearts has always been those who were very tight to organisations like the Chamber of Commerce and the City Council, which up until the mid-1980s was always Tory. If you look back over the board of Hearts compared to the board of Hibs, Hearts was very much, until the 1980s, successful businessmen, lawyers, but also people who were brought in from major businesses like the banks. For Hibs it has always been small businessmen, bookmakers, guys with building firms, and before that, bakers, more artisan successful tradesmen.

So we have this ongoing sense of grievance and it expresses itself in many ways. And we do also ignore the fact that in the same way at Hibs, the majority of Hearts fans are ordinary working-class folk. But we quite like the fact that we can say, 'well you have got David McLetchie [former leader of the Scottish Conservatives], you've got Alex Salmond [Scotland's First Minister] and you have got the boy from the bank, [Romanov]. You are obviously the team of the establishment, the team of the rich, but that's just another one of the various insults, in the same way that we are 'the beggers' to them. We are all jakey's and junkies."

WHILE HIBERNIAN TRIED TO throw off much of their history, Hearts have wrapped themselves in theirs. Its greatest chapter is a story of sacrifice. Regardless of the fact that it all happened almost one hundred years ago, it remains, in many ways, the period which defined Hearts' character and what the club stands for. When the First World War broke out in August 1914 there was a general consensus that the whole thing would be over in months and the troops home for Christmas. When reality struck, Britain realised she was bogged down in a long-term conflict which would be a bloody drain on manpower and resources.

Under this misapprehension, however, league football sailed on as normal, but as the game of the people it came under ever greater scrutiny, with demands the fixture list be suspended. How could it be that thousands of able-bodied civilians turned up for matches every weekend to watch the supreme athletes of the day chase a ball around, while others were playing a much greater game, that of securing the country's freedom? The question was asked time and again. At this stage conscription was nothing more than a concept talked about in newspapers. Going to fight was voluntary, but increasingly expected of all young unmarried and medically fit men. By the end of 1914, the consensus was that the troops were being stretched to the absolute limits of endurance and prospects for victory were bleak.

Football, it was said, had become a national shame, with grounds petitioned but only handfuls of men coming forward to join up. The truth was many at matches were already in uniform and thousands of others were carrying out extra shifts in industry to keep the war effort afloat. Still, it was felt that to have a grand gesture from the football community would turn public opinion back towards the game and boost recruitment considerably. The best way of doing this, it was argued, would be to have the support of players themselves.

Hearts were pushing for the title and, with Celtic, considered to be the best team in Scotland. Their players were to give up that pursuit for the battlefields of northern France when thirteen of them enlisted in November 1914. It was a gesture which prompted telegrams from the Prime Minister of the day, Herbert Asquith, as well as Winston Churchill, Lloyd George, HG Wells and Conan Doyle.

For thousands of Hearts fans has been a much-loved story passed down through the years, a tale partly fostered by the club, that the players simply decided one day to join up en masse – marching through the streets of Edinburgh in their boots, to the recruiting station. Regardless of the bravery shown by these men, it just wasn't the case.

First of all, the players had been stung by those who had derided them as the 'White Feathers of Midlothian' for playing on during the fighting. But also, as Jack Alexander makes clear in his magnificent book, *McCrae's Battalion*, with so much at stake, the Hearts board and players were coming under tremendous pressure from senior and eminent figures in the city and beyond. There were several meetings both inside and outside the club with the aim of getting the team to serve. Leading players were approached informally, in the hope of securing a positive response before going public with the news. They were being backed into a corner.

In the end, the authorities got the powerful recruiting tool they so desired. With the reputation of their club, their city and their sport seeming to depend on their individual decisions, it would have been extremely difficult for the players to say no. By the close of hostilities seven Hearts men had lost their lives.

A monument to their memory was unveiled in 1922 before a crowd of around 35,000. The ceremony was conducted by no less a figure than the Secretary of State for Scotland, Robert Munro, with a host of dignitaries looking on. That forty-foot sandstone obelisk still stands today close to Haymarket Station and remains a source of pride to Hearts supporters.

For three seasons in the decade which followed the war Hearts were the best supported club in the land. Attendances held firm into the 1930s when they continued to attract bigger gates than any club bar Rangers. Football, clearly, was not the reason for this since Hearts, more often that not, finished well down the table. They were loved for the sacrifice of their players and for saving the good name of football. Their reputation had been sealed. They had become 'Hearts, Hearts, Glorious Hearts', with the words of Noel Coward's contemporary song *Mud, Mud Glorious Mud*, altered and sung with gusto.

The problem with all of this as far as Hibs are concerned is that their players and fans also went to the war. At least one player died in combat and another received a medal for his bravery at the battle of the Somme. Yet, there is no mention of their club on that striking monument in central Edinburgh. I asked Hearts fans about this and they made the entirely reasonable point that they alone had paid for the tribute. Hibs' support feels this is bogus, claiming they would never have been able to erect something on a similar scale to their dead. The city fathers, they say, would not have backed it.

There is a war memorial though, not to Hibs fans or players as such, but to the fallen of Leith. It is tucked away in a corner of the Rosebank cemetery. A tall celtic cross with the Lion Rampant beneath, it is dedicated to over two hundred local men who died in the worst train crash in British history. The majority of them would have been Hibernian supporters and no fewer than eight of those who perished had been on the club's books at one time. The accident happened just outside Gretna, close to the border with England and involved three trains. One of these was packed with the Leith-based 7th Battalion, Royal Scots, who were heading for Gallipoli. Many of them burned to death in the ensuing fire. The official censorship of wartime meant the full facts only emerged years later. Even so, Hibs fans who know of the tragedy feel these souls have never been lauded in the same manner as their Hearts cousins. It is striking, given the numbers involved, that a more prominent memorial is not in place.

Don't be fooled into believing any of this to be mere historical detail. Hearts staff, players and hundreds of supporters still gather on Armistice Day to pay tribute at the war memorial and a more recent cairn erected in northern France. They are joined by representatives of the other clubs which sent players to the fighting from the east of Scotland: Dunfermline, Falkirk, Raith Rovers and, of course, Hibernian. Hearts players, in fact, fought in two world wars, but they still describe the sacrifices made during the Great War as 'the proudest moment of a proud club'. In recent times it has been just such sentiments which have led the club, through no fault of its own, to draw in some unwanted elements intent on perverting the story of their fighting footballers.

Far-right groups such as the British National Party and Combat 18 have both been active at times outside Tynecastle, though not necessarily on a frequent basis. A BBC investigation into the history of the BNP in the 1990s named Hearts, Rangers, Blackburn, Burnley and Oxford United as the clubs which the party had targeted. The reasons for this at Tynecastle seem to be bound up in the club's active association with wartime heroics. Defence of the realm is also likely to by the rationale for the small number of their supporters who express support for Protestant paramilitaries in Northern Ireland. Flags of the UDA and the UVF appear from time to time at home games, though some argue that this is nothing more than a direct response to the minority at Easter Road who display the Irish tri-colour.

If Hearts supporters generally tend to associate themselves with Britishness and see themselves as 'British and Scottish', the opposite is true at Hibernian. Generally there, the feeling is of being 'Scottish not British'. I saw this slogan daubed on walls on the way to Tynecastle. It may very well have been the work of Hibs fans. When Rangers visited Easter Road the previous season, streets around the ground had been covered in anti-Union graffiti. There is a large swathe of the Hibs support which tends to be left-wing in character, even radically so. All of this feeds into Hibernian's background and how they are perceived by their rivals as being a bit down at heel, the 'dock-siders', the poor relations. But there is pride, too, in abundance. Although not always the very best team in Scotland, Hibernian have consistently generated interest and often been on the cusp of greatness. They made their most serious impression on the wider Scottish public between 1947 and 1953. During that time Hibs were either league champions or runners-up in all but one season, winning it three times. They were also runners-up in the Coronation Cup of 1953, a competition featuring the best teams from both sides of the border. It was around this time Hibs began their European campaigns. They were successful from the start, basing their style on the much admired Hungarian side of Puskas, which had destroyed England at Wembley in November 1953, and reaching the semi-final of the inaugural European Cup. Between the mid-50s and late-70s there would often be great midweek nights when the likes of Real Madrid, among others, were put to the sword. Whether fleeting or sustained, their successes have been built on sides which went out to play with panache.

The great Hibs sides of the '50s did not go unanswered in Edinburgh. Between the middle of that decade and the early '60s Hearts had the irresistible Terrible Trio of Wardhaugh, Bauld and Conn. It was an attacking combination which scored more than 500 goals in little over 950 appearances. They won Hearts' first trophy in almost half a century, the League Cup of 1955, the Scottish Cup followed a year later. By 1958 they were said to be unbeatable. They broke goalscoring records to win the league that season, but were defeated twice at home during the process by a young Hibernian side. Two years later Hearts were champions again. Add to that three League Cup victories and you have the finest on-field era for the club by some margin.

Remarkably they have finished as league runners-up 14 times, gathering a reputation for being 'always the bridesmaid and never the bride'. For Hearts to be outside the top two and lose the championship on the final day of the season would be painful enough if it happened only once, but sadly for them the debacle of 1986 was uncannily similar to that of 1965. Hearts needed to avoid defeat at home to Kilmarnock to take the championship. They lost 2-0, and the league trophy went back to Rugby Park with the Killie squad by 0.04 of a goal.

Distressing times certainly, but no more so than what occurred at Tynecastle on New Year's Day 1973. That afternoon Hibs fans arriving late were confronted by the extraordinary spectacle of their rivals scurrying from the ground seeking the solace of the pub. Hibs were second in the league and expected to win, but no-one could have foreseen the margin of victory. They were a goal up within ten minutes, two ahead after a quarter of an hour and five by half-time. It turned out to be the biggest win ever in the fixture. Hearts were demolished 7-0, though they have dished out plenty of hammerings to Hibs both before and after that occasion.

For some reason Edinburgh tends to throw up matches which are high scoring, dramatic and feature unlikely fight-backs with greater frequency than any other derby. There are a whole sequence results which can be plucked from the record books to illustrate these points, but perhaps the New Year derby of 2004 is best example in modern times. That day Hibs were heading for certain victory, having scored in the 89th and 92nd minutes to take a 4-2 lead. It almost defied belief that Hearts managed a draw, scoring two goals in the last 45 seconds of injury time.

The fans love it of course and have always played their part in making the opposition feel uncomfortable, even if passions some-times run a little too high. Players need to be aware that history is never out of sight in this fixture and take responsibility for their actions.

Looking back it's surprising the Hibernian captain, Ian Murray, was ever allowed near the pitch for the derby at Easter Road at the beginning of 2003. He'd had a special haircut for the occasion – marking thirty years since the 7-0 defeat of Hearts – with 1973 shaved into the back of his head. This was clearly designed to provoke the away supporters and delight his own. It worked and Murray, who comes from Edinburgh and was a ball-boy at the club, was almost hit by a bottle thrown at him from the Hearts end.

THE MATCH I SAW, WHILE not being a classic in any sense, confirmed the unpredictable nature of the fixture in that a young and inexperienced Hibs side had taken the points, their first at that ground in two years. Such an outcome had seemed remote before-hand; with even the most seasoned observers of capital-city football failing to predict it. That night the road away from Tynecastle was a constant procession of celebrating Hi-Bees who were either crammed onto corporation double-decker buses, or marching in knots through the streets back towards Leith. Any Hearts fans in their path were barracked as 'Hearts bastards'.

On that great boulevard, Princes Street, the sound of bagpipes and drums filled the air. High above, illuminated by arc lights, hundreds of festival visitors were watching the military tattoo at the castle. Even this failed to drown out the sound of the supporters who were singing the name of their goalie ... 'Do, do, do ... Yves Makalambay ...' again and again. Their only distraction was the appearance of the (replacement) Hibs bus. As it slid past, still under police escort, fans rushed to the pavement's edge, applauding. Their team reciprocated behind the glass. As if on cue, great cannons began to blast in salute and fireworks punctured the darkness above the castle ramparts, signalling the climax of the night's Festival entertainment. Hardly. The unofficial partying was underway, and would go on for hours, possibly days.

TYNE AND WEAR:

Across The Frontier

"I dare say Sunderland people think they are better than Newcastle, and Newcastle feel they are better than Sunderland and football is a great way of expressing that rivalry."

Roy Keane – *Sunderland Echo* (8th November 2007)

THE 11:30 TO MIDDLESBROUGH was about to be transformed. Around three hundred of us had been waiting for it to arrive – late – not that my fellow travellers seemed to care. They were too busy singing the *Blaydon Races*, crammed together on the edge of Platform 6, their words echoing around the cold station. Uniformed police had filmed their arrival; some had even been stopped and searched en route. This was not the everyday black and white bar-coded Toon Army, but the Newcastle Lads, the self-styled Geordie Boot-Boys, and this was the last train stopping at Sunderland before their derby kicked-off early that afternoon, 10th November 2007.

When the four carriages at last swung into view there was an almighty scramble for the doors and standing room only once inside for this assortment of men with heavy jowls, shaven heads, scarred faces and Stone Island clothing. Our police escort was left behind as we pulled out of the station, but at the next stop more officers joined us, sending bodies crashing against the windows as they sullenly pushed their way aboard. Someone shouted 'tickets please'. We laughed, the cops didn't. It felt like an old fashioned 'football special'.

We moved through the North East conurbation down towards Wearside, great idling yellow cranes marking the passage of the Tyne in the distance, Newcastle's stadium – St James' Park – dominating the horizon behind us. Here you hardly touch countryside. Those twelve miles to Sunderland are thick with residential streets, parks and motorway. You could be forgiven for thinking it is all part of a single city. It's not. As we went through a Metro station there was a shout of 'hey Mackems ... bastards!' The first opposition fans had been spotted.

Then, as we touched the fringes of Sunderland, the rhythmical chant went up, 'kill the Mackems, kill the Mackems, kill the Mackems'. We slid over the Wearmouth Bridge parallel to thousands of home fans heading in the opposite direction; two snaking lines of red and white. Everyone rose to their feet to look, hands and heads pressed against the open slits of the windows. A moment later, we alighted at Sunderland station to be herded onto a waiting Metro train which took us back towards Newcastle and over the Wear again, same gestures, same sounds, same reaction. Our destination was the next stop, St Peter's.

When we arrived, all hell broke loose. The doors opened and there was a dash for the stairs and freedom; not what had been planned at all. Police at the top of the steps tried to contain us, while to the rear fans continued to pour off the train pushing forward, believing the commotion was a fight with the Sunderland boys. At a run, from both ends of the platform, more officers fought their way into the crowd causing it to slacken before limbs were unexpectedly slammed together again. Those at the front had begun to panic in the crush – there was some hand-to-hand fighting with the police – teetering at the top of a steep, wet metal staircase. It could have been carnage, but eventually things calmed and we were allowed to descend in single file. Ringed by barking dogs, horses and a helicopter, we were marched through backstreets, skirting the river, past factories to the Stadium of Light. We were never within sight of a Sunderland supporter, but they were waiting for us as we arrived, caught behind another wall of over a hundred police.

None of this was surprising. Extra officers had been drafted in for fear of trouble at the match, fans who caused problems were being threatened with a blanket ban from football, the away support was to be kept inside the ground for a time after the game and the movement of fans at Metro stations was being restricted and monitored. These measures had become standard for the match and were not taken without reason. In 2006, mounted police battled to keep rival supporters apart after Newcastle had won on Wearside. Bottles were thrown at away fans and their coaches ambushed leaving the stadium. The last ever derby at Roker Park, in 1996, was considered such a potential flashpoint that Newcastle fans were banned on safety grounds. An organised fight between hooligan groups in 2000 led to several serious injuries and some lengthy prison terms. The battle, which left one man permanently brain-damaged, took place on a day when the teams weren't even playing each other.

If getting to the match had been precarious, things were little different during it, something to which the form of the teams no doubt contributed. Newcastle, after a bright start to the season under new manager Sam Allardyce, had lost their last two matches, one of them 4-1 at home, while Sunderland, under Roy Keane, had failed to win any of their last six. Newcastle were 10th and Sunderland 15th in the Premiership. Neither would welcome the prospect of another defeat.

After twenty-five minutes, during an injury to a Sunderland player, almost the entire Newcastle team came to the technical area to drink. Under slate skies and next to a wet coast, which had just missed the worst effects of a sea surge, further liquids seemed entirely unnecessary, a short tactical discussion may well have been. Certainly Sunderland had looked the livelier in a goalless first half. Newcastle, playing in powder blue, were pretty toothless, failing to get the ball to strikers Owen and Viduka in anything like threatening areas. The only real incidents of note were when the guy next to me got a call on his mobile and answered by saying – "I'm at the match, love. I can't hear you" – before hanging up as fans around him chortled their approval. They weren't so enamoured when, just before half-time, the consistently spiky Joey Barton (recently transferred from Manchester City after seemingly endless problematic headlines) put his studs firmly into the groin of Sunderland's Dickson Etuhu.

Their mood was changed out of all recognition after seven minutes of the second-half. From a corner in front of us, Danny Higginbotham arrived late at the far post to head high past Newcastle's Steve Harper into the net. In a flash he was in front of the Sunderland fans at the corner of the East Stand, arms outstretched, eyes closed, beaming. When his team-mates arrived their momentum took them forward towards the fans, dozens of whom were rushing onto the pitch, leaping on the players. One was grabbed by his shirt as he jogged away, a supporter pulling him into his embrace. Most of the intruders were teenage boys, but the last to appear was a fully grown man, too late to catch the team, but that didn't seem to matter. He sprinted to the edge of the 18-yard box, pint of lager in one hand, knees bent, pumping his arms in celebration, before scampering back into the crowd while the Sunderland fans roared their team's name; it sounded like they were singing: 'Soon-Lun, Soon-Lun, Soon-Lun.'

This exuberant reaction could be put down to the fact Sunderland have an appalling record league record against their rivals, only winning once on Wearside in the last four decades. Then again, perhaps it was prompted simply by a more basic human desire to win. I watched as someone in front of me celebrated by throwing pieces of his pie into the crowd, shouting – "I hate these Geordie bastards!"

With Newcastle desperate for an equaliser and Sunderland stretching the game on the wings, the ball skidded into touch in front of the Newcastle bench, rebounding off a wall. Their manager, 'Big Sam' Allardyce moved for it, but not quickly enough. It was gone, stolen away by a ball boy, and the home crowd laughed as one, enjoying themselves. Sadly for them, it wasn't to last.

Just after the hour Newcastle were level, though it was hardly a thing of beauty. The Sunderland keeper, Craig Gordon, seemed to be caught flat-footed, letting a weak shot from James Milner trickle across his body, off a post and into the net. The Toon Army, fists shaking, urged their players towards them, as police wearing riot hats rushed to prevent this from happening.

'Oh we are Geordies, we are Geordies.'

Some of the Newcastle fans had taken their tops off, and in what has become a ritual, bounced around the away end, showing off their doughy white skin. Fully-clothed or not, the club's billionaire owner, Mike Ashley, was among them somewhere, having been told he would not be able to wear his replica top in the Sunderland directors' box.

Shortly after this, Michael Owen, on another comeback from his almost permanent state of injury, was clean through only for Gordon to save his weak shot. Then, for the final ten minutes, Sunderland pinned Newcastle back in their own half, coming close, but failing to score.

As the final whistle blew there was nothing more than gentle applause for the home side. The Sunderland crowd felt they should have won it; the Newcastle end reacted as if they had. Joey Barton ran to them, taking his shirt off and throwing it into their midst before departing with a gesture towards the home support. Despite this provocation, the PA system broke into Elvis's *Can't Help Falling in Love*. I wondered for a moment if peace was breaking out between Wear and Tyneside. If that were the case it would have been the first time in literally hundreds of years.

IT MAY BE A SOMEWHAT rose-tinted view to claim that this rivalry predates football by centuries, but is also undoubtedly the case. The bitter feeling between the people of the Tyne and the Wear stretches back to the beginning of the coal trade. The old saying about 'taking coals to Newcastle' meant doing something utterly absurd and entirely useless, like selling snow to Eskimos. Between the mid-16th century and early-20th century the Northumberland coal field was consistently more productive than anywhere else in the country and, because London relied upon these raw materials, Tyneside, more specifically Newcastle, had long been given royal patronage and the licence to mine coal.

Other nearby districts, notably Sunderland, which began to grow quickly as a port during the 16th century, were often heavily taxed for any coal they exported. Newcastle, which also had natural advantages over Sunderland in that the seams lay close to the wide and easily accessible Tyne, developed a virtual monopoly on the movement of coal. It grew rich on the trade and was able to control other ports, keeping these rivals in check, and to some degree impoverishing their people. All of this must have had a material effect on the people of Sunderland because at the time of the English Civil War the two towns ended up on different sides. Newcastle, hardly surprisingly, sided with the Crown to protect their own interests, while Sunderland threw their lot in behind the Parliamentarians. These differences came to a head in March 1644 at the battle of Boldon Hill in South Tyneside. There, loyalists raised from Newcastle and County Durham were defeated at the hands of an anti-monarchist Sunderland army backed by thousands of Scots who'd allied themselves with the English Parliament. Newcastle fell into Scottish hands for the rest of the war. Throughout this time Sunderland continued to send coal to London in support of Oliver Cromwell.

Much of the story of the North-East is bound up in coal, as is its football. In an area famously described as 'the hotbed of soccer' it was, more often than not, the old mining communities which powered that reputation, raising countless fine players who made their name at every level of the game, right up to its highest echelons. When people think of 'Big Jack' Charlton as a player it is either of that glorious afternoon in 1966 when he and his younger brother Bobby helped England to win the World Cup or it is of an uncompromising central defender in Don Revie's Leeds United teams, so rangy and hard he could almost have been hewn from the face of the great Ashington pit itself.

"My father was a miner and when I left school I went to work in the pits and I found out what the pits were like." Jack tells me this as we drive through the countryside from Newcastle airport towards the city. He's just come from the doctors where's he's had his annual flu jab (he's 72; it's a wise move). I say I don't want to take him out of his way. "Well you are taking me out of my way." I'm not sure how much of a joke this is. "Anyway, when I saw what I was going to be doing I said 'no, bugger this. I don't want to work in the pits' and I resigned. I went to see the manager in his office and his secretary said 'you can't come and see him, you don't have an appointment' and the door opened and he was stood there and he said 'if you leave now you will never get another job in the pits' and I said, 'I don't want another job in the pit."

After that Charlton almost joined the police in Morpeth, but ended up playing for Leeds for over twenty years instead. While Bobby was prodigiously talented, Jack was more of a battler. Both could reasonably have felt they were destined to become footballers as the game had always been with them. As kids they were taken to St James' Park by their uncle, the great Jackie Milburn – a player without peer in Newcastle – often being passed over the heads of the crowd to the boys at the front.

Jack was hooked. "Oh I was a Newcastle fan. I had an uncle called Tommy Skinner. He used to be a Sunderland supporter and he would only go to Sunderland. From Ashington that was a rarity. He would take our Bob to the matches with him in the car and he used to ask me if I wanted to come and I never would, I never would go to Sunderland. In fact I never went there until I played there with Leeds.

I never even knew where the ground was, I had never been in the ground, I had never been anywhere near Sunderland. Why? Because I am a Newcastle man, I like to go and watch Newcastle. Me and our Bob used to go to watch Newcastle play and he would go to Sunderland and I would go to see Ashington play."

These days Jack is rather fond of Sunderland, though. He still loves Newcastle, but stresses he's always been treated very kindly at the Stadium of Light where he thinks there are fine people doing a good job. I stop kidding myself that he's mellowed entirely when he says: "Sunderland would never have fucking beat us if I had of played (for overwhelming favourites Leeds in the 1973 FA Cup Final) but I didn't." He'd picked up an injury against Wolves in the semi-final.

Actually, Charlton owes Sunderland a debt of gratitude by a rather circuitous route. He'd been appointed manager of Newcastle in 1984, but made it clear he was doing the club a favour. He wanted no contract and was unlikely to stay longer than a single season; the aim being to remain in the First Division after the departure of manager Arthur Cox and superstar striker Kevin Keegan (who returned to the fold once again in January 2008 for a second stint as manager of Newcastle, playing his favourite role of 'Geordie Messiah'). Had they won the league it would have made no difference to Jack. The problem, as he saw it, was that there was just too much travelling involved in the job. Newcastle was too far from most other big clubs and to really keep on top of your opponents they had to be watched, in person, as did prospective additions to the playing staff.

Before the beginning of what would have been his second season in charge he had been trying to buy the Ipswich striker, Eric Gates. Jack, who treated the club's money like his own, felt the player was making financial demands which were 'over the top' and the deal fell through. Gates immediately signed for Sunderland. The following day Newcastle just happened to be playing a pre-season friendly. Jack remembers how "the crowd weren't very pleased with me over this. They were giving me a bit of stick that day and I said 'what's going on here? You know, we have not even kicked a bloody ball in the season yet and they are playing hell about me'. So I said 'okay, you want me out, I'm not having this' and I went to the directors and told them I didn't want the job. I had done what I said I would do and I was leaving."

Charlton doesn't consider Sunderland have ever been as big a club as Newcastle and I wonder aloud if he thinks the fans were angry not so much that Gates, a lad from County Durham, hadn't signed, but rather that he'd chosen to go to Roker Park instead? "I don't know what they thought. I just got an excuse to get out and to leave."

The difference between what Gates wanted at Newcastle and was eventually paid at Sunderland would be unlikely to trouble many Premiership clubs these days. Charlton finds it hard to believe that John Terry can earn over £100,000 a week. A striker like John Charles or Denis Law maybe, but not a defender. He also tells me how he's reluctant to go to Premier League matches now because of ticket prices and wonders how people in the North-East can afford it and indeed what they do for work now the traditional industries of coal-mining and shipbuilding have gone.

QUESTION: WHICH IS THE biggest city situated between Edinburgh and Leeds? If you thought it was Newcastle, you'd be wrong. Sunderland is the correct answer. This was something I heard time and again during my time there and it features prominently on page after page of promotional material about the place. A recent DVD by Sunderland City Council is packed with images of people shopping, surfing or lounging in parks on sunny afternoons. If not, they are making cars or working in high-tech laboratories. Newcastle fans still refer to it as Albania-on-Wear. The promo film, entitled, *In A New Light*, presents an almost utopian vision of a regenerated city. Sunderland has spent the last twenty years fighting its way out of an economic vacuum. It has succeeded, though not without assistance. Along with regeneration the buzzword of the North East is partnership, which when boiled down means Newcastle and Sunderland working together to create jobs and inward investment.

Scratch the surface and it becomes apparent that ferocious battles were and are still being fought to secure the best deal for each city. The Mayor of Sunderland, Les Scott, made this very point. "We ended up in the early 1990s where the Chief Executive of the regional development agency took us to lunch and I suddenly found out what the purpose of the lunch was. Basically he was really asking us to call off our local job hunters. We were becoming a bit aggressive; when One North East as they are now called, went there, we had already been there. If there was a hint of a new development, if there was a hint of a new firm coming, Sunderland was there, laying out its stall. And to be fair there are some areas where you have to think more regionally, but that one was straightforward, you know: 'you are getting a bit too aggressive', but we could see the results. It fuelled regional jealousies that we were probably getting a bigger share of what was out there."

This attitude may well have been sparked by inadequacies elsewhere. For a number of years people in Sunderland were angry that they paid taxes for a Metro system which was based around Newcastle and didn't even reach their city. Then there was the airport, Newcastle Airport, which the people of Sunderland helped to finance. Sunderland, because of its larger population, may technically be the largest shareholder in the airport, but its very name and situation has been key in putting Newcastle – traditionally the administrative and commercial centre for the region – firmly on the map when it comes to business and tourism.

The leader of Sunderland City Council, Bob Symonds, does his best to be conciliatory about these issues, talking in terms of "swings and roundabouts" and "integrated transport networks". But when I ask him how people on Wearside see their partners, the Geordies, he's far more revealing. "Well, they are not friends or relatives. I mean, not friends with a capital F. I think that what we say is we recognise there is a city twelve miles up the road that is part of what the region has to offer and we try to be as cooperative as we can in a number of areas, but I wouldn't say we are all friends and we all embrace each other and love each other to death because that isn't the case."

Even in partnership, it seems, old habits can be rather hard to break. The Tyne and the Wear, even at the height of their industrial power always looked for ways of expressing separate identities, in this football was key. The game became an extension of the collective pride these two great workforces took in their own output. In both Newcastle and Sunderland, when the football team is doing well you can virtually feel the boost it gives to morale.

While Newcastle produced warships and magnificent ocean liners, Sunderland made the more common bulk carriers, but came to be known as 'the largest shipbuilding town in the world' because of its immense work-rate. Such was the rivalry that the demarcation lines were clearly drawn in the yards; there was a Tyne agreement and a separate Wear agreement with the trade unions over what could be built on each river. It was also difficult for men from Wearside to find work making ships on the Tyne and vice versa. The few who did risked their necks since trouble was known to flare from time to time. Roger, a Sunderland fan, recalled how a relative of his would often say that the Sunderland workers had 'strange habits'.

With subtle changes in accents across the region, what you say and how you say it, also matters. Among the crowd at the Stadium of Light I heard several cries of Ha'Way the Lads! The very same thing would be said at St James' Park, but the spelling would be different – Howay the Lads! In both places it has long been a message of support to the team. Translated from the North-East dialect as 'Come on Boys', the phrase has been traced back to the pits where miners would call down the shaft for the cage to move either halfway – or ha-way – up or down.

Then there are the names – labels which fans have come to use for themselves and the opposition. The best known of these is probably Geordie, referring to people from Newcastle. The origin of the term is now obscured, though certainly a derivative of the name George. One theory has it that the George in question was actually King George II, the name reflecting Newcastle's support for the Hanoverians during the Jacobite rebellion of 1745. Given the city's long-held royalist sympathies this seems entirely credible. Others are inclined to believe George Stephenson, The Father of the Railways, should take the credit, Tyneside miners preferring the safety lamp he invented to the more common 'Davy Lamps'.

Regardless, the name has stuck and people around Britain, at least, tend to know where Geordies come from. The same can't quite be said of Mackems, a much younger term which originated in Tyne shipyards as an insult to their contemporaries on the Wear. Sunderland would make the ships – or Mak'em – while Newcastle would often take – or Tak'em – to be fitted out. The implicit suggestion being that only the Tynesiders had the craft needed to finish the ships off and that they were the superior workforce, alone able to create something out of the ordinary, ships of prestige and beauty.

Times have changed. Mackem is still used pejoratively on Tyneside, but it is not always intended as such. People in Sunderland don't necessarily object to the name, though they tend to prefer Wearsider. There's also a feeling that Newcastle has stolen Geordie from the wider region. Some Sunderland people, those over fifty, make the point that they'd once described themselves as Geordies, but no longer do so. The picture is further blurred when it comes to football. I spoke to supporters who remembered being on the terraces at Roker Park in the late 1980s, hearing alternative cries go up – Mackems! Geordies! Mackems! Geordies! – each from the Sunderland end.

NAVIGATING THE MINEFIELD OF North-East terminology can be tricky, but I thought I at least knew the name of the derby, Tyne-Wear. A quick look at the Sunderland website revealed I was mistaken. It was previewing what was described there as the Wear-Tyne derby. I'd never known the rivers to be used this way around, probably because Tyne and Wear is the county which takes in both cities and the national media tends to use this when talking about the match, no matter where it is played. Regional television news bulletins also put the Wear first in this context even when explaining that the Tyne Bridge was to be illuminated in the colours of both clubs the night before the match. Local newspapers, crammed full of daring derby feats from times past, were split. It was easy in Sunderland; there the *Echo* went for Wear-Tyne. In Newcastle things were a bit trickier. *The Journal* did it's best to avoid the phrase, while the *Evening Chronicle* was less diplomatic, tending to carry on with Tyne-Wear as of old.

The clubs are completely aware of the power of a media which, perhaps more than anywhere else in England, seems to thrive on every spit and cough emanating from the stadiums and training grounds. Both communities have long demanded and been fed a constant, some would say unhealthy, diet of stories about the teams.

In September 2007 the *News of the World* made a series of allegations under the headline Toon Spies Exposed. The paper claimed an illegal surveillance operation had been mounted at Newcastle in the 1990s to secretly tap the phones of senior players and officials. Astonishingly Kevin Keegan, Alan Shearer and a local newspaper editor were said to be among the victims.

They were not alone. The paper also alleged that a security consultant, employed by Douglas Hall, Newcastle's vice-Chairman at the time, had been ordered to bug the Sunderland Chairman, Bob Murray, with a view to discovering how he planned to finance the move to the Stadium of Light. Unexpectedly, in the course of that operation, the undercover agent claimed to have come across details of how the club were changing their strip in the New Year, but wanted to keep this quiet in the run-up to Christmas. Fans were effectively buying a strip which would be out of date in months. The consultant said he was then told by Hall to play the tape to a local journalist. The story was front-page news within hours, causing serious embarrassment to Sunderland and a furore which added fuel to the cantankerous nature of the relations between the two clubs.

Sometimes it is less about what you say than what you do. This was certainly the case with Lee Clark. Something of a midfield dynamo, he had grown up on Tyneside as a Newcastle fan and emerged from the youth ranks to spend eight years with the senior side. At the 1999 FA Cup final against Manchester United he was photographed with Newcastle supporters wearing a T-shirt which said 'Sad Mackem Bastards.' As a Toon fan this would hardly have been a problem, but as the then club captain at Sunderland it undoubtedly was. Clark's fate was sealed. Within weeks of that incident, and despite being the most expensive player in the club's history, he was put up for sale saying: "I have to accept that my

---

* Lee Clark, quoted in *The Independent*, 1 July 1999

presence could be an unsettling factor and with this in mind I have reluctantly agreed to go on the transfer list."* Sunderland, with considerable understatement, said the supporters had to come first and would no longer be prepared to back Clark. Fulham, a safe distance from the North-East hothouse, were the club which benefited for the debacle. While at Craven Cottage, Clark reflected that the T-shirt incident had been a "massive regret" in his career, though he had actually been thinking of moving from Wearside before he was forced out. "In hindsight, joining Sunderland was a mistake, a mistake because of my background. Everyone knows I'm Newcastle through and through. When I left Newcastle the prospect of staying in the North East, close to my family, was the big pull in going to Sunderland. But when we won promotion it dawned on me what that really meant. I would have to go to Newcastle the following season as a Sunderland player. I couldn't do that. Not go there and give 100 per cent for Sunderland against the club I love and played for. And if I couldn't do that, I'd have been cheating..."*

To understand how difficult it had been for Clark to contemplate playing for Sunderland against his old club you probably have to have been brought up with the rivalry. History does tell us that only around thirty players, including loan signings, have been transferred directly between the clubs in almost 120 years. Few of these have been names of note, with the exceptions of the former Scotland captain Bobby Moncur and Len Shackleton, the brilliant Clown Prince of Soccer who once said: "I am not biased when it comes to Newcastle, I don't care who beats them."**

The sentiment was typical of the rivalry and has been there throughout the ups and downs which made Sunderland one of the great sides at end of the 19th century, before Newcastle's emergence as a force with three titles and four FA Cup finals in the 1900s in a team which starred the likes of Colin Veitch, Peter McWilliam and Bill McCracken. Newcastle also had the edge in

* Lee Clark, quoted in *The Observer*, 25 November 2000
** quote taken from the Sunderland Programme, *Red and White*,
10 November 2007

the '20s, but Sunderland were again the leading team of the '30s, from 1935 finishing second in the league, winning the title and then lifting the FA Cup in successive seasons. In the 1950s, Newcastle had a fabulously successful cup side, triumphing on three occasions in the first half of the decade, while Sunderland were known as the Bank of England Club, such was their spending power. Since then success has been more elusive. Newcastle have won nothing more than the Fairs Cup back in 1969 and Sunderland just the FA Cup four years later. Both have had their fair share of near misses, runners-up spots and losing final appearances in the last three decades. Over the years Newcastle can be said to have just about had the edge on the silverware front, but the margin is small and certainly disputable.

A MARRIAGE OF CONVENIENCE brought Newcastle United into the world. They were really an umbrella for supporters of Newcastle East End, who'd taken over at St James' Park at the close of the 1880s when Newcastle West End went bust. The formation of United was the answer to a farcical situation in which East Enders were having to travel miles to see their team, while fans of West End were reluctant to watch another side at what had been the ground of their favourites. It truly was an act of unification and good business sense to boot.

Sunderland AFC had a harder fight to claim the prize of senior club of their area. Having been formed as Sunderland and District Teachers Association Football Club by a Glaswegian schoolmaster, they eventually overcame a rival power on Wearside – Sunderland Albion – who almost forced Sunderland AFC out of business during their early days.

If there were once rivalries closer to home it did not take long before the present day article was constituted as a bona fide classic of its kind, one which fans would literally go to lengths to see. On a November morning in 1922, 700 unemployed Sunderland fans gathered in the town in readiness for the derby. What is remarkable is that their team were not playing at home, and with at least another thousand marching alongside them in support these hardy souls tramped together across the countryside to St James' Park. A round trip of almost twenty-five miles on foot, deep in winter, for men who had little in the world must rank as one of the greatest demonstrations of supporter fanaticism anywhere. Sunderland went on to mount a serious challenge for the title that season, but would be sunk, 2-1, by Newcastle in front of 60,000 that particular afternoon.

In steadier economic times the derby remained a must-see, though in 1948 the Tyne-Wear public hadn't had the opportunity to do so for fourteen years. Hard to believe it may be, but queues started to form outside Roker Park from 4pm the day before the match that October. First in line were three women keeping places for their husbands. Soon they were then joined by boys and girls doing the same for their fathers before the men started to arrive during the night and into the early morning streaming out of factories, mines and the shipyards. This kind of demand consistently produced huge derby crowds, numbers which were always capable of causing serious problems. On Good Friday 1901 more than 70,000 tried to squeeze into Newcastle's ground, which had a capacity of less than half that figure. Such was the clamour to see the match, iron gates rung with barbed wire were forced open by supporters. In the end thousands were forced onto the pitch to avoid being crushed. Things turned ugly when it was announced that the game could not proceed. The goals were smashed and the club flag torn to shreds. Supporters, many throwing missiles, fought among themselves and with police; there were several serious injuries, though no-one was killed. It was the precursor to other battles down the years at both grounds which have seen some nasty incidents involving bottles and coins, communal spitting and more pitch invasions. The last of these came as late as 1990 with a desperate attempt by the Newcastle fans to have a Division Two play-off semi-final abandoned as it ebbed away from their side following a late Sunderland goal.

The sight of Sunderland's victory over Leeds in the FA Cup final of 1973 also led to extraordinary scenes among Newcastle fans watching on TV. The local football writer and historian, Alan Candlish, was one of many who saw the game in a working men's club close to St James'. "It was choc-a-block full by half past eleven. I think everywhere in the country apart from on Tyneside people wanted to see Sunderland, as Second Division underdogs, win.

When [Jim] Montgomery made that fantastic save, one of the guys who was sitting next to me, I remember his name, Jim Daley, he jumped up and down cheering because he thought Leeds had scored. I said: 'Jim, it hasn't gone in'. He went: 'what, what, what?' He wanted to fight the whole room for some reason, I don't know why. He wanted to fight everybody, he was so upset about it."

At least no-one actually lost their head at Mr Daley's hands. It has been known, or at least that is what they will tell you on the streets of Newcastle. The story goes that the sight of Sunderland winning 9-1 at St James' Park in 1908 caused the head on the statue of the great Liberal pioneer, Charles Grey, to crash to the ground from his monument in the city centre. Apocryphal? Yes, but not entirely unsusbstantiated. The head did come off years later in a Nazi bombing raid. Had it been weakened over three decades earlier?

The derby has always been capable of rocking the foundations of these cities, the last occasion being the tremor sent through Newcastle by Ruud Gullit's decision to drop Alan Shearer for the home fixture against Sunderland in 1999. Shearer and Gullit were in open conflict; Gullit was the manager but Shearer was the untouchable, local goalscoring hero – The Lion of Gosforth – beatified in the eyes of the Newcastle public. The Dutchman had effectively put his job on the line. Lose the derby and he was finished.

The match came to be known as the derby in the rain, really it was a downpour, with conditions verging on the unplayable. Shearer glowered from the bench as Sunderland levelled the game at 1-1. The Toon Army bayed for their hero, they got him, but two minutes later Sunderland were in front. It proved to be the winner and the reaction on Tyneside was predictably grave – one headline read 'It Doesn't Get Any Worse Than This'. Three days later Gullit was gone and Shearer back in harness, occupying the position of Local Hero until the end of his career. Had Gullit known his history he would have realised that these matches make or break people and their reputations in the North East. Peter Beardsley, that miniature, mercurial attacker scored a hat-trick for Newcastle in the derby on New Year's Day 1985. A Geordie lad aged 23, he became an instant folk hero. "People still talk to me about the game all the time. Everyone wants me to explain what it was like to score those three goals. Amazing. That's all I can tell them. I could have dined out on it for several years – in Newcastle at least.

I had a good career. I have 59 caps for England, I won the league title at Liverpool and I played in a World Cup semi-final. But scoring a hat-trick against Sunderland ranks alongside anything I've ever done in the game. It's hard to explain the feeling – I can't put it into words. Gary Rowell will understand because he scored a hat-trick for Sunderland against Newcastle in 1979, but no-one has managed it since me."*

Rowell's three goals in a single derby made even more headlines than Beardsley's, no Sunderland player had managed the feat since the First World War, an achievement which is unlikely to be forgotten. In 2006 Rowell was voted as the club's all-time cult hero by the fans. There is little doubt that that one moment weighed heavily in his favour; even more than either Montgomery or Ian Porterfield's heroics at Wembley in 1973.

Players will always welcome such adulation, but it is also wise to beware the long memory of the supporter. When the Sunderland manager, Roy Keane, paid £5 million for Michael Chopra in the summer of 2007 it wasn't so much the price-tag for a relatively untested striker which raised eyebrows on Wearside, more that Chopra had grown up as a Newcastle fan and had played for them before departing to Cardiff City where he had finished as the Championship's leading scorer in 2006/07. News of his imminent arrival was met with an almost universally negative response. The problem was exacerbated by Chopra who, while in Wales, had spoken about how he loved scoring against Sunderland; he was also remembered for some highly vigorous goal celebrations after equalising for Newcastle at the Stadium of Light in 2006. What was Newcastle's reaction to their former player heading for Wearside? To put the video of that goal on their website of course.

Bobby Moncur warned Chopra that to succeed he would have to learn from the mistakes made by Lee Clark. Interestingly it was to Clark himself that Chopra turned for advice, being told: "Sunderland is a good club, but make sure you are 100 per cent because if you aren't prepared to work hard and score goals for Sunderland they will turn on you and as an ex-Newcastle player you don't want that."**

* Peter Beardsley, quoted in *The Journal*, 9 November 2007

** quote taken from the Sunderland Programme, *Red and White*, 10 November 2007

Given the circumstances, Chopra could have been forgiven for feeling the pressure of the derby. Not only was he without a goal in almost three months, but Sunderland had chosen to plaster his face across the cover of the match programme. There was also a long interview with him and, if that wasn't enough, a centre-fold poster. If all this was intended to wind up the Geordies it wasn't having quite the desired effect. They were happily singing, to the tune of *Winter Wonderland*:

Oh Michael Chopra, are you listening
You scored a goal down in Sunderland
You're not welcome home
You sold your soul
Now you're just a Mackem arsehole.

Chopra caused his old buddies plenty of problems during the match and almost extinguished their taunts when his header came back off the crossbar late in the second-half. Perhaps it was better all round that he didn't score what would have been the winner; there was little likelihood that he'd have been able to control himself in the immediate aftermath. In two cities which treat their footballers as Gods, players must understand what they, the game and victory in the derbies mean to people. After switching allegiances it's best to keep as low a low profile as possible, something easier said than done.

Sunderland can rightly be criticised for choosing to put Chopra under the spotlight in their magazine. They would say the timing was coincidental, but I doubt it. In the same issue there was also a feature on Sam Allardyce in his playing days at Roker.

Further on in the Wear-Tyne or Tyne-Wear derby programme, an article entitled 'We Are More Alike Than We Are Unalike' struck a more conciliatory note. Great sentiment, but seriously, try telling anyone in this corner of the football world that they are all just the same. I wish you luck.

AFTERWORD

SHORTLY BEFORE COMPLETING this book, a good friend asked me: "so what's it all about then?" Another wanted to know: "what's the most interesting thing you found out about the derbies?" On both occasions I tried, but failed, to formulate what I had hoped would be an electrifying glimpse into my work over the previous two years. Reflecting on this I cheered myself by admitting that the reason for my oral incompetence was that the rivalries I'd encountered were not easy to sum up, in fact often not what I'd expected at all.

I had come to realise that everything in Liverpool wasn't friendly, that Manchester United fans really often do come from Manchester and that the Old Firm were not simply acting on behalf of the two main religious communities. Sheffield's relative isolation and infrequent derby gives the fixture its fervour. The North East bristles with tension born of the need to gain the upper hand economically as well as on the field, while race plays a part in Birmingham. In Edinburgh, class (something most Scots see as an English preoccupation) took centre stage, along with expressions of nationhood. None of these things, not even the way Arsenal fans view Spurs as an inconvenience, rather than a major threat, had been entirely obvious to me at the outset.

Uncovering exactly how rival fans feel about each other raised some problems. Often what I was being told was confusing and even contradictory for the simple reason that, contrary to what today's sound-bite and headline-driven mass media would have us believe, supporters of any one particular football club don't always speak with a single voice. When it comes to affairs of the heart, or more accurately their club, they can hold wildly differing views.

It would be wrong to say all Rangers fans are anti-Catholic, Hearts supporters are not solely members of the middle-class establishment, and there are Villa fans who don't own houses in the suburbs. But, in all cases, many are and do. I was forced to generalise, to have done anything else would have been ridiculous. For that I make no apology.

This book was always about differences, that was its purpose. But it was also hard to ignore the similarities. Consistently fans said that they didn't hate their opponents as people, only the club they followed, though usually that didn't reflect their actions during matches. Certainly, wherever I went, there was no end of passion and general ill-feeling towards 'the other'.

It would be easy to portray these games as nothing more than harsh tribal battles, always on the point of bursting into violent confrontation. They often were, but actually there was much more to them, like the way they constantly provoked acts of mockery. Even in Glasgow, a place where, more than any other, one might have expected to find only bile, the fixture was heavily laced with humour.

Supporters tended in the main to be young white males who, despite the rise of the middle-class pound in football, come from traditional working-class backgrounds. In general they also complained that their views were largely ignored by those running their clubs, while the players were remote or aloof. There was also deep and widespread anger over the cost of matches – leading to fans, from all sides, choosing to watch from the pub rather than the stands. Perhaps this reflects something which fails to come across properly on television. Despite the top clubs in the 21st century being the playthings of fabulously wealthy businessmen and consortiums, there is a grime which clings to the game. The grounds I went to seemed hopelessly at odds with the communities which surround them. Anfield is a good example. Next to the stadium there are rows of houses waiting to be demolished. At Celtic Park and Ibrox they have already been razed.

This echoes the battle currently taking place to make these cities as economically viable as is possible in the early years of this century. In some I discovered a constant and cut-throat pitch for investment, in others a re-building strategy which was cutting away great swathes, to give the appearance of prosperity and renewal.

These tended to be accompanied by major public relations attempts at re-branding and image building for the city at large.

Football fits right in with all of this. Why? Because as we saw right at the beginning of this book in Sheffield and at the end in Sunderland, if the local team is succeeding it transmits a positive feeling, that 'we' – the whole community – are doing well. In times of prosperity the fans want their team, not their rivals, to be the ones reflecting that on the pitch. If the city is doing badly, the same thing applies; the support demands that theirs is the team lifting the spirits. Whatever the circumstances, football remains the focus, a barometer of the life of these cities.

In their most simple form the derbies are about 'bragging rights', about putting one over on your neighbour. They are far more than that, however. They have to be, because these are matches which divide communities and which define people, and shape identities.

To the supporters they are a way of saying our history, our colours, our team, our way of playing the game reflects the spirit and values of a particular place. Yours, the other side, are bogus, incomplete, or even to be despised. But the derbies are also loved as events, something no fan would choose to be without. They provoke continual debate and every fixture, before, during and after the match, seems to be surrounded by a whirl of hype and incident, making mountains of what journalists refer to as 'good copy.'

One thing we can be sure of, these are and no doubt will continue to be, great matches in great cities. They remain the cornerstone of football's intense and unique tribalism.